Best wishes

Denis O'Hare

Friday

July 1, 2011

# RETURN
## to
## 'RETREAT'

— the Minnie O'Hara Memoirs —

*Minnie O'Hara.*

*January 6, 1904-December 3,1996*

PRINTED by Impact Printing, Ballycastle, County Antrim, in association with Glendun Publishing (denisjohn@utvinternet.com).

ISBN Hardback: 978-1-906689-28-5

Glendun
Publishing

# ACKNOWLEDGEMENTS

Editor - Colin McAlpin.

Sub-Editors - Orla Wilkinson, Elizabeth Stewart and Daniel V. O'Hara.

Commercial Consultant - Catherine O'Hara.

Technical Support - Gregory McToal.

Poem transcriptions - Maura O'Hara.

------------------------

THIS chronicle release of June 2011 would not have been possible but for the assistance of Daniel Vincent O'Hara, curator of Minnie O'Hara memorabilia, and Maura O'Hara, widow of Alex O'Hara, Mornington, County Meath. This book was also achievable through the generous co-operation of interviewees - John Blaney, Willie Blaney, John Brogan, Tommy Campbell, Mary Gilligan, Kevin Murray, Emily McAfee, Hugh McCormick (Dunurgan), Fred McCormick, Randal McDonnell, Hughie and Alex McGavock, Dan McKillop, Alex 'Stoots' McKay, Hugh McKay, 'Wee' John McKay, Rosemary McKay, Seamus McNeill, Sean McNeill, Malachy McSparran, Danny McQuillan, Tessie O'Neill and Robin Walsh.

Research included Google.co.uk and newspapers - *Irish News* (Belfast), *Belfast Telegraph, News Letter* (Belfast), *Northern Whig* (Belfast), and with appreciation to the Newspaper Library staff at Central Library, Royal Avenue, Belfast.

Grateful thanks to the understanding folk at Impact Printers, Ballycastle, County Antrim, especially Darren McLean, Peter McCaughan and Tommy McDonald.

PHOTOGRAPH availability - mainly from the O'Hara/McGavock family collection. Thanks also to Christopher Barrett, Bridget and Jacinta Blaney, Willie Blaney, Angela Bryson, John Delargy, Mary Gilligan, Glens of Antrim Historical Society (Dominic O'Loan, Mary Blaney), Paddy Hamilton, Impact Printers, Alan Murphy - Church of Ireland, Cushendall, Emily McAfee, Oonagh McAuley, Rosemary McCollam, Randal McDonnell, Joe and Mary McFadden, Harry McGavock, Alex McKay, Rosemary McKay, 'Wee' John McKay, Dan McKillop, Terence McNeill, Malachy McSparran, Tina O'Hara, Gerard O'Neill, Rector Moreen Hutchinson (Church of Ireland, Cushendall), Philip Sharpe and Robin Walsh. Sketches by Joe McFadden.

# CONTENTS

# INTRODUCTION

MINNIE O'Hara, an original member of the Glens of Antrim Historical Society in 1965, left a goldmine of recollection relating not only to her experiences as a much-travelled schoolteacher but also acute observations on how life was lived in the Glens of Antrim long before electricity or mechanical vehicles intruded on what was a harsh yet conversely idyllic existence.

Born Mary Anne McGavock, at Dunurgan, Cushendun, on January 6, 1904, she died aged 92, on December 3, 1996. A quiet and pious lady of striking humility, there is every indication her profound understanding of life's demands, and also an awareness of everything good, were gifts handed down by her parents, Alexander and Lizzie McGavock. She was blessed with an abiding appreciation and curiosity for the wonders of the world, and all aspects of basic living.

Minnie provides an absorbing insight to the social conditions during parts of the 19th and 20th centuries, not only relating to the Glens of Antrim but also on the other side of the Atlantic where numerous members of her McGavock clan settled into the New World.

Her father, intrepid traveller Alexander John McGavock, was born in July 1858. He was also an amateur poet of interesting yet untapped potential who spent many years working in America's mid-Western States. Minnie took note and record of her father's adventures, sensed and respected his proud connection to the Glens - and also his close attachment to his supportive closely-knit cousins in the USA, until 1902, when, at 44 years of age, he settled to married life on the home farm, at Dunurgan.

Later, she listed in detail her thoughts and interpretation of life in Cushendun, the warmth and renowned hospitality of the people who resided in what outsiders regarded an insular community; her network of relatives; her sacrifices on the way to qualifying as a schoolteacher, and then the rota of employment that took in such diverse places as Dromara, Carnlough, Cullyhanna and Portstewart.

What is truly a special period in Irish history, Minnie penned part of her unique insight as *Pages of My Life*. Her description of the physical demands involved during the growing and processing of flax, the utter necessity of spinning wool, and the summer expeditions of the entire family to cut turf near the famous 'Vanishing Lake' at Loughareema, on Carey Mountain, makes for absorbing reading.

Her narrative on the frugal lifestyle in the Glens of Antrim at the end of the 19th century - from the aftermath of the ghastly Famine, and involving the imperative of emigration or an escape to a life at sea, provide a special catalogue of stringent survival.

In collaboration with my younger brother Daniel, who supplied a mountain of material left by our mother, hopefully I have preserved this treasure-trove of yarns, and made that distant time come alive in the pages of this special recount of trials and tribulations in the face of extreme adversity. Minnie included a wickedly witty catalogue of nicknames and explanations of how people somehow cheerily survived the endless grinding poverty to scratch out a living on small hill farms.

# RETURN to RETREAT
## - a TRAIN of EVENTS

ALEXANDER John McGavock breathed a sigh of relief as the narrow gauge railway train pulled into the final passenger stop at Parkmore, high in the County Antrim hills. He was almost home again in Cushendun, following a third spell of rewarding work in the United States. Less than ten miles to go.

Normally this stocky and sturdy wanderer, who survived numerous scary incidents, including dangers on the high seas and severe frostbite while in America, came back to his native Dunurgan along the then often tortuous Antrim Coast Road route, arriving from his Atlantic endurance test via Glasgow and on to Larne Harbour.

This time, in the year 1901, it was another testing maritime journey from New York harbour to Liverpool. It needed a change of boat at Liverpool docks to reach Belfast, then onto the railway link, and on board the train that chugged down the line to Ballymena, and beyond to the Antrim high ground.

The uneven rocking motion of the steam train pushed it on to skirt Trostan mountain, and then it veered north to snake towards the green Glens.

Born in Cushendall, in late July, 1858, and baptised in St Patrick's and St Brigid's Church at the The Bay, Glenariffe, County Antrim, on July 31, 1858, McGavock knew all about train trips. This one was a cinch. Didn't he spend a back-breaking stint on the Acheson and Topeka railway line in Kansas! His first cousins, Hugh and John, of Beloit, Illinois, were also in the railway business, building track in Wisconsin, Kansas, and apparently they also laid the the first tracks through what was then known as Indian Territory, now Oklahoma.

Those were the pioneering days in the 'New World', with Alexander McGavock eventually moving up with the Longhorn cattle imports from the 'Wild West' area, such as the Texas Panhandle, to secure employment in the giant meat processing plants of Chicago.

Again, he brought back to his beloved Glens the usual bunch of letters, and more importantly much-welcomed financial help from the USA for respective relatives of kinfolk in the Cushendun, Glendun, Cushleake and Torr Head areas. During his three return journeys from the States, he was a much sought and appreciated courier . . . almost like a modern-day postman bringing good news to the Glens, from immigrants who were fortunate to secure rewarding working conditions in America.

This was the general manner of communications back in those tough times, an age of acceptance, an era when there was practically no electronic means of communicating across the wide Atlantic. There was no e-mail, no texting; indeed no telephone means of contact whatsoever, and little chance of a letter arriving. The old 'bush telegraph system' proved the most reliable method during the late 19th century.

If it wasn't the seemingly restless, but utterly reliable, McGavock arriving for another short holiday, to bring hard-earned dollars to help his own family at Dunurgan, it was someone like him. Many folk, young and old, made the hazardous move across the Atlantic Ocean to escape the constant uphill struggle of the small farmer and the shoreline fisherman's battle to try and ease above the poverty line that existed in those years - not long after the dreadful 'Great Famine' that devastated the Irish nation.

McGavock was due to step down from the rickety, lurching train at the small Parkmore halt that rested above one of the most breathtakingly beautiful areas of north Antrim - the Waterfalls and Glenariffe, known as the 'Queen of the Glens'. The secluded Station opened on September 1, 1888, and closed on October 1, 1930. It was part of a narrow gauge line launched by the Ballymena, Cushendall and Red Bay Railway Company.

The train ran from Ballymena through Parkmore to the end of the line at the isolated station house, gloriously named *Retreat.* It was later absorbed by the Northern Counties Railway and then by the LMS/NCR. The line covered a little over 16 miles between Ballymena and *Retreat.* It operated from 1875 to 1940. The railway line was incorporated in 1872, and when it opened in May, 1875, it was the first narrow gauge railway in Ireland to be sanctioned by Parliament.

The railway system was installed mainly to service iron ore outlets in the north Antrim area. The mines were connected by sidings and branch lines, some of which were owned by the mining companies. By October, 1884, the iron ore market collapsed. The line was taken over by the Belfast and Northern Counties Railway (BNCR), and the sale had to be approved by Parliament on July 14, 1884.

In 1886, the first passenger trains were introduced. This facility terminated at Parkmore, just short of three miles from *Retreat.* The trip from Ballymena lasted almost one hour, in most cases 50 minutes best, because the train had to battle against the gradient. It was quicker on the way back, the journey lasting 40 minutes. The 1,045 feet summit at Essathohan siding was the highest point achieved by an Irish railway. The route from Ballymena had stops at Ballygarvey, Ballycloughan, Rathkenny, Clough Road, Knockanully (renamed Martinstown on July 1, 1920), Cross Roads (formerly Carrowcowan), Cargan, Parkmore and *Retreat* - a total coverage of 16 and one quarter miles from Ballymena.

At the start of the enterprise, three Black Hawthorn 0-4-25T engines were used, but these were replaced by the BNCR. Passengers were transported in tramway-type bogie carriages. Generally, the train driver was a Mr Charles Kingston. To reach the tourist areas of Cushendun, Cushendall and Glenariffe, customers had to hire road transport from the Parkmore terminus, where the Station Master for a good portion of the railway line's lifespan was a Mr John McCollum. Passenger traffic ceased in 1930, and the goods traffic ended in 1940. It is believed the last person to reside at Parkmore Station House was a Mr Billy McQuitty.

The end of the passenger line meant McGavock needed to 'cadge' an unofficial lift, and remain on board the train over the last small leg of his rail journey. The train moved on with 'goods-only' on board, the parcels for shops, and the bottles and barrels for the pubs to be left at the end of the track. The final destination of the train was *Retreat* Station, where the Station Master was a Mr Seamus McKinley. The last folk to live there were the members of the family of Tommy and Maggie McNeely. Remnants of this lonely perch remain on the south slopes of Glenballyeamon.

The view from *Retreat* is spectacularly stunning, the isolated yet tree-sheltered house majestically looks directly down the Glen towards the holiday seaside village of Cushendall. From the other side of the valley there's the hypnotic view across the Irish Sea of some Scottish islands, the bedroom slipper-shaped Sanda and further down Gault's Road the pimple-like outline of Paddy's Milestone or Ailsa Craig comes into view.

The panorama at *Retreat* swings to a northward sweep along the Scottish coast. There lies the Mull of Kintyre, and further up the North Channel it is on to the western Isles. Nearer to McGavock's home is the joint of Glenballyeamon and Glenaan. Closeby rests the 'fairy mountain', Tieverragh. To the left, the vista unwraps Glencorp, and the welcoming downward trip to quaintly cosmopolitan Cushendun. In the distance juts the proud headland at Tournamona.

The area was opening up now, following the creation of the Coast Road. It was not the old boxed-in enclave that once relied purely on trade with Scottish neighbours from Kintyre. Once there was a regular boat service from Dunaverty, on the tip of the Mull of Kintyre, to the Rockport side of Cushendun Bay. The white-walled single-storey Custom House building is still there, and so is the nearby hurling pitch, named 'The Rigs' - but once better known as Liganergat . . . 'the money field', where all the bartering and purchasing took place after a ship docked with varied goods.

During the 18th and 19th centuries, the spoken language in the Torr, Glendun, Glenballyeamon and Glenariffe areas was mostly Hebridean Gaelic. Further down the Antrim Coast, where Alex McGavock's father, Hugh, came from, in the Glenarm and Cairncastle district and heading towards the crucial sea artery port of Larne, the dialect was closer to Lowland Scottish - later to be termed Ulster Scots.

Anyhow, Alexander McGavock managed to get a lift with John McGowan, a neighbour from Tromra Cottages near Dunurgan. McGowan was a driver for O'Hara's of Knocknacarry. The necessary transportation for the village of Cushendall, and surrounding area, was generally in the hands of Robert Mort. The O'Hara's looked after the needs of the next valley and Cushendun. The 1911 Ireland Census includes a 40-year-old John McGowan living at Tromra on the main track between Cushendun and Cushendall.

Tromra townland also featured 60-year-old Alex McKeegan, Elizabeth McCambridge (75), Mary McAuley (73), and a family named McLeod, who worshipped in the Church of Ireland. Down the road a few yards, at Mullarts on the junction of the Cushendun and Ballycastle highways, was the Gillis family - Presbyterians headed by 80-year-old Jane. Next door lived the McFetridge family, devoted Church of Ireland followers and led by Richard (40). One of the daughters, Greta - a close friend of Minnie McGavock, was then listed as seven years of age.

McGowan controlled the reins on two Clydesdale horses that pulled a heavy wagon featuring four metal-covered wooden wheels. There was a touch of irony in McGavock's final journey home, in that he was helped over those last seven miles on the back of an O'Hara cart. Thirty four years later his first-born, Mary Anne (Minnie), would marry Alex O'Hara, the eldest son of Alexander O'Hara, who ran the haulage business with his brother Daniel.

McGavock was not to know it then, that his days of wanderlust were about to end. He was never to cross the briny to America again. He was on a special private mission now, planning to marry Elizabeth McCambridge from the next townland of Carey, near Ballyvoy, Ballycastle, and take his bride back to Chicago. But, there was to be no fourth experience of life in the States as Lizzie McCambridge steadfastly refused to leave her north Antrim roots.

The move from the Parish of Culfeitrim, at Carey, to live near the charming little Catholic church at Cregagh, at the foot of the perfectly formed 'Glen' - Glendun, was all the distance the new Mrs McGavock would make from her family home at Crook, close to Murlough Bay. Neither the bright lights of the Windy City nor the panoramic offerings of nearby Lake Michigan would lure this strong-willed woman out of the Glens. So, it was down to working on the McGavock farm at Dunurgan, and raising a family.

# THE GREAT ESCAPE

MINNIE always took great delight in recalling the early exploits of her father, before he had to settle as head of a new family. The opening adventure of the young tearaway had a touch of the Huckleberry Finn's about it, a script Mark Twain would have been happy with when Alexander John decided to run away from his Dunurgan home for a demanding life on the ocean wave.

Her writings richly illustrate that dramatic first phase: "My father and Johnny Dinsmore of Gortacreggan were great pals, first going to 'The Turn' school - built by General Cuppage, the landlord. At that time, the teacher was a Dublin girl named Julia Murray, who later became a Catholic and married John McCormick of Innispollan. Tom McCormick of Callisnaugh was their son. The school at 'The Turn' was very convenient for the Gortacreggan and Dunurgan children, but, as it was a Protestant school, the parish priest made them come to Knocknacarry School, which was opened in 1851.

"In their early teens, Alex and Johnny decided to run away to sea, against their parents' wishes. In those days many owners of the poor small strips of farms went to work at sea in Summer, and in Winter they attended night school to try to better their livelihoods for themselves, wives and families.

"So, the pair of boys heard a lot about the sailor's life, and thought they would have a try. When Alex's father learned of their intention to walk to Larne, and look for a job on one of the small tramp ships that came in and out of Larne Harbour, he yoked the horse and cart, took his youngest son Hugh with him, and followed the pair of miscreants. But, the boys recognised the horse and cart following them in the distance, and slipped behind rocks on the seaward side of the road at Garron Point. I don't know how far the pursuers continued, but the pair of boys reached Larne without being caught.

"They were there some time before getting a job, remaining at the Harbour looking for a vacancy for a cabin boy on one of the in-coming boats. When a ship's Captain would ask where they were from, during an interview, Alex would say 'from Dunurgan' - and Johnny would say 'from Gortacreggan'. As none of the Captains ever heard of those places they didn't think these boys would make good sailors, and so were not chosen. But, on complaining to a Mr Agnew of Larne he told them to say 'Red Bay' (Glenariffe) the next time. Red Bay produced many great seamen, and so by naming that place it was assumed they were supposed to know something about the sea, and this got employment. They gained jobs on separate vessels, as cabin boys."

Life on the ocean wave, however, almost turned to instant disaster for the adventurous McGavock. He was on a small vessel carrying potatoes and other farm goods between Larne, Derry, and Glasgow. "My father used to tell of one time in the harbour of Derry he was heaving a bag of potatoes from the boat to the pier," mentioned Minnie. "The ship moved slightly, and he and the bag fell in between the boat and the pier. By good luck he surfaced straight up, and was rescued, whereas he would have drowned had he come up under the vessel.

"I suppose he made some money, came home for a break, and went to school where Master Joseph Duffy was the Knocknacarry Boys' School Principal from 1875 to 1902. Master Duffy, a relative of the Lynn's, died in Kilnadore House, Cushendall, in 1905. He taught Alex 'all branches of navigation' (to quote my father) with the intention of going back to sea as mate, and perhaps captain! BUT - mother was very much against his going again to face the perils of the sea, and as luck would have it a sister of his father's, married with no family and living on a good farm in Illinois, sent for young Hugh to come to America to inherit the place.

"His mother always opposed my father's determination to be a sailor, and when a letter came from Aunt Elizabeth, and I suppose a ticket to America for young Hugh, she coaxed Alex to go instead. Thus the mother prevented him from being a sailor. At that time it was sailing ships that crossed the Atlantic, and it must have taken many weeks to cross the ocean, and then travel so far inland."

It seems he landed in New York, at Castle Garden Immigration Department, in Manhattan, South Ferry. Castle Garden, later to be known as Castle Clinton, was the official recording depot for immigrants from 1855 to the end of 1891. The more famous Ellis Island, at the mouth of the Hudson River, took over from January, 1892, and lasted until November, 1954.

Under such strange circumstances, the roving Alexander John McGavock, who died in Dunurgan on March 19, 1940, and is buried in Cregagh graveyard, emigrated, aged 18 in 1876, to Illinois. The farm was on the outskirts of Waukegan, on the shores of Lake Michigan. The town, 40 miles north of Chicago, was founded in 1829. It is one of the oldest communities in Illinois, starting out as a French trading post, and first known as 'Little Fort'. It became a city in 1859. It is the birthplace of famous comedian Jack Benny (1894-1974).

McGavock's arrival coincided with Centenary celebrations for the United States. That July 4, the city of Philadelphia celebrated the 100th birthday of this fresh Nation. There was also an on-going Centennial Exposition, a display that began on May 10 and ended on November 10. The extravaganza included the launch of the first Alexander Graham Bell-patented telephone and the first typewriter. The jollifications were tempered, however, when news filtered through from the Wild West, from the Black Hills area of south Dakota and Wyoming, of the 1876 massacre of Lieutenant Colonel George Armstrong Custer and 300 men of his 7th Cavalry, including County Louth-born Major Myles O'Reilly, at Little Big Horn by bands of Native Americans led by the famous Hunkpapa Lakota Sioux chief Sitting Bull.

In his journal, McGavock insisted: "I am an Irishman by birth, and an American by adoption, and I feel proud of it." While obviously elated to be given a chance to improve his status in the United States, his first days in the mid-West proved difficult. It was no fun for the youngster when he experienced sub-zero temperatures for a first time, and at a cost.

Minnie related: "The winters in the centre of the continent were very severe, and during his first winter he didn't keep his ears covered when going on a message into Waukegan. The ears were frost-bitten. He told me of going to the town, walking on top of the frozen snow and keeping himself from sinking by using two sacks - stepping on one first, placing the other in front, then stepping on it, and lifting the first one for the next step. It was a slow process. But, worst of all, he was not protected properly from frostbite, and lost the fleshy part of both ears.

"Aunt Elizabeth was married to a County Down man. They and many other McGavock's emigrated to America probably after the Famine. They owned a large farm, but had no family, so the indication was her brother's son would have a good chance of owning it after their day. I don't know exactly how long he remained on the farm. He got on extra well with Aunt Elizabeth's husband, but when he died my father had a row with his aunt, and left. He said he discovered he would not inherit the farm, that she wasn't going to leave him the place, as 'she was corresponding with the head nun of a convent, in Kildare, I think'. I suppose he understood nuns would inherit the money from the sale of the farm."

His Aunt Elizabeth married John Fearon, and to some of the McGavock 'in-laws' Minnie's father was known as 'Little Alick' - to distinguish him from the other Alex McGavock's. It was later claimed, in another family record, that Elizabeth Fearon included in the Will her sister Margery McKeaver (McKeever) of Carnlough, County Antrim, and a Sister Mary Frances of County Clare.

*Alex John McGavock in Chicago during late 19th century.*

*Bishop Alex McGavock*

*Train stop at Parkmore, County Antrim*

*Knocknacarry Boys Primary School, 1905.*

*Minnie seated right with her sister Lizzie, and grandson Sean Blaney.
Standing are Alex O'Hara, Archie McSparran and Hugh McGavock.*

*1905 Knocknacarry Girls' Primary School students.*

*Ballycastle McCaughan's Chemist shop, first right, where Minnie once lodged when it was known as the 'The Mug Shop'.*

*Lammas Fair scene at Ballycastle*

*Feis na nGleann hurling match 1905.*

*Anna McSparran (nee McArdle) is flanked by the McGavock sisters, Lizzie and Minnie.*

*Minnie sits on her brother Hugh's motorbike.*

*Minnie's parents, Lizzie and Alex McGavock pictured at Dunurgan during the 1920's*

*Atlantic Liner of 1881*

*One of Minnie's American cousins, Hugh McGavock, who built railroad in the late 19th century through USA mid-Western states. He died in Beloit, Illinois, aged 74, in December 1935. His father, also Hugh, left Glenarm for America in 1847.*

*Alex McGavock once had to endure a stormy sail to the USA in the 'City of Rome'.*

*Mass Rock Procession at Innispollan, Cushendun, includes canopy bearers Archie McSparran (front right pole) and Alex O'Hara, back left.*

*Minnie in a fur-collared coat during her teaching stint at Portstewart*

*Cushendun Sports Day on Glenmona Lawn.*

*Minnie McGavock and a cat*

*Hugh McGavock's wife Kathleen, and Minnie.*

*Minnie's brother Hugh McGavock with Archie McSparran.*

*The brothers McGavock, Alex and Hugh at Dunurgan.*

*Mrs Lizzie McGavock in front of her open hearth fire at Dunurgan, circa, 1930.*

*Minnie's was a teacher in 1928 at Ballynacloshe Primary School, near the County Louth border in County Armagh.*

*Jim McMullan, John O'Hara and Dan McCormick seen at Knocknacarry in 1930*

*Artist Joe McFadden's impression of St Patrick's Church.*

*July 1928. Ready to start ploughing at Dunurgan - Minnie's younger brother, a 22-year-old Hugh McGavock.*

# RIGHT on TRACK

DETERMINED McGavock, who seemed to adopt a phlegmatic approach to the unfortunate experience on his aunt's farm, and get on with life's great challenges in the 'Land of the Free', found work with the Sante Fe railway. The Atchison, Topeka and Sante Fe Railway, more often abbreviated to Santa Fe, was charted in 1859, and with the first track section starting at Topeka, Kansas, in April 1869.

In September 1872, the railway line reached Dodge City. The last section of track, between Topeka and the Colorado-Kansas border, opened on December 23, 1873. It pushed into Pueblo, on March 1, 1876, and finally the Sante Fe track arrived in New Mexico on December 7, 1878. The industrial advances were well under way in America, a burgeoning country and a land of immense opportunity. McGavock appreciated the exciting challenges, spending the bulk of a quarter of a century there.

Minnie wrote: "Milwaukee was another placename my father mentioned. He spent time there, in a city that is the largest in Wisconsin. Famous for brewing beer, initially through enterprising German immigrants, it is situated on the south-western side shoreline of Lake Michigan. Chicago, however, soon became his main place of work. During the spell with the Sante Fe railway, he was aware of the huge shipments of Longhorn cattle coming into Chicago by rail from the Texas Panhandle. With plenty of work there, he moved to the famous stock yards of Chicago, a city since 1837 in the Prairie State of Illinois.

"He was quite a while in this gruelling job. The heat was excessive. He told me the workers cooled themselves by drinking from a tub of water with salt added. The Union Stock Yard featured meat packing on a massive scale.

"The 'Yard' era of Chicago opened in 1865. At one time 500,000 gallons of water a day pumped through from the Chicago River into the Stock Yards. Apparently my father worked for the Armour meat packing company, founded by Philip Danforth Armour. Other meat packing companies concentrated at 'The Yard' included Swift, Hammond and Morris.

"My father used to talk of Alex John 'Bawn' McAlister, who shared digs with him. Alex John was the father of Arthur McAlister, a butcher in Ballymena.

"In his later years in Chicago, my father was on the street cars as a driver. One conductor who worked with him he named 'The Roaring Tip from Nenagh'. Mary McAuley had photos of him with a great uncle of hers - Henry McAuley, who stayed in the same digs. Chicago Street Cars were first horse drawn, from 1858 to 1861, and run by the Chicago

City Railway Company and the North Chicago City Railway Company. The owners became Cable Cars in 1881, and later converted to electricity powered 'Trolleys' by the mid-1890's.

"He was in America until the beginning of this century (20th), but was home on two visits before the concluding trip to the Glens. Once he travelled back from the States, in the 1880's, on a trans-Atlantic sailing ship named the *City of Rome.* He said the *City of Rome* was supposed to be the 'last word in ocean travel' but he claimed she sat so high out of the water that she got a mighty tossing. The ship, even though it looked well, took a lot of battering from the waves. It was his worst voyage."

The SS *City of Rome* was once reckoned the fastest passenger ship to journey the Atlantic towards the close of the 19th century. It was built in 1881, and the four-mast ship was one of the first lit entirely by electricity. Originally it carried 520 1st Class passengers, and 810 Steerage. Plying out of Glasgow to New York, it was later altered to accommodate 75 1st Class, 250 2nd Class, and 1,000 Steerage. In September 1898, the *City of Rome* was used to repatriate Spanish naval POW's captured by the United States. In 1899, it was in a collision with an iceberg, and in 1900 it was used to transport troops involved in the Boer War before being sold in 1901 to a German scrap firm.

In 1896, McGavock's address in Chicago was 2031, West Lake Street. From here he recalled a great sporting occasion in New York. He referred to the buzz that followed an international athletics match in the 'fall' of 1895. "A great London Athletics team came over here, with full expectation of carrying some great honours back to John Bull, but ended terribly disappointed at finding many young Irishmen fully qualified to retain those honours with Uncle Sam.

"Little Tommy Conneff, the Greenhorn Irishman, came over here and joined with New Yorks in order to help America, and his equine-like powers can beat the world from one mile to three. And brave young Michael Sweenie, the champion high jumper of the world, when he cleared the six foot mark the Englishmen all looked at each other, but when he winged over six foot three inches the Englishmen went off and sat down. The Londoners went home disappointed, and they can honestly attribute their defeat to young Irishmen."

The proper surname spelling of the high-jump ace was Sweeney. Irish-American Michael F. Sweeney is regarded the first of the World High Jump champions. He used what was then known as the 'Eastern Cut-Off' technique, a scissors-like style of run up. In 1895, he also cleared 6 feet 5.625 inches. Conneff, born at Forge, Kilmurry, County Kildare, in 1866, was described as the World's double 'foot-running' amateur champion at three-quarters of a mile and the one mile.

He became a member of the Manhattan Athletic Club, and later joined the American Army. He represented New York against London, and clocked a new World mile record time of 4 mins 15.6 secs.

Eventually, he became an officer in Company B, 22nd Infantry, stationed at San Antonio, Texas. It was reported he made a return to Ireland for a short visit in January, 1911, before his death during Army duty in Manila. The G.A.A. ground at Clane, close to Naas and also the K-Club at Straffan, is named in his honour - Conneff Park.

Minnie added: "My father also mentioned a journey back to the States in 1899, aboard the SS *Nebraska*. He wrote, in mid-ocean on July 1, 1899, a four-verse poem about the trip, after departing on June 24 from the Port of Derry for New York. He also recorded a one-week fishing trip at the end of July 1899, from Chicago to lakes at Libertyville, a place where McGavock cousins, including the Bishop (McGavock) purchased a house at the start of the 20th century. The 1899 junket was hosted by Illinois County Commissioner Iain Mack, who had a house rented for the holiday.

"He (my father) mentions another Cushendun man, Dan Magee in the group, and also the names of Connolly, Nap, White, Dunne, and Quinn. Upon departing Libertyville he decided to give the house a name - took a card, and wrote 'Castlegreen' on it, and hung the card above the front door.

"His third trip home to Cushendun proved to be the end of his adventures in America. His sister Kate was the first to marry. She became Mrs Daniel McKendry of Ballypatrick, Carey, and my father would visit her when home. I think that is how he met his wife, Lizzie McCambridge of Crook, in Carey, and married her in 1902 with the intention of returning to America.

"But Lizzie refused to leave Ireland, and so they settled in Dunurgan where his father Hugh, over ninety then, lived alone. Mary, the youngest of the family, had just left to become the wife of Archie McKenty of Aughalum, Carnlough."

# THE RUNAWAYS

**W**RITING in 1984, Minnie recalled the 'elopers', a family incident that created great excitement, much ado at the time throughout the parish of Cushendun.

She wrote: "My uncle, Hugh McGavock married Etta McCambridge, an aunt of Mrs McIlgorm and auctioneer Pat 'Valdy' McCambridge, and went to America where they settled in Tacoma in the State of Washington. That was long before my father married.

"Here's how a local funeral stirred my memory on that adventure. Last Wednesday, the 29th of August 1984, my son Daniel, who was here for a week's holiday from Dublin, brought me and Maggie McKinley (Gore) to Mrs Maggie Butler's funeral.

"Before leaving the graveyard at Ballyvoy, we were speaking to Pat 'Valdy', and he mentioned that Don McGavock and his daughter were over from America, and staying in Cushendall. He said Don, a nephew of Hugh, brought his daughter to the Lammas Fair on the day before, to show her where his grandfather - my uncle Hugh McGavock, sold the mare, unknown to his parents, to enable him 'run away' with Pat's aunt Etta. But, my neighbour in Knocknacarry - Mary MacCormack, says it was in Armoy, a few miles inland from Ballycastle, that he sold the mare, and her father Charles was with him. Charles was his best man.

"When my cousin Leo was in Cushendall some years ago, my sister Lizzie Blaney brought him to McCormick's house at Bonavor to see the kitchen to which Charles brought them after the marriage. You see, on the day they were married Etta was to have married a widower from Cushleake, named McCormick, who later married a sister of George McIlheran of Ranaghan. Pat 'Valdy' said one of the McDonnell's (Randy's) was sent to tell McCormick not to come up.

"My uncle and Etta were at a lint-pulling some days before in Laney, on the road to Cushendall, and decided to run away. I suppose her father had arranged the marriage with the widower. After she was married to Hugh - they were both very young, he brought her to stay with his aunt Katie, Mrs McBride, in Cushendun. Maggie Gore said her mother told her that our granny (Hugh's mother) sent her down to bring them up to Dunurgan.

"I don't know how long they remained there, before heading to America, and I think their initial intention was to go to the Klondike. On our mantelpiece in 'the room' at Dunurgan there was a lovely wedding photograph of the pair. There was also one of my father and mother. Hugh had the same features as my father, but was much taller. He played the fiddle, and was in a group of fiddlers who played in the church choir. He became known as Hugh 'Fiddler' McGavock. I think it was Master Duffy who taught the fiddlers. Master Duffy was Joe Lynn's grandfather.

"At the time of Hugh's wedding, my father was already in America. I never heard exactly how the young bride and groom made it to the West of America. It was the time of the 'Gold Rush', and apparently they were heading north in the State of Washington, and in the company of a gentleman who owned a ranch and asked my uncle Hugh to work for him. So, instead of going to the Klondike, as was believed at the time, they left the wagon train with this gentleman at Tacoma."

The Yukon or Klondike Gold Rush began on August 1896, at Bonanza Creek, outside Dawson City, with the main stampede of gold diggers in July 1897. There was also a theory Hugh 'Fiddler' McGavock may have targeted the tail-end of the British Columbia gold rush at Kamloops, the last stop before Vancouver and one that created the main mining town of Barkerville. In the first frenzy there was the Frazer River Gold Rush, followed nearby by the Caribou Gold strike at William's Creek in the south-central area of the Canadian province.

Minnie, from varied discussion with her father and also Pat McCambridge, stated: "After crossing most of the American continent, and moving in some conveyance north through the State of Washington, they left the wagon train and remained at Tacoma for the rest of their lives. Louisa McGavick, daughter of Hugh and Etta, was apparently named after the wife of the ranch owner. The other children were Hugh John, James (born 1902, died 1932) and Leo (born 1904, died 1994)."

Leo became a Lawyer in Tacoma, Washington. A former State Senator, he visited the Glens of Antrim on a number of occasions, generally on his way back home from playing golf in England with his friend, apparently ever since Primary School days, crooner Bing Crosby. Leo stayed with Lizzie Blaney at The Bridge, Cushendall. During Leo's first visit to seek out his roots he joined in a McGavock family re-union in the old Cushendall Hotel. Those present at the dinner included his first cousins Minnie, Lizzie Blaney, and Hugh McGavock, who travelled from Belfast with two of Minnie's sons, Alex and me.

Somewhere along the trail, the surname changed to McGavick. Some members of the McGavock clan in North America reverted to the old Scottish spelling of MacGavock. Leo's Attorney-at-Law business was listed at 1102, Broadway Street, Tacoma. He was elected to the State Legislature three times. He was also a Trustee of the Tacoma Country and Golf Club.

Born in Rosedale, on the Gig Harbour peninsula, Leo graduated from Gonzaga University and Gonzaga Law School. He became a senior partner of the firm of Murray, Scott, McGavick, Gagliardi and Graves - one of the most reputable law firms in the State. Gonzaga bestowed upon him the honorary degree of Doctor of Law, and the Gonzaga University Law Medal. After 62 years of practice, he retired from McGavick, Graves, Beale & McNerthney.

In the State Legislature, Leo stood for good government and clean politics. He was a Board Member, Chairman and General Counsel for

State Mutual Savings Bank of Tacoma for 22 years. He served as the first President of the Tacoma Junior Chamber of Commerce. His other accomplishments included being past President and past Trustee of the Tacoma Athletic Commission; past President of the Tacoma Eagles; member and past President of the Tacoma Pierce County Bar Association; member of the Washington State American Bar Association; member and past Trustee of the Tacoma Chamber of Commerce; past Trustee of the Tacoma Country and Golf Club and past Trustee of the Washington Athletic Club.

Minnie added: "Hugh's eldest son was Hugh, the father of Don. James, the second son, had very red hair, and not unlike my eldest son Alex's eldest son - Peter O'Hara of Mornington, County Meath. The McGavock's of Tacoma sent pictures of the family to Dunurgan, and to the Gores. I remember a lovely one of Leo, in his robes when he graduated. He is the only one of the family alive. James was married with one child when, in 1932, he was in a boat with friends fishing on a lake when he fell in and was drowned. His companions were going to jump in to rescue him, but he shouted that he could swim.

"Tragically, he had on rubber boots which filled with water, and brought him to the bottom. We were sent newspaper cuttings of the sad event. My neighbour, Mary MacCormack then informed me that Mrs McBride, who was Etta's sister Elizabeth, sent for her father (Charles) to tell him that the bride he helped to run away with Hugh McGavock was dead. Leo visited the Blaney's and McCambridge's in Cushendall, as did a nephew named Don.

"Descendants of my aunt Annie, the Gore's, live in New York, and her daughter Rosie's family - the McNaughton's, live in Vancouver, Canada. Aunt Mary's daughter, Mary Agnes, became Mrs Esler in Carnlough. Mrs Maggie McKinley (Maggie Gore) of Carey. Mary Agnes Esler, my sister Lizzie Blaney and me are the only cousins left of that generation. I forgot to say that my grandfather was still living when I was born, and lived for a few years afterwards. He had red hair, as I and many of his descendants have. Many of my grandchildren have red hair."

# MEMORY LANE

DURING his stints in the States, a touch of homesickness surfaced when Alexander J. McGavock took to writing poetry. While working in Chicago in 1893, he penned *Adieu to Antrim Glens.* This deserves a special place in the Minnie memoirs.

### *ADIEU TO ANTRIM GLENS*

*In Antrim Glens amid my friends*
*I've spent my boyish days*
*In flowery dales and pleasant vales*
*I've joined them in their plays*
*But, I feel at last such joys are past*
*My mind is on foreign gems*
*In them, in fields gold, my arms I'll fold*
*Yet far from Antrim Glens.*

*Oh, Sweet Glendun where-on shines the sun*
*It's water and purest rays*
*I've walked your hills from peak to rills*
*I've climbed your steepest braes*
*On your bridge so grand where l love to stand*
*In company with my friends*
*My name in full is on you still*
*Sweet Viaduct of the Glens.*

*Glenariffe too, I've walked it through*
*To your mines of iron ore*
*By your verdant fields the burden wheels*
*Does trumble to your shore*
*From your mineral hills the rolling mills*
*Their brightest sparks ascend*
*To man and boy you give*
*Rich mineral of the Glens.*

*Amidst your rills and shamrock hills*
*My young heart proudly fills.*
*And sweet Glenarm I've oftimes scanned*
*It lives between two hills*
*Our market town for all around*
*Its fame now wide extends*

*It's known by all as Cushendall*
*In the bosom of the Glens.*

*To Cushendun I'll yet return*
*I love your tranquil shore*
*Through your cave I oft have roved*
*In good old days of yore*
*Cranaugh's Peak I've climbed so steep*
*To view your brightest gems*
*And to take a sight of Scotland*
*From the hills of Antrim Glens.*

*To leave such scenes and daisied greens*
*The thought I can't subdue*
*Your sparkling rills and shamrock hills*
*I now must bid adieu*
*The neighbouring cots I'll never forget*
*Where musical praise ascend*
*Were it fortune will I might live still*
*Amidst you in Antrim Glens.*

*Young friends so kind still bear in mind*
*The youth that shared your joy*
*Across the Atlantic foam I passed to roam*
*to the shores of Illinois*
*And when I'm sound in slumbers bound*
*And dreaming of my friends*
*I oftimes sigh and in fancy fly*
*Back to you sweet Antrim Glens.*

FOOTNOTE - A.J. was apparently registered McGavick, not 'ock' in the U.S.A, just like his brother Hugh in Tacoma. At the back of the typed sheet it is signified he wrote this poem in Chicago in March of 1893. In a flamboyant handwriting style it reveals . . . Mr A.J. McGavick of 748 750 63rd Street. 'Dear Cousin, I write to let you know that I am well, hoping to find you and friends the same. Your Cousin. A.J. McGavick.' (He signs it 'ick').

In 1893, he would have enjoyed the famous Chicago World Fair, officially known as the World's Columbian Exposition in memory of the discovery of the New World 400 years earlier by Christopher Columbus. The great occasion began with a Dedication Ceremony on October 21, 1892, but the fairground did not open for business until May 1, 1893, and ended on October 30, 1893. On October 9, 1893, the Fair event attracted an amazing outdoor attendance of 716,881.

The main focus was the giant Ferris Wheel, built by a Mr George Ferris. The wheel was 264 feet high, and featured 36 cars with each carrying 60 passengers. The World Fair also highlighted a special exhibition by Irish-American landscape artist J.P. McMeekin. His product mainly portrayed

Western USA landscapes. Outside the Exhibition area was the famous Buffalo Bill Cody's 'Wild West' show. More than likely the stunning 'Wild West' production included a lone Irish rider in the cast. Born in Mallow, County Cork, George Rowe became a cowboy in the United States, and, for years, was a trick rider in the Buffalo Bill extravaganza. Rowe, who toured America, Canada, England and Europe with the show, returned to Ireland to launch Fossett's Famous Circus.

There is no doubt Alex McGavock was happy in the 'home of the brave' until thoughts strayed to the Antrim hills, yet I felt he also seriously missed the buzz in America once he was settled again in the Glens. Another of his poems reflects that mood. It is a short story-cum-poem titled *You'll Come Back To Chicago Again.* He wrote: 'Being a resident of young and everfair Chicago for a period over ten years, witnessing life in almost every form, and the wonderful growth in population and industry.'

### *YOU'LL COME BACK TO CHICAGO AGAIN*

*Chicago in reality*
*Is a wonderful city*
*It's young, it's proud and it's fair*
*It's great drawing powers*
*Will haunt you by hours*
*That's when you once have been there.*

*You may tour the West*
*In the East do your best*
*And try to forget it in vain*
*It don't matter from home*
*Where you chance for to roam*
*You'll come back to Chicago again.*

Here is further example of a little bit of home sickness, when he writes *AMONG THE WILD FLOWERS OF THE GLENS.* His introduction states - 'the following verses I have written while in my room on the 14th of March, 1892, at No. 1327, Park Avenue, Chicago.' He pens 12 verses, the first of which reads . . .

*Tonight I think of Cushendun*
*Its lovely hills and dales*
*Where I was bred a farmer's son*
*Amidst its shamrocked vales*
*Tonight I wander back again*
*in fancy among the ferns*
*Where pleasant evenings I have spent*
*Among the wild flowers of the Glens.*

# GOING WEST

EMIGRATION took on many forms and targets. The exodus from the Glens of Antrim, heading to foreign fields from as far back as the 17th century, was mainly to North America.

Young men and women, indeed complete families such as another section of the McGavock's from Glenarm, became trailblazers in helping to shape the future of the new nations of north America. It is believed some early members of the north Antrim McGavock clan emigrated out of Larne, bound for Boston, in 1717.

The early McGavock settlers to the Antrim Coast, it seems, were originally septs or sub-divisions of the Clan Douglas from Lanarkshire, Dumfriesshire and Galloway, Highlanders arriving there from the Western Isles, and in some old Scottish historical records were named MacGuffock. They moved on to the Antrim Coast, to lands between Larne and Glenarm, and arrived as of the Presbyterian faith. Some married into the local Irish Catholic population, and became converts, while other strains of the McGavock bloodline stayed non-Catholic.

Prominent from this latter section were those who first emigrated to America during the pioneering days. A brief stop in Ireland was to be, for many, the first leg of that journey across the Atlantic. Randal McGavock, one of the first officers to die in the American Civil War, was a descendent of another James McGavock, who left Glenarm to open up land tracks and a wayside Inn along the famed Cumberland Gap.

Colonel Randal McGavock, a Harvard Graduate who featured the trademark McGavock flaming red hair, led the 10th Tennessee Irish in a battle charge against Union soldiers near the town of Raymond, and was killed in May 1863. Before the Civil War, the aristocratic McGavock made a tour of Ireland, England and Europe, and compiled his experiences in print, a hardback book named *Pen and Sword.*

There is a McGavock 'Confederate Cemetery' at Franklin, Tennessee, and a McGavock Cemetery in Nashville, Tennessee. Carnton Plantation, named after Cairntown, Glenarm, and built by Randal McGavock in 1815, was south of Franklin, and the main house served as a hospital during the 1864 Battle of Franklin. The McGavock's arranged the removal of the Confederate dead from battlefield graves to an organized cemetery that lies beside the family graveyard - established in 1818.

There seemed an almost endless exodus of McGavock family members to the United States. The origins of Alexander John McGavock have been traced to the mid-18th century, including Jack 'John' McGavock, born in 1770, and his brother Patrick McGavock, born in 1763. The latter died in 1843. Jack married Catherine Mulvenna, who was born in 1795. Jack and

Patrick had a farm in the Saint Cunning area at Mullaghsandall - between Cairncastle and Glenarm, before Jack and his son Hugh (Alexander John's father) moved up the Antrim Coast to Dunurgan, Cushendun, where they bought a farm.

Hugh, also Minnie's grandfather, was born in 1815 at Mullaghsandall, and died in 1906 in Cushendun. He married Anne McAlister, daughter of Charles McAlister and Nancy Shannon. She was born in 1815, at Carnahaugh, Cushendall, and died in Dunurgan in 1905. "My maternal great grandmother, Nancy Shannon, came from Glenariffe - where the Sharpe's live. Nancy's husband, Charles McAlister was married twice," explained Minnie,

"His first wife being McAuley - Dan Mick's connection. My great-great-great grandmother was Anne McAuley of Bannside. Hugh McGavock was a dealer in Highland ponies, imported on ships from the Mull of Kintyre, Scotland, and brought ashore either at Red Bay, at Layd - near Cushendall Golf course, or at Cushendun - beside 'The Rigs' hurling pitch at Rockport.

"In those days, Fairs were held in Cushendall eight times a year, and at Fair Days many Highland ponies were on offer. Girls as well as men attended, and many matches were made. So, it is assumed that was how Hugh McGavock met and married a Cushendall girl. After their marriage, they lived in Gortacreggan and Straid before buying a small farm in Dunurgan. It had been owned by relations of Hugh Murray, named Walsh. Mr Walsh died, and I think his son was lost at sea . . . so, his widow and daughters moved to Cushendun, where they kept boarders.

"I think Miss Wilde boarded with them when she first came to Cushendun, to teach in Knocknacarry School. Two of the Walsh girls, Mary and Kate, moved to Belfast, and used to come and stay with Miss Wilde when she lived in Innispollan. They later had a wee house in the Milltown area of Cushendun."

The McGavock's operated a small shop in 'the room' in Dunurgan, and the father gave up trading in ponies. Alex was the eldest of the family. He had a young brother Hugh, and sisters Annie, Kate and Mary. There was also a baby named Charles, for Anne's father, but he died in infancy. Alex would be named for a McGavock relation, as no near McAlister relation was an Alex.

Minnie added: "Anne married Ralph Gore, Kate married Daniel 'Tinker' McKendry, and Mary married Archie McKenty of Carnlough. Annie and Ralph's children were Mary (born 1897, died 1975), who married County Mayo man Martin Sweeney. James died in New York. Maggie (born 1900) married Dan McKinley of the Ballycastle Line at Ballypatrick. Maggie was reared by her Aunt Kate and Daniel McKendry, who had no children. Maggie inherited their farm, where she and her husband Dan lived. They also had no children. The remaining children were Rosie and Annie Gore - the latter a teacher in Cushendall Primary School.

"Many members of the McGavock clan emigrated to America, and took the name Alexander with them. My father used to tell of how he played cards at a table in America at which there were four Alex McGavock's, all cousins."

Back to the earliest phase on the family signpost she explained it was a Patrick, who died in 1843 in the Glenarm area, who reared a family of six. This included another Alexander McGavock, born in 1791, who emigrated to Beloit, Illinois, in 1847. He died there in 1861. Apparently, this Alex McGavock sailed on the *Tallerand* out of Glasgow for America. He married Sarah Devlin in County Antrim. She died in 1854, in Beloit. Sarah's relatives emigrated to U.S.A. in 1798, during the rebellion in Ireland. Alex, Sarah, and family eventually settled in Fox Lake, Illinois. Their children included youngest son Hugh, who was born in 1828 in County Antrim, and died in Illinois in 1901.

Hugh married Catherine Buckley in 1857. He worked on railroad construction for 20 years, during which he built the Chicago and North Western railroad from Afton to Beloit, Illinois. In 1852, he bought 444 acres in Beloit, and increased it to 800 acres. He was a Democrat. A great uncle fought under Washington in the Revolutionary Army, while another relative in the South, General John McGavock was an officer in the Confederate Army.

Hugh and Catherine, whose parents emigrated to Janesville, Illinois in 1849, reared a family of 10 children . . . Alex, John, Hugh (born 1861, died 1935 Illinois), William, Patrick, Thomas (who became a merchant in Chicago), James (married Alice McMiniment, and was a contractor in Chicago), Edward (involved in the meat trade in Chicago), Charlotte, and Mary Margaret, known as the 'Sweet Wisconsin Girl' from a short poem, written in January of 1896 by her cousin and Minnie O'Hara's father - Alex McGavock. He wrote on a single sheet, following a visit to Beloit.

### A YOUNG WISCONSIN GIRL

*Have you ever been to Beloit, boys*
*Or did you cross the line*
*That divides Wisconsin from Illinois*
*If you have, you will bear in mind*
*those sparkling sceneries there so grand*
*would cause your brain to whirl*
*and the most charming flower in all the land*
*Is a sweet Wisconsin girl.*

*I have heard of those shady bowers*
*of some enchanted dell*
*Where young love spend happy hours*
*and many sweet nothings tell*
*And the heart that's won in some abode*
*Where cupid finds no churl*
*But let me stray along a country road*
*with a sweet Wisconsin girl.*

*Their magnetic power where a dimple lies*
*And a heart still free from care*

*With ruby lips and laughing eyes*
*They don't use powder there*
*And when you come to say goodbye*
*How that love-lit eye does whirl*
*I could ever stray through a field of rye*
*With a sweet Wisconsin girl.*

*Now you boys that wish to live on charms*
*And lead a happy life*
*Just wander through those rural farms*
*Get a country girl for a wife*
*For lucky will be the young man*
*Who a tale of love can unfurl*
*To win the charming heart and hand*
*Of a sweet Wisconsin girl.*

Three siblings of Minnie's grandfather Hugh were the first members of the Mullaghsandall family to emigrate to America - James, Elizabeth and John. Other members of this family of nine children, were Catherine, William, Mary Ann, yet another Alexander, and Margery 'Rose'. James and Elizabeth settled in Illinois. On the way to America, James, born in 1816, met Catherine Watt, born in Loughguile, County Antrim, on an emigrant ship.

Originally they went to Wisconsin, and then moved to Fox Lake, Illinois. They had seven children. The boys attended Kankakee College, which is situated 60 miles south of Chicago. Eldest son James E. (1861-1936) became a priest, followed by Alexander Joseph (August 22, 1863 - August 25, 1948), who also joined the priesthood and served as Bishop of La Crosse from 1921 until his death. The latter went to local primary and public schools before entering St Viator College at Kankakee in 1879. He graduated in 1887, with a Master of Arts degree - and on June 11, 1887, was ordained to the priesthood by Archbishop Patrick Feehan.

He served as a curate at the All Saints' Church, Chicago, until 1887. He became pastor of St John's, before being appointed auxiliary Bishop of the Archdiocese of Chicago on December 2, 1898, and titular Bishop of Markopoulos by Pope Leo X111. He received his Episcopal consecration on May 1, 1899, from Archbishop Feehan. Serving as co-consecrator at Holy Name Cathedral, he also became pastor of Holy Angels Church, Chicago, in 1900.

After the death of Bishop James Schwebach, Alexander McGavick was named the fourth Bishop of La Crosse, Wisconsin, in the Archdiocese of Milwaukee, on November 21, 1921. He was founder of La Crosse's Aquinas High School. In 1945, he was succeeded by John Patrick Treacy, another Irish-American who was born at Marlborough, Massachusetts, and who died in 1964. Bishop Alexander McGavick died, aged 85, on August 25, 1948. By the way, the city of La Crosse, twinned with Bantry, County Cork, lies alongside the Mississippi River - the area opened up by French fur traders in the late 17th century.

Incidentally, John McGavock's whereabouts remain a mystery. There is no trace of him in the 1850 U.S. census. It is speculated he headed West in 1849, to the California Gold Fields. The famous 'Gold Rush' began at Sutter's Mill, near San Francisco, where placer gold was discovered on January 24, 1848. The real 'Rush' was in 1849, hence the 300,000 panning for gold were known as the 49ers. Gold was also found at Yreka, northern California, in 1851. John McGavock may have perished in the West, as the gold diggers faced deadly hazards such as typhoid, cholera, and regular attacks by native Americans, angry after they were displaced from their fishing and hunting homeland.

# ONLY in AMERICA

DURING his early days in the U.S.A., Alexander John McGavock's pen became very active. He seemed to be a man who closely observed how the nation had to overcome growing pains.

He placed a personal take on the strike of 1894, in the Pulman Car shops, the strikers backed by members of the - 'flourishing young society known as the American Railway Union, led by the union President E.V. Debs.'

Forthright McGavock stated: "The strike was doing well, with public sympathy on its side, until Grover Cleveland, who was then President of the U.S, ordered out the regular army in defiance to the Governor J.P. Altgeld. Men were shot down on many occasions. The President, not being satisfied even with his regular army, called together his High Court which issued an order of injunction that placed the leader of the American Railway Union in jail, and demoralised the strike."

The biting chorus to his hard-hitting poem *The Strike Of '94* reads . .

> *To strike for their rights was no dishonour*
> *Their children shall know no shame*
> *For the trouble existing throughout this country*
> *George M. Pulman was to blame.*

On January 4, 1895, he writes a note from his digs at 2031, West Lake Street, Chicago, to a James Norton regarding his view on a forthcoming vote on proposed Civil Service reform. However, Alexander J's writings generally ooze a romantic trait. After all, he became an adventurer at a very early age. It seems one of his happy places was a lover's rendezvous named Garfield Park, Chicago. Before penning a poem on the subject *Out in Garfield Park*, in April, 1895, he explains: "Garfield Park is a beautiful Park on the west side of Chicago, and is noted for the number of young lovers that frequent it, and after dark you could scarcely find a park seat in the shadow of an evergreen hidden from the rays of the electric lights, without a pair of young lovers whispering some sweet nothings there."

He was a witness to a mixture of all sorts of excitement, sadness, hardships, and the euphoric changing trends to mechanisation. One example is a poem about the alterations in his work - *The Electric Motorman* - written on March 15, 1896, and depicting the progress from horse-drawn trams in Chicago to electrically driven vehicles. He also noted some political change. On March 25, 1896, he mentions George B. Swift, the Republican Mayor of Chicago, replacing Democrat John P. Hopkins.

On July 15, 1896, he highlighted a Democratic National Convention held in Chicago. Nominated was 'Silver' Bill Bryan. On September 12 of that year he took an interest in sailing, and wrote: "The following verse was written on the first heat or race for the American Cup, between the *Valkyrie* and *Defender*, but being disgusted with the outcome of the race dropped my pen!"

> *We must admit Dunraven's grit*
> *With his gallant little sloop*
> *Who crossed the wide Atlantic*
> *To contest the American Cup*
>
> *But, our brave champion Defender*
> *She winded it like a bird*
> *And proudly showed her tail*
> *To Valkyrie the Third.*

On September 5, 1896, he writes about the latest craze in Chicago, bicycle clubs in the city with girls on bicycles - and wearing bloomers. The poem is named - *My Girl Has got a Wheel.*

During a trip home McGavock stitched together four verses of his eye appreciation of the wondrous *Glenariffe Waterfalls*. Here is a flavour of the theme - the opening stanza, written on July 31, 1897 . . .

> *Along these falls I come to stray*
> *Their pretty sights to see*
> *With a sweet Glens girl on every side*
> *Ain't that fine company*
>
> *I am told young love is plenty*
> *Along these cliffy walks*
> *Still whispering sweet nothings*
> *At Glenariffe Waterfalls.*

On a somewhat sombre reflection, he recaptured the horror of a drowning tragedy at Loughareema, calling the area 'Carey Lough'. The tragedy unfolded on September 30, 1898. Apparently. the bridge road crossing the 'Vanishing Lake' was much lower then than it is today, and was always considered a danger when there was flooding.

Heavy rains for over two days had the lough waters spilling onto the road. It was now in a dangerous state, and it was reported people attempting to return from Cushendall Fair to their homes at Carey and Ballycastle decided to sit out the storm, and not risk crossing. There were also slower ways, walking around the lough.

It appears 60-year-old Colonel John Magee McNeill, a retired Army Engineer who had been staying with his cousin, Captain Daniel McNeill at Cushendun House, took an ill-fated gamble that resulted in two deaths. He was keen to catch a train at Ballycastle.

Another theory is that he, also known as Jack McNeill and a cousin of future Lord Cushendun, Ronald McNeill, was still in the British army and anxious to return to his regiment in India.

The Colonel and a coachman, David McNeill, set off from Cushendun in a two-horse carriage, and in the attempt to cross the flooded road the horses and carriage slipped over the edge and into the Lough. It seems the Colonel managed to extricate himself from the overturned carriage, but was weighed down by his heavy great coat, and perished along with the coachman and the two horses.

It was reported that Ronald John McNeill came down from Craigduun on the next morning, and also the Coastguards at Cushendun managed to transport a boat inland by cart to drag the waters of the Lough. The two bodies were recovered late that evening. Here is a report of the tragedy from the Belfast *News-Letter* issue of Monday October 3, 1898. The headings read . . .

SAD ACCIDENT NEAR
BALLYCASTLE.
A CARRIAGE SUBMERGES.
TWO MEN DROWNED

"A sad fatality occurred on the 30th ult. on the mountains between Cushendall and Ballycastle, and through which the post road runs. There is a place on this road called the 'Lough'. On ordinary occasions this is a small pool of water, surrounded by marshy ground. During the season of heavy rains, however, it assumes large proportions, being fed by several mountain streams, and often becomes a regular lake.

"The rains of the 28th and 29th ult. filled the 'Lough' to an enormous extent. So much so that the road, which runs right through the marshy ground at a height of ten feet, was completely submerged and in some parts there was four feet of water. It appears Colonel McNeill, son of the late celebrated preacher, Dean McNeill of Liverpool, and nephew of Captain Daniel McNeill JP, of Cushendun House, had been staying with his uncle in Cushendun for the past few days.

"He left Cushendun House on the 30th ult. at one o'clock pm to drive to Ballycastle to catch the 3pm train. Captain McNeill's coachman drove him in a covered two-horse brougham. On reaching the 'Lough' the coachman hesitated to go through the water, as the horses were very high-spirited, but at last determined to make the effort. A surface-man named McKendry watched the passage, and says that when in the middle of the waters the horses took fright, and suddenly reared, turned half round, and made a plunge. Their four feet got over a small ditch, and the impetus carried the carriage clean over into the lake. The coachman jumped off into the water, but was only able to swim a few strokes 'till he sank.

"Colonel McNeill, on the contrary, was a splendid swimmer. He jumped out of the carriage and at once made to swim the road. The horses and carriage were between him and the road. The horses were making fearful plunges. The Colonel made a detour to avoid being struck. McKendry rushed up to his waist in the water, and held out a short stick to him. Colonel McNeill was on the point of grasping it, when he sank and never rose.

# SAD ACCIDENT NEAR BALLYCASTLE.

## A CARRIAGE SUBMERGED.

## TWO MEN DROWNED.

A sad fatality occurred on the 30th ult. on the mountains between Cushendall and Ballycastle, and through which the post road runs. There is a place

"In the meantime, the horses also had ceased to struggle, and in fact disappeared with the carriage underneath the waters. The horses and carriage were pulled out about two o'clock on the 1st inst. A party was busy at work searching for the bodies, and in the afternoon the body of Colonel McNeill was found. It was discovered at the spot where he disappeared. The slimy bottom eluded the search parties, who had procured boats from coastguards at Cushendun and the fishermen at the quay Ballycastle.

"The coachman's remains were got about an hour afterwards. One arm was in and the other out of his coat. He evidently had endeavoured to throw it off before he was flung into the water. The remains of Colonel McNeill were taken to Ballycastle by the police, those of the coachman to his residence in Cushendun. Both await an inquest, which will be held today."

A day later, the *News-Letter* reported on the findings of the inquest. The story heading was -

THE ACCIDENT AT
BALLYCASTLE.

"An inquest was held yesterday on the remains of Colonel McNeill, one of the victims of the sad fatalities at the Lough, near Ballycastle, on the 30th ult. Dr Camac, Coroner for North Antrim, presided. Sergeant Doohan represented the Crown. James Duncan McNeill, son of deceased, was examined and identified the remains as those of his father, who was a colonel in the Army.

"Dr John Ewing deposed he had made an examination of the body, and that death resulted from drowning. The body bore no marks of violence. Patrick McHenry stated that he was the surface-man on the road at the Lough. On the 1st inst, the Lough was greatly flooded, the road being submerged fully 4 feet. About 1.30pm the tourist car came in sight, and after some hesitation the driver put the horses through the water. Witness afterwards saw Captain McNeill's coach come in sight, and stopped to see how it would come through.

"Witness knew the horses were very spirited. On coming to the water the coachman hesitated for a time, and at last urged the animals forward. When they reached the bridge, which was the shallowest part the horses were quiet, but in getting down the little incline from the bridge the water was up to the horses stomachs, and they got nervous and plunged. The coachman coaxed them, and at last struck the off horse, which at once reared in fright.

"Suddenly both horses rose in the air, and abruptly turned and made a plunge sideways, and carried machine and occupants into the water. The coachman gave a wild scream, and the Colonel at once struck out. The plunging horses being between him and the road, he swam across the lake. Witness ran along the side and encouraged him all he could.

"The Colonel spoke to witness and asked him to help. When near the shore he sank and never rose. When the horses were down they never rose, as the pole of the carriage kept their heads down. The coachman made only a few strokes and sank. The Coroner proceeded to address the jury, and referred in feeling terms the loss of deceased.

"The jury returned the following verdict - "That the deceased at BALLYVERMACHT LOUGH, in the Parish of Culfeghtrim, on 30th September, 1898, came to his death accidentally by drowning as the result of the carriage in which he was driving going into the Lough."

They added the following rider:- 'And we would wish to add that the notice of the County Surveyor be directed at once to the dangerous and unprotected state of the fences on the road and the proper drainage of the Lough to prevent flooding.'

"It should be added that the affair has caused great commotion in the district and universal sympathies are felt for the relatives of the deceased, who was a member of a very popular and leading family in Antrim. On the same evening an inquest was held on the body of David McNeill, coachman, at his residence at Cushendun by Dr Camac.

"Sergeant McNally (Knocknacarry) was present on behalf of the Constabulary, and examined Patrick McHenry, whose evidence was similar to that given above. A verdict of accidental drowning was returned."

Here are McGavock's eight verses of the . . .

# CAREY LOUGH DISASTER

Today we think of Cushendun
Its lonesome hills and Glens
Where every honest heart does mourn
A true and manly friend
With sorrow we look on Carey mount
Where its cruel waters lie
Where our good friend met a sad end
No time to say goodbye.

It was in the year of '98
On the 30th of September
When the sad news spread through the Glens
We always shall remember
At two o'clock in the afternoon
Of that unlucky day
One we esteemed so highly
In Carey waters lay.

He left the grove of Cushendun
Driving two in hand
And he was master of the art
The lines he could command
He was advised not to go that way
But friendship seemed in vain
Being urged by an Englishman
Who thought to catch a train.

He glided by those gloomy hills
With a light and manly heart
It was beneath his lofty views
To act a coward's part.
It was a wild adventure
I have heard some people say
With those black waters flowing high
Across the king's highway.

His horses baulked when in the ford
And would not heed his call
Regardless of whip or lines
Went o'er the water wall
He had a chance his life to save
Though danger all around
But he was faithful to his trust
And with his team went down.

Once he raised above the surf
And struck out for the shore
But seemed entangled in the lines
Went down to rise no more
Two bodies now enveloped were
In that watery main
And the Englishman we understand
Never caught his train.

Now the peaceful vale of Cushendun
Wears a sad look today
He is spoken of with due respect
As you pass along the way
For he still was a favourite
And always shared our joys
He was called by all who knew him
A man among the boys.

And some we know will miss him
Among those he left behind
For he was a faithful husband
And father true and kind
They have our truest sympathy
Their loss we deeply mourn
May they always be provided for
In the grove of Cushendun.

# MAN of LETTERS

ALEXANDER McGavock was a natural wordsmith, and perhaps this gift is something he passed on to his daughter Minnie. His wife Lizzie was also noted for writing stories. He was pretty much a self-educated man, and at one stage of his life in the U.S.A. was invited to become a schoolteacher.

Minnie noted: "His cousins recognised the talent. The McGavock clan at Fox Lake tried to entice him to move to the blackboard." Fox Lake was a settlement founded in 1707. The area was settled by the French in the 1600's. It was a noted summer holiday spot for people from Chicago - keen on boating and fishing. Notorious Chicago gangster Al Capone often took a vacation there during the 1920's. Fox Lake's most distinguished citizen was Alexander Joseph McGavick, the R.C. Bishop of LaCrosse.

"One of the two priests in that family wanted my father to come and teach in his parish, but he refused," added Minnie. "These people all visited his aunt Elizabeth, during his sojourn there. A couple who also visited included a man, a native of Loughguile, who had taught in Culraney school in Cushleake, and was married to a McCaughan from Glenshesk. This man joined the Fenians, and had to emigrate.

"His wife's sister was a Mrs McKinley, who owned a public house in Culraney. The ruins are at the bottom of the hill before you reach the Church coming from Cushendun. Her daughter was Teresa McKinley, whose daughter was a nurse in Ballycastle some years ago. My father came home from America a few times, and each time he went to Culraney to visit the McKinley's, and to bring them word of their relations in America."

Minnie moves on to tell of her parents setting up home, and the day a visiting American clergyman, who was also her cousin, arrived unexpectedly at Dunurgan. Her flowing narrative holds distinct colour: "One day when I was young, it was before the First World War and we were all - mother, father, and children, working the harvest in the big holm which is half-way down Dunurgan loanin. Father James McGavock, accompanied by his cousin Watt from Loughguile, with whom he was staying, came down the lane to the field to visit my father.

"My mother and father went up with them to the house, which was not very tidy, I'm sure, for the unexpected visit of an American priest. They travelled from Loughguile in a horse and trap, and then went to visit our parish priest, Fr Skeffington. I remember on Fr Skeffington's next visit to our house my mother saying to him that she was 'in a stew' on the day of that Rev McGavock's visit.

"My father worked very hard on the farm, until a year or so before he died, on the 19th of March, 1940, the feast of St Joseph to whom he had special devotion. He was very strong, and prided himself on being ambidextrous, and could use each hand equally when playing ball in a ball alley. He also told us that he played caman (hurling) in his youth, with sticks made from tree branches - and a ball made of wood, which was 'turned' by Susanna McIlheran's father, who was a wheelwright in Straid.

"A wheelwright made and mended spinning wheels which were a 'must' in every house in the Glens for spinning lint to make sheets, and wool to make blankets, trousers and jerseys. The McKeegan's of Tromra Brae were weavers, and my father told me that he brought spun woollen yarn to them to have blankets made, and a man up there taught him how to weave creels from sally rods. That was how he knew how to make a wicker cradle for me when a baby, and it served the other three children as they came along. He would also make little 'carrier bags' of rushes for us to gather fruochs up the braes, and bring home to eat.

"After being so long in America, my father spoke with a Yankee accent. Indeed, while the neighbouring children all called their parents 'daddy and mammy' much to our humiliation we had to call ours, 'papa and mamma', after the American fashion. My father also said 'noo' for new, and when my young brother Alex was a child he imitated him. A new suit, bought for our yearly visit on the jaunting car to Carey, he called 'my noo Carey suit.'

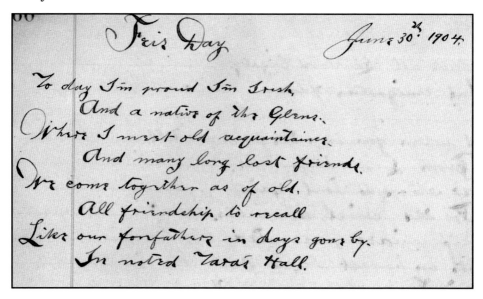

"The only kind of curse words my father used were 'Beats Hell'. He'd say: 'Beats Hell, you couldn't get that right', and he also used 'son-of-a-bitch', just like Harry S. Truman in 'Plain Speaking'. Bill O'Mullan, as a boy, worked for us in Dunurgan. My father called him 'The Youth', a nickname that stuck to Bill over the years - and Bill retaliated by calling my father 'Beats Hell'- and the name stuck."

When Alex McGavock settled into married life as a small farmer in the Glens he didn't put his pen to the sword. On September 24, 1911, he made a personal allowance for the occasional hitch in grammar. Rightly, he declares the story-telling is the important issue, and wrote: "When a farmer puts his plough aside for a short time to shoulder the pen, he is expected to make many mistakes in the line of grammar and spelling. However, it has always been my belief that such mistakes should not prevent learned people from understanding the ideas of the writer, and it is my belief also that a person without ideas should never lift a pen."

Glendun Hurling Team.

All his friends of the nine Glens
Come from far away
To increase the fame of the hurling game
On the second day
Twas whispered round by the sports of the town
Though early was their claim
That the Hero's Shield stood on the field
For the Glendun Hurling Team

He always found time to record his observations, compelling compositions that included milestone and rare microscopic records of the sinking of the *Titanic*, the first Feis na nGleann Day of June 1904, and a Glendun (Cushendun) hurling team winning the Feis title for the 1905 Shield of Heroes. Here is a verse from the prolific poet's recall of the first *FEIS DAY*. Beside the fluent and flowery handwriting is the date - June 30, 1904 - six months after Minnie was born:

### FEIS DAY

> *Competitors all with right good will*
> *To their superiors yield*
> *Both in the industrial section*
> *And on the athletic field*
> *And may they proudly hold*
> *The badge their merit sends*
> *And wear it long in memory*
> *Of the Feis of Antrim Glens.*

Dignitaries present at the inaugural Feis, on June 30, 1904, included Sir Horace Plunkett (founder of the agricultural co-operative movement), Eoin MacNeill, Francis Joseph Bigger and Miss Evelyn Gleeson of Dublin. Those who subscribed and supported the great occasion, one that focussed on cross-class and cross-community, included Lord Cushendun (Ronald MacNeill), Sir Daniel Dixon, Dr Douglas Hyde (later the first President of Ireland), Mr Francis Turnley, Sir Hugh Smiley and Lord Macnaughton. The Feis Committee was represented by Roger Casement, Miss M.E. Dobbs, Miss Ada MacNeill, Miss Barbara MacDonnell, Miss Rose Young, Miss Johnstone and Francis Joseph Bigger.

McGavock's praise of *The Glendun Hurling Team* was written on June 27, 1905, and is of special historic value to the Parish of Cushendun.

### THE GLENDUN HURLING TEAM

*All Feis friends of the nine Glens*
*Come from far away*
*To increase the fame of the hurling game*
*On the second day*
*'Twas whispered round by the sports of the town*
*Though early was their claim*
*That the Heroes' Shield stood on the field*
*For the Glendun Hurling Team*

*How that great throng did move along*
*When 'twas made known to all*
*That the boys so bold the ball did roll*
*Just at the sportsman's call*
*The betting lords did change their odds*
*Quite early in the game*
*And every man put two to one*
*On the Glendun Hurling Team.*

*Though untrained they stood, they always could*
*Play like the boys of old*
*They had in mind to work the line*
*With three points to the goal*
*And that great crowd did shout aloud*
*Their friendship still the same*
*As the ball did roll from point to goal*
*For the Glendun Hurling Team.*

*'Twas Glendun style all the while*
*To respect their opponents' skill*
*Who for to seize that courteous prize*
*Fought with puck and pull*
*But that sad fate which caused defeat*
*They were outclassed in the game*
*And that day on field went the Heroe's Shield*
*To the Glendun Hurling Team.*

*Now sportsmanlike they've won their stake*
*And the same will still defend*
*But will not neglect to show respect*
*When they meet the beaten men*
*By the Glendun rose that buds and blows*
*None can dispute their claim*
*And the nine Glens wide will look with pride*
*On the Glendun Hurling Team.*

It is interesting to note the Cushendun hurling side is listed as Glendun by A.J. McGavock. The team contested the opening two finals. Eminent Glens of Antrim historian and Cushendun Emmets' G.A.C. President, Malachy McSparran tracked down the beginnings of the 'Shield of Heroes' competition through the late Dan McCarry of Carey Faughs: "Dan vividly remembered the first Feis nanGleann of 1904, when Carey beat Glenarm in the semi-final while Cushendun defeated Glenariffe. In the final, Carey beat Cushendun, and during the game Dan claimed he suffered a broken nose from a clash with Maurice Finlay. A year later, Cushendun made amends by winning the prestigious title."

# CHANGING WORLD

WRITING in 1984, Minnie reflected on the transformation from olden times to the present. Unashamedly insular in her love of the golden Glens she remarked: "Such a change has taken place in those eighty years since I was born and since my young days working on the family farm. Modern mechanisation brings the milk every morning, left on my doorstep, coal once a week - on a Friday, and on that same day the bin men call to collect my rubbish, while the baker and the butcher call in the afternoon.

"Whereas, when I was young we had to work off and on during the summer. We had to cut and save turf for the fire, to milk the cows and produce milk. Obviously the cows needed a lot of attention if they were to produce milk at all. Each day griddlefuls of large farls of soda bread had to be baked on an open turf fire. Flour from the 10-stone bag in the corner and the buttermilk from the plunge churn were used in the breadmaking. Hens produced eggs, and a young rooster or an old hen would be killed each week to be boiled in a pot hung from a crane over the turf for the Sunday dinner. Fowl could only be boiled, as there was no means of roasting. Water for the tea would be boiled in a heavy metal kettle, and this water was carried in a can from a Spring Well some distance away.

"Tea was considered a great luxury. I once heard a story of a visitor complaining that she was fed every day on 'tea & eggs' and 'eggs & tea' - and the neighbour replied: 'You're very lucky to have such a diet for I have to sell the eggs to buy the tea.' Porridge was the main food both for breakfast and supper. It was made from oatmeal, which often had some 'seeds' in it. The meal was ground at the mill from oats brought by the farmer. He had to bring some turf in the cart along with the bag of corn so that it could be dried and roasted before grinding. Potatoes and corn were the main crops. Some turnips and cabbage for the animals were also grown.

"Harvesting the oats in September brought the whole family into the field. The youngest child could 'powl' - hold a pole or strong rod against the face of the sward - while the father mowed rhythmically with a scythe. Behind him came an older child making straps, while the older ones lifted the mown corn stalk into sheaves. The mother would come at mid-day with a can of tea, and a basketful of buttered bread - and remain in the field until tea time, when she would have to think about getting in the cows to the byre for milking. About half-an-acre would be harvested and stooked in one day. I remember my father praising my lifting and leaving a few stray stalks on the ground. He said: 'Take your time, and do it well - for no one will ask how long it took you to do the job.'

"Four to six cows were about the number kept on these small farms. Milking by hand and the buttermaking took a lot of time. The fresh milk was strained into shallow crockery pans placed on the wide cement floor of the milkhouse to cool. A cloth curtain was always drawn across the milkhouse window, for light had a deteriorating effect on milk, and would spoil the taste of the butter. Next day, the cream was skimmed from the top of the pan, and put in a crock to sour. The skim milk was given to the pigs and calves.

"After a few days the sour cream was poured into a well-scalded plunge churn, and a half day was occupied by two or more members of the family taking turns to churn the cream into butter by means of a churn staff - a circular piece of wood with big holes on it was attached to a long wooden handle or shaft. A Glenaan man, named Dan McAlister, could make the 'heads' for churnstaffs. Because he was a carpenter he was called 'Dan Chip'. When the churned cream formed into big yellow molecules it was ready to be lifted out into a wooden butter tub and slapped well to extract all the buttermilk. Salt was added and then water was poured over it to ensure that every last trace of buttermilk was removed. It was then beaten into blocks of about a pound each by wooden clappers, and put in the cupboard for future use.

"If there was more butter than was needed by the family the extra amount was put into a wooden butt. Week after week more butter would be added until the butt was full when a wooden lid would be placed on it - and it would be taken to Stevenson's and the weighbridge at Cushendall Market House. After being weighed it was usually bought by a merchant, who brought it to Glasgow, to be sold to shipping merchants for the crews of tramp ships."

# THE GREAT WAR

THE HORRENDOUS happenings of World War One, and the massive loss of lives, brought understandable sadness to all parts of the globe, including the Glens of Antrim.

Minnie, at Primary School when the War started, had some chilling recall of that traumatic time. She wrote: "I was about ten-and-a-half years of age when World War One broke out in 1914. John Redmond came North from Dublin to campaign for young men to join the Forces, and fight for Britain, thinking that the Home Rule Bill, which had been placed on the Statute Book, would be granted should Britain should win the War."

John Edward Redmond, born in Kilrane, County Wexford, on September 1, 1856, was a Barrister, an MP in the House of Commons of the UK and Ireland, and an Irish Nationalist politician. He led the Irish Parliamentary Party from 1900 to 1918. In 1914, he secured Irish Home Rule, under an Act that allowed an interim form of self-government to Ireland. Unfortunately for Redmond, regarded a moderate and conciliatory politician who died aged 61 on March 6, 1918, in London, the implementation of the Act was suspended because of the outbreak of World War One. His brother, Major Willie Redmond, an MP in East Clare, died at the 'Front' during June 17 - at the start of the Battle of Messines in Flanders.

Minnie stated: "John Redmond's orations apparently had young men spellbound when he addressed recruiting meetings all over the country, and after one in Cushendall, in the Glens of Antrim Hotel, three young men responded to his eloquence by joining. Pat McAlister, a brother of Arthur and Dan, Denis McCollam, a brother of 'Johnnie Joe', and another whose name I forget, joined - but none returned."

The information handed down to Minnie is partially correct. With the help of Cushendall schoolteacher and part-time historian Tommy Campbell, husband of Joan McAlister who is a relative of Pat McAlister, I traced some of the young men who left the Glens during that dreadful period.

Tommy Campbell explained: "Patrick McAlister was 42 when he died in 1917, not a young man, unlike most who went away, when he joined the 7th Enniskillen Fusiliers in 1915. He died in February 1917, and was buried at Kemel Chateau Cemetery, just inside the Belgian border with France. The 7th was involved in the Battle of Somme, the Battle of Luges, and also moved to Messines.

"Denis McCollam, of Johnny Joe's, was born in 1897, but was not in the Forces, He was a merchant seaman who was murdered on board his ship near Marseilles. Denis was shot on November 6, 1920. Apparently he was taking home a gift of diamonds or the suchlike, and had them under his pillow in his bunk."

John Blaney of Mullarts, Cushendun, and a direct relative of Denis McCollam, confirmed: "Denis McCollam was buried in Glenariffe Graveyard, alongside his brother John - my grandfather, who was born in 1884 and died aged 66 in 1949. Denis joined the Merchant Navy. He was murdered on board his boat. It was said he had some valuables in his bunk, under his pillow. He got up to tackle the thief, and the assailant shot him."

Tommy Campbell added: "The third person Minnie couldn't remember was likely to be Arthur McCarry. In 1915, others to join up from the Glens included Michael O'Connell, Pat Crawley and Pat McAuley. I believe five men joined the 7th Irish Brigade, in response to Redmond's plea. They signed on at Glenville. Inside the Church of Ireland in Cushendall there is a memorial tribute to locals such as two Humphrey brothers, Denis and John from Layd, one of whom was in Canada and joined the Ontario Brigade. He died in France.

"One of the Humphrey men was buried close to Kemel Chateau. Alan Morrow of Ballyeamon died in the south Atlantic. He was the son of a former Rector. He was a Major, a Master of Languages, and died in Mesopotamia. The Protestants joined the Royal Irish Rifles earlier, and fought side by side with their Catholic neighbours from the Glens during the Battle of Messines."

The plaque inside the Church of Ireland reads. . .

*To the glory of God and undying memory of the following connected with this Parish who gave their lives in the Great War 1914-18*

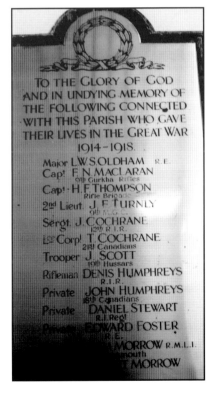

*Maj L.W.S. Oldham RE; Capt Francis Nairne MacLaran 9th Gurka Rifles killed in action in Mesopotamia (modern day Iraq) on 15th April 1916; Capt H.F. Thompson Rifle Brigade; 2nd Lt J.F. Turnly 9th MGC; Sgt J. Cochrane 12th RIR; Lt Corp T. Cochrane 21st Canadian; Trooper J. Scott 19th Hussars; Rifleman Denis Humphries RIR; Private John Humphries 18th Canadian; Private Daniel Stevens RIR; Private Edward Foster RE; Private Adam Morrow RMLI HMS Monmouth; Gunner Robert Morrow*

*RFA. Two headstones in the adjacent C.O.I. Graveyard reveal - Pvt D. Stewart. R Irish Reg. Aged 31.16th Feb 1916, and Asst Engineer RNR E.S. Manning. HMS Clementina 20th Sept 1915.*

The Great War claimed many other lives of young men from the Glens. One particular tragedy was that of sea Captain James McKeegan of Falmacrilly, Glenaan, drowned on December 25, 1914, off Scarborough where his ship, the S.S. *Gem* sunk after hitting a German mine. It appears he returned to his sinking ship to try and retrieve personal valuables. Also to perish in that incident was the ship's cook, James McNaughton of Glenaan.

The 464 ton SS *Gem* was a coaster built in 1887 in Glasgow. It was steaming to Tyneside from Mostyn with a cargo of 460 tons of salt cake. The ship broke in two after striking a mine, and sank. The Captain and nine of the crew perished, including some from Glenaan, Carnlough and Glenarm. The first mate and one ordinary seaman survived. The Germans bombarded from gunships along the east coast of England. While two German battlecruisers bombarded Scarborough, their light cruiser - *Kolberg* - laid what proved to be the densest minefield ever known in the history of naval warfare. During that awfulness at and off Scarborough 19 people were killed and 80 injured. Several small ships - coasters, merchant boats - were sunk.

Minnie's recollection of this particular painful passage in the uneasy history of Ireland is a mini-milestone, and a signpost of how times and opinions changed so rapidly. She said: "We were very pro-British then, and in school the senior girls knitted pulse-warmers for the troops, and we all sang marching jingles like *'Tipperary'*. Another one was -

> *Belgium put the Kibosh on the Kaiser.*
> *Russia took a stick and made him sore.*
> *On his throne he hurts to sit*
> *And when John Bull starts to hit*
> *He will never sit upon it any more.*

She added: "I don't remember any tightening of the belts, for we in the Glens were self-sufficient. We had our own eggs, milk and butter, and also corn for oatmeal. Perhaps flour was a bit hard to obtain. Tobacco was definitely scarce during World War One, as I remember pipesmokers smoking tea leaves! And, I recall clogs being worn by farmers and children, so perhaps leather was scarce. As we (the McGavock's) had no radio in Dunurgan then, the only information of the War came via *The Irish Weekly* newspaper from Belfast."

# FOR THE RECORD

AMERICAN interest in the past inevitably surfaces from time to time, with people searching for their Irish roots. On March 7, 1988, Minnie replied to a letter she received from a distant American cousin, Elizabeth Glos Larkin, who was attempting to trace her McGavock ancestors.

Mrs Larkin, whose address was 246, Forest Avenue, Elmhurst, Illinois. 60126, tracked down Minnie following her contact with Mrs McIlgorm of Larne. Minnie wrote: "Mrs McIlgorm was a sister of Pat 'Valdy' McCambridge. Their aunt ran away to America with my uncle Hugh. I informed Mrs Larkin of all the history I was aware of relating to the McGavock's, including the trading in Scottish ponies. I explained to her I was the eldest of five children of Alexander John McGavock and wife Lizzie. There was a boy who died at birth in August, 1910, and was named Alex.

"The second oldest was Patrick Hugh (Hugh), born on the 20th of February, 1906. I believe the spouses at his christening were Susanna McIlheran of Straid and Neil McGavock of Glenarm. Next was Elizabeth Catherine (Lizzie), born on the 2nd of June, 1908, and then Alexander John Jnr - born on the 11th of February, 1912. Hugh inherited the farm, and married Kathleen O'Boyle from Glenarm. After the Second World War, he bought a farm at Culcrow, Aghadowey, near Coleraine. My mother went with them, and lived until 1960."

Mary Gilligan, the eldest in the family of Hugh and Kathleen McGavock, holds vague recollection of her grandfather Alex J. He was 44 when he married a 32-year-old Lizzie McCambridge. He died aged 81, leaving Lizzie a widow for twenty years.

"Believe it or not I was able to read before I was three years of age, long before I went to the Primary School at Knocknacarry," said Mary Gilligan, "It was all down to the old man. I was merely three years old when he died, but before that happened he taught me how to read. He sat me on his knee and showed me how to read newspapers, the *Irish News* and *Irish Weekly*. From that, I never stopped reading, and still love to read."

She held close affection for her grandmother Lizzie. They were together for Mary's first eight years of living at Dunurgan, then at Aghadowey, and finally, for a period, at Hughenden Avenue, Belfast. "My grandmother was a great woman. She maintained a terrific work ethic," added Mary, "It was speculated she met her husband at Maggie Gore's house near Ballypatrick Forest in Carey. He was looking for a wife, I was told. Perhaps they met before he came back from America for a last time, but we know she would not return there with him. I held the feeling he was a bit of a daydreamer, always keen on writing poetry.

"I don't believe Granny McGavock ever had a holiday. She considered going to stay for a short spell with her daughters, Minnie and Lizzie, as her holidays. She lived through many hardships. I recall all she ate in the mornings, around 10am, was a slice of buttered bread and a mug of tea. Then she ate the tea leaves, and that habit went back to the frugal days when living was really difficult. That was why she ate the tea leaves that were lying at the bottom of the mug where the leaves mixed with melted sugar there. She maintained this habit right through her life. Of course, this started long before teabags became the common thing.

"Later in the day she had her dinner, but not a full one as we know it. Her main meal, also a carry-over from olden times, was made up of spuds (potatoes), butter, salt and buttermilk. I also remember granny making nettle soup. For a time, she stayed on her own in the old McGavock home at Dunurgan. I lived with my parents across the road, in what was once Hyndman's house."

There was an even closer bond between Mary and her granny after the McGavock family moved to farm at Culcrow: "When we went to live in Aghadowey she picked me to sleep in her bed. Her room was off the kitchen, very warm. She also had her own fireplace in that room. My younger sisters, Ann and Frances were not at all pleased when I was the one to be selected, as granny always had sweets stashed below her pillow and often gave me sixpence."

Also moving with the McGavock entourage from Dunurgan to Aghadowey were Josie Mackin and Willie McIlwaine, a master tractor man. "Working for us was Josie (Mackin), who was taken, I believe, from the Good Shepherd orphanage on the Ormeau Road, Belfast," added Mary, "She later joined the Montague family, owners of the Montague Hotel at Portstewart, and worked in their home at Cromore House, outside Portstewart. Later Josie became Mrs O'Connor. My sister Frances stood for her daughter, also named Frances. Josie went to live at Scunthorpe. Willie McIlwaine from Cloughs, Cushendall, also worked for us. One of his sons became manager of the Brown Trout Inn at Coleraine."

Mary's brother Hughie, who left Dunurgan at two years of age, recalled his grandmother's unwavering devotion to an almost frugal work ethic: "I never knew my grandfather, but was fortunate to get to know how fine a woman my grandmother was. She was a very smart lady. However, she didn't believe in the new milking system my father installed after we went to Aghadowey. She never trusted the milking machines, insisting they didn't complete the job. She felt the old ways were the best, and would go around stripping the cows after milk time. One day we went into the byre to find she had been kicked by a heifer, and knocked out, cold. That didn't bother her. One of her great habits was to take a billhook and a bag, and go out along the ditches at roadside to cut what is the sweetest of grass. She believed this was the best way to feed calves."

Willie Blaney, a son of Lizzie (McGavock), remembered the ever resilient and resourceful Granny McGavock: "I was a very young boy when she stayed for a short spell in our house at The Bridge. I believe she moved on to rejoin my uncle Hugh, who was settling in at Aghadowey. She was an amazing lady. One thing that sticks out in my mind was after she drank a cup of tea, then made from loose leaves, she chewed the tea leaves. Another memory was being with her when looking out a bedroom window to watch an incident at the bottom of the road, where a horse belonging to the Gore family was killed in an accident."

Willie's aunt Minnie added: "My mother was over 90 years old when she died, on 28th March, 1960, in Belfast. Hugh sold out in Aghadowey, and went to live in Belfast. His family of ten is scattered. Two sons and three daughters went to Perth, Australia. Kathleen, their mother, went to Australia. My youngest brother was named after his father. Alex was born on the 11th of February, 1912, and died on August 2, 1979. He lived in Belfast for a time, where he was a barber. He came back to live at Knocknacarry, become a bus driver, and then moved to Larne, County Antrim.

"He married Lizzie Redmond of Ringsend, Dublin, who was born on the 5th of May 1915, and died in Larne on the 8th of December 1983. They had one child, Emily, who was born in Cushendun on March 21, 1948. Both Alex and Lizzie are buried in Larne Cemetery, at Craigyhill. Emily married Kevin McAfee, a house painter from Ballycastle, County Antrim. They lived at Larne for a number of years before settling at Glentaise Drive, Ballycastle. Their son is Stephen, born on August 30, 1971, and daughter Teresa was born on the 22nd of October 1973."

Emily held a vague recollection of her grandmother, Lizzie McGavock, during a visit to Culcrow: "I remember going to Aghadowey as a six year old, with my daddy and my aunt Lizzie (Blaney), and seeing my granny McGavock for a first time. I recall meeting this old woman who was wearing a black shawl. She was walking along the roadside, outside the house.

"My father never mentioned a lot about his days when growing up at Dunurgan. He was very young when he left home, because he didn't like the farming. He must have been trained to be a barber, because he worked as one in Divis Street, Belfast. Mammy and him lived there - over or beside the barber's shop. After the barbering he drove lorries, and then went to drive the UTA (Ulster Transport Authority) buses.

"He took early retirement from the time of the changes in the UTA, and took a job with the Water Board. My father was a very good swimmer. Ironically swimming, I feel, contributed to his death. He was swimming on holidays in County Wicklow with us, when he was stung by a jellyfish. Poison went through his system. He never recovered, and inside two years died at 68."

Despite the tragic circumstances of Alex McGavock's death, Emily holds a strong connection with the sea and sport. Her young grandaughter Megan Morrow is an Irish Outdoor Bowls international, while her grandfather was the chief pilot for boats in Dublin Harbour.

During a chat in her Ballycastle home, in late October, 2010, she said: "My mother's father was Captain James Redmond, head of the pilot boats for Dublin Port and Docks. I recall my grandfather, who had a direct link with Cushendun, taking me down to see the big liners coming in at

Dublin Port. Born at Arklow, County Wicklow, Captain James's wife was Elizabeth O'Drain from Cushendun. They lived at Ringsend, Dublin, and had three daughters and one son.

"Mary was the eldest, then my mother Lizzie, aunt Suzy, and uncle James, who was a very good soccer player in his young days with Ringsend United. Living in Cushendun were the brother and sister, Alex and Mary O'Drain. My mother came to Cushendun during summer holidays to stay with her aunt and uncle in The Square. My aunts, Mary and Susan also came up. Susan once played for Cushendun's camogie team.

"Because my mother's mother died very young, my aunt Mary took on a lot of the family responsibilities, including coming up from Dublin from time to time to look after Alex and Mary O'Drain. My father met my mother when she was staying on holiday in Cushendun. My uncle, James Redmond Jnr, also came up and when he was here on holidays he played hurling in Cushendun. He became a docker in Dublin Harbour, and also played football, soccer, to a high level in Dublin. One of the teams he played for was his local side, Ringsend United. Peter North's pub in Ringsend was a favourite place for James, opposite the chapel."

Emily and husband Kevin McAfee are understandably proud of Megan Morrow: "Absolutely," added Emily, "My granddaughter Megan, now aged 13 (last week), was 12 when she got her first international cap this summer, at the end of June (2010) when she made her Irish outdoor bowling team appearance. She is the youngest to do so, and also the first player from Ballycastle to play bowls for the international Irish team. The match was in England. She is a student at the Dominican College, Portstewart, and is one of three children of my daughter Teresa, who is married to Fred Morrow, and live just up the street from us. The other children are Jennifer (6) and John (5). Megan's father first took her to indoor bowls in Ballycastle when she was nine years of age. The interest took off from there."

*Minnie, second left, enjoying some frolics with schoolteacher friends at Portstewart.*

*The Immortals. Hugh McGavock helped Cushendun Emmets to a first Antrim Senior hurling title in 1931, beating Belfast O'Connell's in a replay. BACK (l to r)-Denis McKeegan, John Gore, Archie McSparran, Jim McBride, John 'Packer' McLaughlin, Harry Scally. MIDDLE-Hugh McGavock, Jim 'Chip' McAllister, James 'The Bear' McDonnell, Jim McHenry. FRONT-Neal Delargy, Paddy McQuaige, Dan McCormick (Capt), Alex McKay, Alex Delargy.*

*Kennedy's Row in old Knocknacarry.*

*Moyle Hospital's Nurse Hanratty sitting up front in the jaunting car during a holiday in Killarney, County Kerry. Back right is 'Auntie' Mary O'Hara, and second right is Miss Mary McKillop of Glendun, who was manageress of the King's Arms Hotel, Larne.*

*Minnie's husband-to-be Alex O'Hara (vertical striped jersey, right) with 1929 Cushendun hurling team colleagues.*

*Taking a tea break from cutting corn at Agolagh are Hugh Cunningham, Bill O'Hara, Mary Brogan, Alex O'Hara and Eddie Brogan.*

*Minnie's sister-in-law 'Auntie' Mary O'Hara and nursing colleague Miss Quinn of Derrylaughan, County Tyrone.*

*'Auntie' Mary O'Hara (back second left) during the official opening of Moyle Hospital, Larne.*

*North Antrim hurling team of 1937, before playing a South Antrim selection on Feis na nGleann day. BACK (l to r)-Hugh Osborne (Carey), Willie McNeill (Ballycastle), Arthur Gibson (Glenarm), Dan McDonnell (Cushendun), John Butler (Ballycastle), Bob Hunter (Carey), James Maguire (Ballycastle), and Team Manager John Kearns (Ballycastle). MIDDLE-Charlie Jolly (Carey), Alex Butler (Ballycastle), Dan McKillop (Glenariffe), Harry McKendry (Cushendun), Moore Dunlop (Ballycastle), Dan Gibson (Glenarm), Bob Graham (Glenariffe), Paddy McGarry (Loughguile). FRONT-North Antrim Secretary Seamus Clarke (Ballycastle), James McDonnell (Cushendun) and Hugh Mulholland (Loughguile).*

*John O'Hara, Alex's brother, sporting one of the first automobiles in the Glens.*

*Alex O'Hara, standing left, with sea-faring colleagues during a stop-off in Rio De Janeiro.*

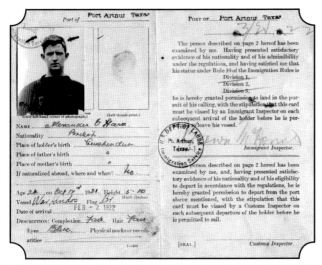

*Alex O'Hara at Port Arthur, Galveston, Texas, in 1922.*

*Teenager Alex O'Hara pictured in Glasgow in 1916, before embarking on a career at sea.*

*Mary 'Auntie' O'Hara with grandsons Denis and Alex at Cushendun strand in 1939.*

*Granny Catherine O'Hara with first godson, Peter Alexander.*

*Denis Lavelle of Cullyhanna with daughter Nan.*

*Mairead McLaughlin of Ballymena, a schoolteaching colleague of Minnie.*

*Minnie McGavock (centre) during a nature ramble with St Mary's Training College, Belfast, student colleagues. Right is Lecturer Miss Duff.*

*March 17, 1928, portrait of Minnie's student colleague Sadie McFadden.*

*Greta Magee, a student with Minnie at St Mary's Training College.*

*The McGavock clan pictured at Dunurgan in the 1920's - Hugh, Minnie, Mrs Lizzie McGavock Snr, Lizzie, Anna McArdle and Alex McGavock.*

Minnie's youngest brother Alex McGavock.

The iconic Rope seller at Lammas Fair.

The wedding day of Kathleen O'Boyle and Hugh McGavock.

Milltown, Cushendun, 1914. Taking a break from playing hurling with make-shift sticks are Brablagh and Milltown youngsters, supervised by Mrs John McKay (back row second right). BACK (l to r)-Denis McVeigh, Francis O'Grady (son of Rose McKillop), Alex McKay and Danny McKay. FRONT-Dan McDonnell, Mary McKay and James McDonnell.

1928 gathering of friends and neighbours at Dunurgan. Minnie is front right with her close pal Mary Jane Murray (front left). Back row features Maggie Murray, Denis McKay, Lizzie McGavock and Denis Black.

Anna McArdle, left, with Hugh McGavock, Lizzie McGavock and Mrs 'The Crane' O'Mullan.

*Minnie on the rocks with her school-teacher pals at Portstewart.*

*A teenage Catherine Brogan of Glasgow, who married Alex O'Hara, Minnie's father-in-law.*

*St Mary's Training College student teachers Miss O'Hare, Cissie McCollam (Cushendall) and Miss Hughes*

*Minnie, back left, joins nurses including 'Auntie' Mary O'Hara and Miss Quinn on a day at the seaside.*

*Minnie, second left, outside her boarding house at Portstewart.*

*Alex O'Hara, left, with Cushendun strongman Jim O'Neill. Out front is Alex's cousin, Eddie Brogan.*

*Student teachers perched on a bridge across a stream at St Mary's Training College in 1927.*

*Minnie McGavock (second left) seen taking a bite from Mairead McLaughlin's apple, while Anna McArdle, left, looks on. Others in the group of student teachers at St Mary's Training College are Annie Bannon, Sadie McFadden, Winnie Hickson, Genevieve Galley and Kathleen Boylan.*

*Mrs Kay Walsh (nee Mann), right, wearing driving gloves before starting as entry No 40 in the Ulster Rally of Easter 1935. She is pictured with her three siblings. The Mann sisters from Bangor were noted for racing cars in Pre-World War Two events, and became known as 'The Four Graces'. Pictured with Mrs Walsh are Mrs Eileen Cooper-Chadwick, Miss Stephanie Mann and Mrs Gwen Wills.*

# BLOOD LINES

MINNIE marched through the family card, relating when she married Alex O'Hara on the 30th of December, 1935. She was aged 31. She mentioned her sister Lizzie's marriage, to John Blaney of Cushendall, in August, 1930, when aged 22. Hugh married Kathleen O'Boyle in the Spring of 1937, and Alex to Lizzie Redmond during Easter, 1938. Her parents were buried at Cregagh, Cushendun.

Alex O'Hara, Minnie's husband, died on the 11th of September, 1955. Her brother Hugh died on the 15th of September, 1970, and was buried at Killavalla, Cregagh. Minnie's youngest son, Hugh O'Hara, died in Dublin on the 10th of December, 1983, and her eldest son, Alexander, died at Mornington, County Meath, on May 28, 2004.

Incidentally, when Hugh McGavock gave up farming in Aghadowey he became a publican in Belfast, living at Hughenden Avenue off the Cavehill Road. His first pub was the 'White Star' on the lower end of the Newtownards Road, and later the 'Roughfort Inn' at Mallusk, County Antrim. In his younger days he was a member of the Cushendun Emmets' 1931 Antrim Senior Hurling Championship winning team. Wife Kathleen, a music teacher born in 1908 in Glenarm, was a sister of Glenarm publican, milk retailer, and old-time hurler Charlie O'Boyle. Kathleen emigrated to Perth, Australia, in 1972, and died there on February 26, 1981.

The eldest child of Patrick Hugh McGavock and Kathleen O'Boyle is Mary Josephine, born March 31, 1938, at Ballycastle. She married pharmacist Barney Gilligan of Garrison, County Fermanagh, who was born on December 7, 1937. They set up home in Lisnaskea, County Fermanagh, and named their bungalow 'Glendun'. Next was Anne, born on May 25, 1939, also in Ballycastle. Married to Belfast-born Reggie Taggart, she emigrated to Perth, Australia, in 1965. Sadly she died, after illness, in Perth Hospital, on Saturday, April 16, 2011. Frances, born July 2, 1940, also emigrated to Perth, Australia, in 1972, and married Australian Bill Matheson. In 2010, they lived 200 miles outside Perth at Wongan Hills, Western Australia.

The eldest boy, Alexander John, was born on October 22, 1941, in Ballycastle, and quickly became a prominent athlete. He was Ulster Junior cross-country title-holder at 15, and the Irish Junior Mile champion of 1959. Once 'mine host' of Daly's Bar on Belfast's Falls Road, he ran for Ireland against Olympic champion Herb Elliott in 1960 at Ibrox Stadium, finishing fourth. In amateur boxing, he represented Ulster when winning the 1966 provincial Senior Light-heavyweight title, shortly after plundering the Irish Junior Championship. Alex also followed his father's footsteps in hurling, when he assisted Cushendun Emmets in the winning of the 1963 Antrim Junior title.

Next in the pecking order, and also to become an occasional pugilist, was Hugh Charles, born on January 18, 1943. He was an Irish Universities' boxing champion, a Midland ABA finalist, and lost the 1965 Ulster Senior Welterweight final to Billy Turkington of Doagh, in the Ulster Hall. For a number of years he ran a successful tarmacadam firm in the greater Belfast area. Henry Oliver, better known as Harry, was born on July 3, 1944. Also active in amateur boxing, he won a County Antrim Light-heavyweight title in 1962, became a noted M.C. for amateur and professional fight shows, was once a publican in Belfast, ran a landscape gardening business, and was prominent as a disc jockey known for his 'Big Bopper' show.

Noel, a motor mechanic and one-time Stock Car racer, was born on December 26, 1945. He emigrated to Perth, Australia, in 1979. Also in Perth is Patrick, an electrician to trade and born on September 4, 1946. He left Belfast in 1965. Kathleen, the baby of the family born on January 20, 1953, also moved 'Down Under', to Perth, in 1972. She qualified as a nurse. Married with two children, her husband Kevin Conoulty died of a heart attack.

Elizabeth 'Lizzie' McGavock was born on June 2, 1908. She died on May 10, 2002. She married John Joe Blaney, one of north Antrim's prominent sheep farmers, who was born in Cushendall in 1898. He died, aged 78, in 1977. They had ten children. The first child is Dr Sean, born on June 21, 1931. He began his medical career in Dalriada Hospital, Ballycastle, County Antrim, then moved to Germany, and later to England. He resides in Chester with wife Jennifer (nee Smith, Lancashire). They have a family of four.

Second in line is Sea Captain Alex, born on March 14, 1933. Tragically, he died following illness on February 22, 1982. He was married to Ballycastle, County Antrim, schoolteacher Margaret Black. Next is Eileen, who entered the nursing profession. She is followed by Mary, who married Pat McCarry, an extensive sheep and cattle farmer from Murlough, County Antrim. Fifth member is Elizabeth. Born on September 26, 1939, she emigrated to Sydney, Australia, and married Benito Perusicha. Bridget resides in the family home at The Bridge, along with the second youngest, Jacinta. Nearby are Willie and Brendan, the latter a prominent sheep and cattle farmer at Cloughs, Cushendall. He married Kathleen McCormick of Glenshesk. Willie, born on May 5, 1943, married Christine Graham of Ballymena. He spent some years in Australia, as a sheep farmer, before returning to the Glens to combine sheep farming and auctioneering with an Estate and Insurance Agency. Tragically, the youngest member of the family, Ruth died aged 51 in 2005.

Branches of Minnie's bloodline spread far and wide, and mainly because of a high head count of females in two family units, one originating in Loughguile and the other from Cushendall. She remembered the strong link to the Kinney family: "The Kinney connection began with my great-grandmother Mary, on my mother's side. She was a member of a family of many sisters and one brother. They were Kinney's of Loughguile. Mary was the eldest, and she married Billy Butler of the Watertop, Carey - a long, long way from Loughguile. Billy Butler lived to be 100. There was one son, John, who remained a bachelor.

"Mary Butler's name is on the Butler headstone, just round the corner on the Ballyvoy side of Carey Church. Her sister Katie was married to Patrick Butler of Doon, near Fairhead, and her sister Grace was married to his nephew, Paddy McBride of Cross. Paddy's sister Mary was married to Hugh McCarry of Murlough. Therefore, Mona McCarry's granny was Butler of Doon. Billy Butler and Mary Kinney's daughter Mary married Patrick McCambridge, and became my grandparents - as their daughter Lizzie was my mother.

"The Butler's of Doon had two daughters, Mary and Anne. Mary didn't marry. Anne married James Darragh, and lived at Drumavoley, a short distance up the Glenshesk Road from Ballycastle. Their son James lives nearby. Son Charlie lived in Drumavoley, while John inherited Doon.

"Unfortunately, John was badly maimed by handling an object which he found on the shore of the Lough at Fairhead, and which he thought was a reel from a fishing rod. Instead, it was an unexploded bomb which had been left by soldiers practising exercises during the First World War. Annie Darragh, a sister, married Joe Devlin, a cousin of John Blaney and an uncle of Rita Sheehan. I remember Fr Fred McSorley telling me they, the McSorley family of Belfast, used to spend their summer holidays at Drumavoley. I visited there in my time in Ballycastle. I also visited in 'The Magistrate's' before Rita was born. It was Mary Butler of Doon who brought me to Ballycastle to board with Mrs McAuley - nee Annie McCaughan, as they were second cousins, as was also my mother Lizzie McCambridge through 'the Kinney connection'.

"At that time, I knew all the McBride's, McCaughan's, the O'Loan's of Glenravel. The O'Loan link used to come and stay during summer holidays. I remember one of them, newly married to a Master Carey, being there, and Fr McBride making fun of her as she was knitting socks for her new husband. I saw the lovely, and funny, snapshot that Fr McCaughan took and developed. One was of his aunt Elizabeth (Mrs McBride) seen stooped when feeding hens.

"The Glenshesk folk, when they came to Ballycastle, stabled their horses in the yard behind Mrs McAuley's house. The entrance was between Thompson's, the saddlers, and the watchmaker's shop. My uncle Daniel and Aunt Catherine McCambridge lived at Black Park, and I often stayed there at week-ends. I remember going with Aunt Catherine along the tops of farms, and climbing fences to visit her Aunt Katie in Doon - and then up a bit to visit her Aunt Grace and Paddy McBride in Cross. Such very, very friendly people! That was only a few years after their son, Alex was murdered in Belfast during the Pogrom. I remember seeing a stone circle, like Stonehenge on a smaller scale, in a field on the clifftop not far from uncle Daniel's farm."

"The McBride's of Cross had several children, including John, the father of John McBride the veterinarian. There was Dan who bought Watertop Farm when old John Butler died. His son was only four months old at the time. He is now a veterinarian in Antrim. Kate McBride married Alex Scally - Harry's parents, while Grace McBride married Jim McAlister of Glenavy - James McAlister's parents. Maggie McBride married Hugh Boyle of Dunloy, and died in the Spring of 1982. It was their grandson, John who was shot dead by soldiers in a graveyard near his home. He was only 16 years of age.

"Back to the marriage of Billy Butler and Mary Kinney. They probably met at the famous Lammas Fair in Ballycastle. In olden times, the Lammas Fair lasted for a whole week. Mary's other sisters were married - one to McAlister of Corkey, whose daughter Nancy was married to Joe McCollam of Cushendall. She was known in Cushendall as 'Nancy Joe', and was the grandmother of Mrs Annie Blaney of Mullarts.

"Another sister was married in Aghadowey to a man named Dempsey. Their son was a famous doctor in Belfast, who became known as Sir Alexander Dempsey. A daughter married a man named O'Hara, and their daughter, Miss O'Hara the Brown Trout when Hugh McGavock and my mother went to live in Culcrow in the mid-1940's. Miss O'Hara let my mother know she was a second cousin of hers. Her nephew, Bill O'Hara of Bangor inherited the 'Brown Trout' pub from his aunt. At the time of this writing the manager of the Brown Trout was John McIlwaine, son of Willie, who went from Glenballyeamon and Cushendun to Aghadowey with Hugh McGavock.

"Another Kinney girl married a McCaughan of Glenshesk, and one of their daughters married Randal McDonnell of Glenariffe. One of the McDonnell daughters became a Mrs O'Loan of Glenravel, and another became Mrs Dowling of Ballymena. Their daughter Annie became Mrs Molloy, whose son Father Archie Molloy used to teach in Garron Tower. Descendants of the Kinney sister's brother live in Glenariffe and Layd, as well as some in Loughguile. Johnny Kinney of Foriff, Glenariffe, would have been a son of that only Kinney son in Loughguile. Pat Kinney of Layd was a second cousin of my mother."

The fascinating ramble down the years, including all the complicated connections, continued with recall of another sisters' act: "My grandmother, Anne McAlister, had four sisters and one brother. Her sister Rachel was married to Donal McKay, a shoemaker in Dunurgan. Rose was married to Delargy of Glenariffe, who was the grandmother of Mrs Pat Harvey - Rose Anne Coogan. Kate was married to McBride of Cushendun - Randal McDonnell's great grandmother.

"The fourth sister was married to a McAlister of Omerban, Loughguile. I used to meet a son of theirs in Mrs McIlwee's in Ballymena, and he looked like a twin brother of my father! Their only brother was Donal, and because he was the youngest of the family, and I suppose a bit spoiled, they called him 'Donal Dear' - and his descendants are called 'The Dears' to this day. He married Charlotte Black of Carey. They had three sons, I think - some resembling my father, and one sister named Mary Dear."

The family tree spread over almost every Glen in north Antrim, and always proved vital and a source of great pride as far as Minnie was concerned. In later life she was regularly taken along with her great friend and neighbour Mary McCormick to funerals of relatives. There were more 'tree trails'. Something triggered Minnie's mind on the Sunday night of August 28, 1983, into an almost frenetic need to explain another passage of who was who, and what was what, in the lengthy family lineage. It proved fascinating stuff.

"Mrs Josephine Macaulay (Mrs Archie 'David') was a daughter of Frank McCaughan of Glenshesk. Frank's wife was McBride, nicknamed 'the Vigs', and a brother of hers was the Parish Priest of Glenavy, whose housekeeper was an old Knocknacarry lady named Annie McLarnon - an aunt of Mary MacCormick. Another McBride sister was married to Frank McCaughan's brother John, nicknamed 'The Magistrate'. John had one son, James, who married a Mary Devlin from Armoy, whose mother was Blaney - and an aunt of John Joe Blaney at The Bridge, Cushendall. James's son Frank is a chemist in Ballycastle. He is married to a girl from Galway, who taught in Ballycastle's Cross & Passion Convent. Rita, a daughter of James, married Tim Sheehan.

"As well as James, the 'Magistrate' had two daughters. Annie, who was married to a Willie McAuley of Glenshesk and occupied the shop in which her nephew, Frank (McCaughan) has the chemist's shop. When I was at school with Master Cullen I stopped in the 'Mug Shop', as it was then called. Mary Clarke of Murlough also boarded there. Mrs McAuley was a second cousin of my mother, through the Kinney connection. She also had a sister Lizzie, who had a shop in Glasgow, but wasn't married. Mrs McAuley had no family. A baby girl tragically died in infancy. The husband, Willie lived on the farm with his brothers and sisters, and came only occasionally to Ballycastle to stay.

"Frank and John McCaughan were each married to a McBride girl, and their sister Elizabeth was married to Patrick McBride. Frank's son John became a priest, and Elizabeth's son John also became a priest. I remember Father McBride was a curate in St Mary's Parish in Belfast when I was in St Mary's Training College (1926-'28), and going to confession there. He asked me where I was from, and when I said: 'Cushendun'. He said: 'I'm from Ballycastle. My name is McBride.' I said: 'You are from Glenshesk'. I knew he was a cousin of Mrs McAuley, with whom I had stayed, and many a time met his mother 'Aunt Elizabeth' as she was called."

Closer to home, the lesson on relatives continued, with Minnie in full flow: "Charlie Murphy (Archie's father) of Cushleake and his brother Johnny of Cushendall were second cousins of my mother. Therefore, Charlie and Johnny would be third cousins of mine. The McKay's of Corrymeela were also second cousins of my mother, so that would mean Robert in Agolagh would be a third cousin of mine. The McHenry's of Cushleake were also related. Father Noel's father was my third cousin. Bob McLister is my second cousin, as his mother, Kate McCambridge was a first cousin of my mother. The other McLister's are third cousins of mine, for their mother was a niece of Kate's.

"The McCambridge's of Iscard originated in Glendun, and through that connection my mother was a second cousin of Charles McCormick (Mary's father), and also of Annie and Alex McKay's mother, whose granny was McCormick of Glendun - and was married to McKillop of Tyban. Annie and Alex McKay's father was also a second cousin, all through the McCambridge connection. I have a note that Big Sarah McKay of Agolagh sent me with one of the girls who was delivering *Far East* magazines from the School, asking me who was my great grandfather's wife. I was able to write back and tell her that she was Esme McCaughan from Drumaridley, near Ballycastle. I learned that from my aunt Catherine McCambridge of the Black Park, above Ballyvoy.

"My friend and neighbour Mary MacCormack recently remarked that in a McCambridge family in Glendun there were seven sisters. One was married to a McCormick, therefore Pat 'Casey's' and Charles MacCormack's (Mary's father) granny was a McCambridge. They were second cousins of my mother. One married Archie O'Hara (or O'Harra) of Knocknacarry. She was an aunt of Mickey McCormick of Ballyteerim, an uncle of Pat 'Casey'. His daughter Cassie told this to Mary MacCormack, who said Archie and wife 'went away' - but I don't know where.

"A Robert McCambridge from Glendun, probably a brother of the seven sisters, married a widow Hamilton, who owned the Iscard farm in Torr, where Bob McLister now lives. Bob's mother Kate McCambridge inherited her grandfather's farm and married Randal McLister. Kate and my mother were full cousins, her father being Robert. Their mother was Esme McCaughan, on the road where the Casement's live - near the Glenshesk Road. I think their grandmother would be the widow Hamilton, and that Archie O'Hara's wife would be a full cousin of my grandfather, Paddy 'Robbie'.

"To sum up some of the family connections, my mother was a second cousin of Charlie Murphy, 'Big' Sarah McKay, Pat 'Casey' McCormick, Charles MacCormack of Knocknacarry, Pat McCormick of Bonavor, the McKillop's of Tyban - whose sister was Annie McKay's mother. Annie's father - John McKay, was also a second cousin, as was Jim 'Bach' McMullan's mother - nee Rose McKay, and Charlie (Duncan) McKendry."

# THE EARLY YEARS

INFORMATION from an Ordnance Survey report on the Parish of Layd for 1830-1840 provides interesting information. Detail was collected by Mr James Boyle in 1935.

He claimed: "It is probable that the earliest improvements in this Parish took place in the 16th century, when the Scots migrated in considerable numbers to this part of the country, and from the prevalence of a few surnames - McAuley, McAlister, McKillop, Harvey, McDonnell and Hamilton, it is probable that the original occupiers of the soil were dispossessed by them.

"The people of the Parish of Layd are almost a distinct race from their more southern parishes, both in their features, manners and accent. They are remarkable for their honesty - theft being wholly unknown. They are apparently simple and primitive in their habits, though they are said to be very canny. Many neither speak nor understand English language, and all speak the Irish. Those who do speak English speak it well, and free from provincialisms or any peculiar accent.

"A strong desire exists to make a decent appearance on Sundays and at Funerals, Fairs etc; and the young women may be seen walking until a short distance of the town with their shoes and stockings in their hands when they put them on and wash and dress themselves. Many of the men have but little agricultural labour to perform during the winter, but spend that season knitting stockings. Cushendall has eight Fairs in the year. They are generally well supplied with cattle, and ponies are imported in great numbers from the Highlands of Scotland. They are brought in boats and landed in Cushendun."

Writing on May 14, 1991, Minnie digs deep into the past: "The ordinary people of this Parish (Cushendun) were mostly of Scottish descent, with names like McKay and McNeill. The landlords were mostly of English descent, with names like Cuppage and Turnley. The residents of Cushendun village made a living by fishing and gathering seaweed to dry and burn into kelp. They also helped in the running of the Ferry, which plied between Cushendun and Scotland once or twice weekly. Some young men preferred the sea, and some emigrated to America.

"In olden times, most of the farm houses were thatched cottages with clay floors. Sows with young pigs were kept in a corner of the kitchen, and hens were fed on the floors. There was usually a half-door which was kept closed to keep out dogs and other animals. Subsistence farming was then the order of the day in the Glens. In the small holms and the fields between the River Dun and The Line potatoes and oats were grown. Many farmers hadn't even a horse, and worked with spades to make rigs for the potatoes. What crops were grown were turned into food for the family and the animals. The corn was ground at the local water-powered mill into a meal for porridge - or gruel for the calves."

She takes time out to expand on the cornmills in the area, and said: "There were cornmills at Carey's - near Tyban, at Glenaan, and in Cushendall. The corn was brought by cart, and heated before being crushed into oatmeal. This was used for porridge, and also cattle feed. Part of the grain was made into 'smash', to be spread on the pulped turnips for the milk cows, and maybe one or two fatteners. The only bags of 'bought stuff' to come to the farm would be bran, pollard and yellow meal of which a very little was required to mix with the mashed potatoes for the hens. Of course, the 10-stone bag of flour for the soda farls was a must.

"In Dunurgan there was a row of small, slated houses built in 1828. This date is still in a tablet above the door of one of these houses. At this time Cuppage was dividing his land into small farms of about 10 acres, running from the River Dun right up to the mountain. There was a small plot of good land at the river, named a holm, then the fields of less good land between the river and 'The Line'. The fields of rough grazing went right up to the mountain, where the fence was called 'The Head Ditch'. Outside the Head Ditch was a stretch of heather for community grazing. The strips of farms were called rundales. The men who built the fences, at a loaning paled off along their right, lived in these slated houses.

"The fence at the Head Ditch would be made of stones, probably mixed with scraws . . . pieces of grass or heather-covered earth. In the English dictionary a ditch is a trench. We would call a trench as 'shough'. There were 'shoughs' left by potato 'rigs' and these could be seen in the field below the Head Ditch, close to the mountain. These are called 'famine ridges' where the potatoes were rotten and were not dug. They are now overgrown with heather and whins.

"Half-way between 'The Line' and the mountain is the ruin of a small house which was called a 'boolie' house. Here some members of the family would live during the summer, herding and milking the cows. Above Cushendall is the sharp-pointed hill Tieve Bulliagh, which means the hill of 'boolie' houses. An opening into a field was usually filled by a 'slap' which was a branch of hawthorn or other bushes.

"Looking inland from Cushendun one gazed on the beautiful Dunurgan braes rising majestically between Glendun and Glenaan. The land on the brae face is divided into those long strips, reaching from the valley to almost the rounded top of this broad hill. There was a delightful view of the valley, looking down towards the sea from the top fields. In Summer, the cows would graze up there until late in the evening. I remember going up there to bring them down for milking, and being so touched by the stunning view that I knelt up there and said my night prayers."

Minnie adored Glendun, one of the fabled Glens of Antrim: "Glendun," she insisted, "is most certainly the most beautiful of the nine Glens. The River Dun flows down this steep glen, with the road along its side. The hills are covered with all kinds of vegetation. The best time to explore it is in the Autumn, when the red berries are on the rowan trees. Holly abounds too, and many beautiful birches. The road joins the Glenaan and Loughguile road at Orra. In my young days a trip on a jaunting car 'up Glendun and down Glenaan' was a must in the Autumn. The first stop on the road would be under the wonderful Glendun Viaduct.

"The River Dun, of course, is famous for its salmon and trout, and fishing for them was an ideal way of passing the time on a Sunday while the young boys would be playing hurling. Young women also spent many pleasant hours chatting and telling yarns while making patchwork quilts. These gatherings were called 'quiltings'. Often, after a hard day's work, the farmer would go for a ceilidh to a neighbouring house. Here he would meet others, and discuss sport and farming news. The teenagers would enjoy a barn dance, where a fiddler was always available. He would play in a corner, while they danced the quadrilles."

The Griffiths Valuation of 1848-1864, the first survey of property ownership in Ireland during that period, listed a Hugh McGavock at 'Gortaghragan', and a John McGavock at Parkmore. The Dunurgan area, spelt Dunourgan in the list, included Charles and George Murray, while down the road a piece lived Alexander and John O'Hara at Knocknacarry, and Donald and John O'Hara at Agolagh. In a list of householders in the area of Knocknacarry and Dunurgan (this time the spelling is Dunorgan) in June of 1881 include farmer Hugh McGavock (aged 50), wife Anne (40) and family Anne (21), Catherine (19), Hugh (17) and Mary (15). Eldest son, Alexander John went to America five years earlier. The neighbouring Murray family was listed as farmer Margaret (48) and seven offspring - Hugh (12), Mary (10), Patrick (8), Neal (6), James (4), Sally (3) and Elizabeth (1). In Knocknacarry there was Alex O'Hara (60) his wife Sarah (57) and two sons - Daniel (34) and Alexander (18).

The Ireland official ministry list of 1911 had Dunurgan again named as Dunourgan, and also had the McGavock family registered wrongly as 'McGarock' - and headed by Alex (50), wife Elizabeth (40), daughters Mary A. (7) and Catherine E. (2), and son Patrick H. (5) - with servant Jeanie E. Ross (16). The McKay's had James (73), Mary (76) and Alex (50). There too was the Church of Ireland family of John Hyndman (71), his brother Robert (68) and sister Sarah (77). Also listed was the Murray family of Hugh (40), wife Mary J. (30), daughter Mary J. (7), Margaret A. (4) and Hugh (3). Annie O'Connor (66) was also registered.

# OVER THE MOUNTAIN

ONCE upon a time a large portion of the Glendun and Cushendun area belonged to the Parish of Culfeitrim, Carey. Minnie took a wry look at her perceived differing attitudes of the inhabitants on either side of Carey Mountain. I suspect there was a touch of tongue-in-cheek in the article she named 'Over the Mountain', which was an oft-used expression of the Carey people in the 1920's.

Minnie's penned opinion was: "The 'Over the Mountain' remark denoted, I felt, the remoteness of the Glens from their own prosperous parish. The two districts were only a few miles distant, but the inhabitants were as`races apart'. The thrifty Carey people were up before the dawn, and as each farmer had a 'sarvant man' - who in winter was handed a hurricane lamp at 6 o'clock to go out to pulp turnips and feed a byreful of fatteners before breakfast, his farm was a hive of industry. After breakfast, the horses were yoked, and - hail, rain or shine the ploughing, reaping, or potato digging progressed until dusk.

"A very different pattern prevailed 'over the mountain'. The small farmer, who had no need of a 'sarvant', rose with the sun, took his breakfast, went outside to have a long look at the sky and predict the weather. If the weather looked favourable he'd head for the field to do a leisurely day's work. No job was so urgent as to prevent his having a chat with a neighbour over a hedge, or to join in conversation with a passer-by, if his small field adjoined a road. At potato-digging time, he would often be seen leaning on his spade and chatting with his gatherer - usually his wife, as she sat on the up-turned 'washer' having a break in the October sunshine.

"In Carey, there was no time for sitting. Horses yoked to a digger were steadily turning up rows of potatoes for six to eight nimble-fingered gatherers who worked in pairs. Each pair raced with full 'washers' to the pits, competing not for a prize but to be able to boast the most potatoes gathered at the end of the day. The Glens folk went 'over the mountain' in reverse, to the Lammas Fair and the Hiring Fairs in Ballycastle. They travelled on horseback, in jaunting cars, and in carts to make merry, and often called on the way home to 'treat' their friends in Ballyvoy or Ballypatrick.

"Turf cutting began in May, and it was such a family affair that usually the schools closed for a fortnight, as men, women and children 'took to the mountain'. What a hub-bub there was in the morning - father going out to catch the mare in the high field, mother packing the basket with eatables, the children feeding the hens and driving out the cows after milking. Maybe, by nearly noon the cart and its load of people, spades, forks and barrows, would set out on the long trek to the Lough or below. The occupants of the slow-moving cart enjoyed every minute of the journey, and waved to the tourists in the faster-moving char-a-bancs as they sped their way to the Giant's Causeway or the sea-side at Portrush. But no day at the sea could be so enjoyable as a day on the mountain at turf-cutting time.

"The mare was taken out of the cart, given some hay and tethered to the shaft for fear she would stray to a soft part and 'bog'. One member of the family got the much-coveted job of lighting a fire, usually from heather and left-over turf, going to the spring well at the Lough for water, and boiling it to make the tea. Father would have previously pared the bank, so now when he had 'hands' he'd start to cut. Some of the children would carefully wheel the wet sods on the flat turf barrow some distance back, where mother would fork them out in rows to dry in the sun.

"There was never any rush to work after the meal, and one could sit and drink in the beauty of the sea at Ballycastle, with Rathlin Island in the distance. Usually the man working the neighbouring bank would come over for a smoke and a bit of craic. No one objected to resuming work for an hour or so, until tea time when the same delightful respite was experienced. After a short spell, all the families on the mountain headed for home to take in the cows, milk them, and after supper, retire to bed for a well-earned rest.

"This turf-cutting and saving business continued on a similar pattern, off and on, throughout the summer. The sods, turf moss cut into blocks, were spread out, and when dried they had to be first castled, then footed, and then rickled. Before the corn harvest they were built in a big stack on the mountain, and later in the Autumn they were carted home to make a pleasant winter fire in the open hearth. The soothing sound of the heavily laden carts and the rhythmic sound of the mill wheel are now only nostalgic memories."

In Minnie's eyes, Dunurgan in the old days was the centre of the planet. That special charm remains. One 'converted' resident, Hugh 'Tom' McCormick was born in Glasgow in 1923, but became a 'native' of Dunurgan. He remembered Minnie with affection, especially when she came home for a few days from her schoolteaching duties.

He said: "During school breaks, such as Halloween, she would be home and always bringing Big Denis (McKillop) and me jotters and pencils. That was about 1932. There was one particular time when I didn't get a present from Minnie McGavock, nor apples. There used to be apple bushes down the back of McGavock's house.

"One produced eating apples and the other had apples for cooking. We were called over by Minnie. She asked if we were two good boys. Big Denis once clashed me, because I had been cursing. I got no apples. Big Denis did. He was older than me. The McKillop's lived then at Dunurgan, and in the house presently owned by Jim McPeake. People called Hyndman's lived there before that. Big Denis and Jim were born where the McPeake's live, while Dan McKillop was born where I am living now. Later they moved to live at the Big Bridge.

"I came here from Scotland, to go to school at Knocknacarry. You didn't start in school until you were seven in Glasgow. I stayed in Calisnaugh with my aunt, Caroline McCormick, before she became Mrs Charlie Graham. I had a sister, Mary Margaret, who was also born in Glasgow, but died young and was buried in Maryhill, Glasgow. My brother Paddy was born here. My mother ran a boarding house in Glasgow, along with her sister Mrs McKenty. It was mainly for deep-sea sailors. My father's name was Hugh. He was a sailor, and went deep sea with Alex O'Hara, later to be Minnie's husband. When I was 14, I moved the few hundred yards from Calisnaugh to live in Dunurgan. There was a Hostel there, owned by old Alex 'Beat's Hell' McGavock, and it was running for a number of years - especially during Second World War. In 1945, the McGavock's left Dunurgan, and I have a special reason for remembering the date."

Hugh, whose grandfather was Tom McCormick, hence the nickname of Tom, added: "On the 6th of March 1945, Hugh (McGavock) sold out. My mother bought the former Hostel, which is now our house. She paid Hugh McGavock £250. Everything was sold then, including the McGavock original house and the home farm to Peter McAuley of Glendun. Peter's son, John McAuley now lives there. Hugh McGavock lived then in what is now McPeake's. The old McGavock barn is still there. There was a byre and stables underneath the barn. There was another old barn up above the house. After school hours I used to help out on McGavock's farm, especially during lint-pulling time. Many schoolchildren gathered to help. It was great fun. I also remember Hugh McGavock with his milk run, and also old Mrs McGavock. She was a good hearted woman."

Incidentally, the McCormick family had to deal with a double family tragedy, both connected to seafaring. Hugh's father and younger brother Paddy were killed. Paddy 'Tom' drowned in Drogheda harbour on November 30, 1960. Apparently he slipped and fell into the water between his ship and the quay. Many families along the Antrim Coast had to endure such fatal setbacks when loved ones were lost through drowning or accident at sea. It was a hazarduous occupation. What made the Paddy 'Tom' tragedy all the more poignant was it was the second bodyblow to strike the same family. In March 10, 1937, Paddy's father Hugh, married to Mary Anne McAlister, died in horrific circumstance in Glasgow. He was painting down the side of a ship on the River Clyde when an incoming ship struck his vessel and crushed him. He was 49.

Dan McKillop of 'The Big Bridge', who was born in the house where Hugh McCormick now resides, said: "The death of Paddy Tom was reckoned one of the wildest tragedies to hit Cushendun, and one of the biggest funerals ever held at Craigagh. When news of the awful accident reached us I remember going down to Drogheda with my brother Jim. On the Sunday we went out to Trim, County Meath, to see John James McKay. He was a brother of Alex and Ellen Jane at the Mill, Dunurgan. John James was in America for a time, along with Jim O'Hara.

"When he returned from the United States he bought a big farm in County Meath. Old Mrs McKay gave us the address of John James, and to make sure we went and visted him. There was a Brogan farming out there also, near Trim. Indeed, I believe it was through advice given by Eddie Brogan he (John James) went there and purchased the farm. Jim O'Hara, who came home from America with John James, married Mary Sharkey and went to live in Rasharkin."

McKillop believed old Mrs Lizzie McGavock may have helped to deliver him, when he was born in what became a Hostel owned by the McGavock family: "I was born on December 13, 1926, and was reared in the house at Dunurgan where Hugh McCormick now lives, the former once owned by the McGavock's. I believe that old Mrs McGavock helped to deliver me at birth. That was the way it was in the country in those olden times.

"My father's name was Denis, and his father was also called Denis. My brothers, Denis and Jim and my sister Mary were born and lived for a time in what was known as Hyndman's house at Dunurgan. The Hyndman's were nailers. Robert Hyndman and his famly lived there before my family did. Then it was Alex McIlhatton, who was a shoemaker there, in one half of the house. The other half was occupied by 'The Crane' (Mrs McMullan). Some time after that the place was renovated and lived in by Hugh McGavock, and in more recent times by the McPeake family.

"Before we lived in the house that became the Hostel, a shoemaker was in it. I started school days in Glendun Primary at six years of age, walking with my sister Mary from Dunurgan. Minnie McGavock stood for my sister Mary at Baptism. I recall playing games of hurling during the lunch break at school, the ball was made out of wood and called 'Nigs' and the sticks were taken from a hedge.

"Shortly after that, in 1933, we moved up here, to live with my mother and father beside the Big Bridge. After we left Dunurgan I remember Hugh McGavock up at the door, probably completing the rent. The thatched house was taken up by the Youth Hostel Association, as was a house of Archie David's near Glenaan, and another one up near Glenville, Cushendall.

"The house where I was born was rented from Hugh McGavock. Mary Anne (McCormick) then operated it as a Hostel. She lived in the house on the other side of that entry. The holidaymakers were cyclists from all arts and parts, and especially Belfast people. I'd say it was a Hostel from around 1933, and right through the Second World War - and still a Hostel after McGavock sold it and left for Aghadowey. Hugh McCormick's mother kept it going as a Hostel after that. The barn outside the wee house was also used as a part of the Hostel until a house was built where the Hostel was."

Dan retained sketchy recall (in September 2010) of the McGavock family, adding: "I remember being told old Alex McGavock, as a young man, carved his name on the side of an arch at 'The Big Bridge'. I may have met him when helping to gather potatoes, but don't recall much else about him. As a very young boy I attended the wedding of Minnie's sister Lizzie to John Joe Blaney. The wedding was in McGavock's old house, where John McAuley now lives. I remember asking my mother when was the wedding due to start, because I thought it would be along the lines of a procession."

Another dignatory of Dunurgan, a major part of the history and folklore of the area, was the most remarkable person I 'grilled' in a search for any little nugget of background to the McGavock family history. She was the ever charming and impressively alert 96-year-old Tessie O'Neill. Born Tessie McIlhatton at 'The Windy Gap' in Skerry East, Newtowncrommelin, she retained high praise for old Mrs Lizzie McGavock.

During my interview of Friday, October 1, 2010, she said: "She was very hard working. She never stopped working. She was a great old woman. I recall meeting her on occasions, and after a quick conversation she'd say, 'Got to be moving on. There's work to be done, and I can't be wasting time.' I knew old Alex McGavock, a very clever person. He kept pretty much to himself, I felt. He was a quiet man. I knew Minnie well, and her brother Hugh, who was a good hurler. He also played the violin. I also remember Hugh's wife Kathleen. She was strict. Minnie's youngest brother Alex was a nice fella, easy going. Minnie's sister Lizzie and me were very great. She was a nice person."

Tessie once published a little gem of a book on the harsh life and times in the Glens of Antrim during the early 20th century. It is called *The Windy Gap. Memories of Skerry East,* where she was reared. She moved from Newtowncrommelin to Dunurgan at 14 years of age. "I came from a family of eleven children, six boys and five girls," she said, "I was born in 1914, and went to Omerbane Primary School, in the parish of Cloughmills. I think my father wanted to support the teachers there. We lived a similar distance for the school in Cargin. My brother Dan and I walked the three miles there and back every day, and walked barefoot during good summer weather.

"My grandmother was Mary Jane McAlister of Glendun and a relation of the 'Mors' at The Viaduct, and my mother was Mary Jane O'Hagan. My father Michael was a shoemaker, and my brother Alex was the one boy in the family to learn that trade. My sister Jean, who will be 103 in November, 2010, and me are the survivors. Jennie married John Duffin, also from Glenravel, in Glasgow. She came back to live in Glenariffe. They had one boy and one girl. The girl is dead. The boy, Pat often comes over from Scotland to Waterfoot during holiday times.

"I followed my brother Alex to Dunurgan. Alex, a shoemaker, lived in McGavock's old house where McPeake's now live. Alex set up the shoemaking when he was 19. He died aged 78. The Hyndman family used to live there before that. I never knew them. The McGavock's lived there some time after us. In 1940, I married here, in Dunurgan, to Ned O'Neill of Unsinagh, Glendun, and had six children - 4 girls and 2 boys. Dunurgan was a wee town all on its own, great neighbours, everyone helping each other when necessary.

"Sometimes after a day's work in the fields, maybe lint pulling, there would be a bit of a party. My brother Alex played the accordion by ear. Mickey was a fiddler. Who didn't know Mickey? He became very famous. My brother Dan was very clever. The teacher at Primary School said he knew more than she did. It was a shame he never had a chance of learning - an awful pity there was no way then of getting further education. He died aged 78."

Mickey McIlhatton was the most colourful and charismatic member of the family. He started out as a shepherd. In the 1920's he was imprisoned without trial on the prison ship *Argenta*. A fluent Irish speaker, the flamboyant Mickey, who became part of the butchery business in Waterfoot and was a fiddler in the Glenariffe Ceili Band, was best known for making the finest poteen in the land. However, this cottage industry of Mickey's, in the Newtowncrommelin-Skerry region, created constant brushes with the Excise Men. He was once locked up for a spell in Crumlin Road jail for his illegal antics. The larger-than-life McIlhatton died, aged 77, in June 1975.

# HIRING FAIRS

KEVIN Murray, the last survivor of a long line of the old-time Dunurgan family friend and neighbour of Minnie, retained many memories of a time that seemed full of a mixture of happiness and hardships. He provided a fascinating insight to the ghastly and cruel business of the old Hiring Fairs of the 19th century. Kevin, born on March 6, 1921, recalled his father was once involved in what was little more than a disguised form of slavery.

On Tuesday May 4, 2010, Kevin delved into his memory bank. "My father was six weeks at school, he claimed, because he was taken from school, and hired out. The reason for this I trace back to what happened my grandfather, Hugh Murray. He was a horse and cattle dealer. Some people here at Dunurgan were being evicted, and he went guarantor for them. Unfortunately, they couldn't pay it, and he was then almost evicted.

"He took ill, was taken to the Fever Hospital in Ballycastle, and he died there. He was married twice, the first to Carol Blaney, and then to Margaret McGee of Unsunagh. He already had six kids, but there is no trace of them now. They went to America, and lost touch. Poor Margaret was left with the family. The landlord, came and took the cattle away. They cleaned out the farm to get their money back, and she was left with the six kids.

"My father, also named Hugh Murray, who was born in 1868, said he was hired to a family in Glenshesk, and paid £5 for six month's work. He recalled having to be up at 5 o'clock in the morning, was given porridge, worked to 11 at night - more porridge, and then five hours sleep, at most." The process adopted at a Hiring Fair was akin to a scene from the film *Roots*, but with underage Caucasians involved.

Kevin added: "He was taken to Ballycastle to attend a Hiring Fair. He joined a lot of other young people. They were lined up at the top of the Tanyard Brae, just off the Diamond in Ballycastle. My father said the hirers felt your muscles, and looked at your teeth. It was slavery. He told us all about the procedures. He had two sessions there. Generally he didn't talk a lot about the old times, but it was tough going. They took that for granted in those days. You had to be tough to survive. He went to sea for a while. In 1901, he was missing for a spell, while my mother, Mary Jane, was the farmer when he was at sea. In 1953 and '55 my father and mother died.

"Mary Jane, my sister and the oldest of the family, died in January 1979. She was rushed to the hospital in Ballymena with a suspected stroke. There was snow on the ground. I came over from Glasgow for the funeral, and I recall heavy snowfalls as a plough was needed on the road down to Stranraer. Mary Jane, Minnie's great friend, was married to Pat 'Archie' McNeill. Another sister, Margaret Anne or Maggie Anne - or better known to us as Nan, went to America in 1928. I remember well the day she left. She was in London training to be a nurse, and then got a job as a Governess to a family in New York, looking after two kids.

"There was a Trust set up for the two children, with the wee boy worth half-a-million dollars and the girl worth $250,000. Her job was to take them to school, look after them, but the job lasted hardly a full year. Wall Street crashed in 1929. She lost her job, because the family she worked for lost everything, except their house and the Cadillac sitting outside. The family money was lost in the share market, wiped out. She moved out of New York, and got employment with a rancher. Her job again was to look after kids. She loved the life, and then married a Flanagan from Scotland. Nan died in America, up in Maine. She had three sons - Jim, Kevin and John."

Kevin also recalled close contact with the McGavock family. The Murray's at one time owned the property taken over by the McGavock's. "When the McGavock's came from Glenarm they took over that place my great, great grandfather George Murray had," he added. "He was the father of Charles Murray who, I understood, built our house in 1828. Maybe Cuppage, the landlord, gave the ground. They had this from the time the strips of farms were made. I remember hearing about Charles, who was a dealer too, having a boarder in from Donegal, a worker at the making of the 'Big Bridge' (The Viaduct).

"Moving on, I recall a story about Alex McGavock and Lizzie getting married. They walked down to the Chapel at Craigagh, got married and walked back. Getting the ceremony over was the main thing. There was no big 'do' then, because folk couldn't afford it, and in most cases it was back to work. I remember Lizzie well. I recall times when Harry McKendry and others were pulling flax for Hugh. She put up good feeds for us, and always walked through the floor of the kitchen while we were eating. At the same time she ate a spud, and talked away. My mother did the same thing in our house. I don't remember my mother sitting when the rest of us were eating. That was the way it was in those days."

Tales of yesteryear came easy for Kevin Murray. He recalled helping the McGavock's with potato picking, and listening open-mouthed to 'Beat's Hell' relating a hair-raising incident he was involved in while living in the United States. "I was gathering spuds for him and Hugh. Old Alex told us of Two-Gun Charlie, a bank robber in Chicago where Alex stopped him by putting a spoon in his back. Two-Gun Charlie was in the process of robbing a bank when Alex came into the building. McGavock had a spoon in his pocket, stuck it into the back of the robber, and said - 'Drop your guns'.

"Alex happened to arrive right at the time of the robbery, and Two Gun Charlie surrendered, thinking there was a real gun in his back. Charlie gave in, and Alex McGavock was highly commended for his action by the Chicago police and City Hall officials. Alex also got a good write-up in the Chicago papers. That day in the potato field he also he recited one of his poems for me. It was *The Homespun Jersey From Home.* The early memories stay with you. It is a funny thing, certain happenings stick out, like that day in McGavock's potato field." The bank stick-up drama may well have provided the inspiration some years later for a hilarious scene in a silent comedy film.

Alex 'Beat's Hell' McGavock had his 'jersey' poem, one that again appears heavily tinged with homesickness, printed in Chicago. Composed on May 14, 1894, while residing at 1327, Park Avenue, Chicago, he announced the special work and with reason for writing it. Heading the signed introduction was *A Present from Home,* and he stated: 'The poem herein contained is composed with respect to a present from home, in the form of a handknit jacket. It is a most peculiar gift, and I doubt very much if there is another young man in these United States in possession of one of its kind, because it was father who shore the sheep for it, mother spun the yarn, and it was constructed by a most worthy little sister, and the great respect which I hold for it is fully explained in the following verses."

### A PRESENT FROM HOME

*Now the dress that I'm in I do love I declare*
*Though my costume may cause you to smile*
*And the reason this same I wish for to wear*
*Is because it's the old country style*
*It's a jersey that came from far o'er the sea*
*A gift that I'm proud for to own*
*And the reason why it's so dear to me*
*Is because it's a present from home.*

Chorus
   *It came from a sheep that a kind father shore*
   *And a yarn that a fond mother spun*
   *as a token of respect it has to be worn*
   *It's a present they sent to their son.*

*It was carefully knitted by a sister so kind*
*It's a proof of her hand-working skill*
*She sent it to me to bear her in mind*
*A respect I intend to pay still*
*It's in memory of times we spent together*
*Long before that I thought for to roam*
*It shows the respect she still holds for her brother*
*In sending this present from home.*
*(CHORUS)*

*When at night she sat knitting how she felt contented*
*Gazing out at the stars that shone from above*
*Her girlish ability is well represented*

*Every stitch in the garment is embroidered in love*
*How her young heart did wander while plying her needles*
*Wondering why her brother was so given to roam*
*Of her present surrounding then she was heedless*
*Just thinking of sending a present from home.*
*(CHORUS)*

*I never was ashamed to wear it*
*For my life I don't see why I should*
*And the reason that I so become it*
*Is because I ain't built like a dude*
*Sure their heart and their brain is all notion*
*They never could fill it alone*
*For it's made of the old country fashion*
*And sent as a present from home.*
*(CHORUS)*

*Now the boys all do wish they had a sister like mine*
*It's talked of by all of my friends*
*And the reason they say they think it so fine*
*Is because that it came from the Glens*
*But my respect is of a different nature*
*It's the love of a brother alone*
*It's because it was knit by a sister*
*And sent as a present from home.*

Kevin Murray enjoyed relating a brief glimpse of other incidents he experienced as a youngster: "Like every child at Knocknacarry School I brought a couple of turf to the school for the fire. Master Doherty had a big blackboard. He used to scratch his nail on the board. It was a bit sickening. I didn't like that noise he made. Michael Doherty, a son of the Master, sat beside me at School. John was a teacher in Armagh. His sister Mary died in Donegal. Michael died in Birmingham. He was with the Henry Cable company in Belfast - and moved with the firm to Birmingham. It was draughtsmanship. Michael was marvellous with his hands."

Other incidents flooded back, as Kevin added: "I remember the most famous day at the Rigs very well. I was standing there in the old hurling field, in 1931, when the Emmets beat O'Connell's for the Antrim Hurling Championship. My Da took me to the game, and we stood on the Glendun side of the field. Archie McSparran, who played the hollow on the pitch, was very speedy. I also recall a fuss about a disputed goal, with James 'The Barrister' McSparran involved. I think the O'Connell's players argued a ball was going wide, but suddenly went into the net, apparently off the 'Barrister', who was not a player. He was standing beside a goal post. He was a great Emmets' man long before he became a Glasgow Celtic man."

Kevin then listed two key elements of his young life - a period when motorbicycles 'plagued' the Parish of Cushendun, and the glorious balmy days of the summer holiday when the valley was awash with Scottish visitors. "There was an explosion of motorbikes at a time. I remember six or more bikes in the Dunurgan district alone, including one my brother Hugh had. Fr Blacker used to give lectures on the subject, giving off about having women on the pillion seat. Hugh McGavock had a wee Excelsior, with a sidecar attached.

"I recall standing behind my father and my sister Nan in our doorway as McGavock went round and round what was his circuit - up by the Big Bridge, on to McFetridge's, and round again to Dunurgan - but with nobody in the sidecar. He was trying to get Nan into the sidecar. My father said - no way will she get into that box. What chance would she have if you hit the ditch.

"McGavock eventually lured a cousin of mine and near-neighbour, Alex 'Jazzus' McKay, into the sidecar - and next time round he skidded down the sand at Dunurgan, near a holly bush, and crashed the machine. McKay got the worst of it - not a hair left on his arms - all skinned. Hugh was also hurt, bleeding . . . but he ran away. However, he left a blood trail back to his own house. I don't remember the police doing anything about it. The first priority for both was to run, if able, and get away from the scene of the crime as quickly as possible. That must have been in or around 1928."

The Excelsior motorbicycle started in production at Coventry in 1874. After the First World War the Plant moved to Birmingham. The small bike became famous in 1935, when the company produced the Manxman model, available with a 246cc or 349cc engine. In the Cushendun area, heavier and faster bikes became the rage, mostly the B.S.A model.

Kevin Murray said: "Hugh's brother, Alex McGavock had a really good big motorbike, so too had Francis McKillop, both B.S.A's. In the late 1920's and early 30's they got the habit of riding motorbikes. O'Hara's had a petrol pump at Knocknacarry, and there was also one, I'm sure, then at McFetridge's of Castlegreen."

Summertimes were idyllic, particularly during the years leading up to the Second World War, according to Kevin. "I remember when there might have been up to sixty young people around the area during evenings in the summer time. People came here on holiday, mostly from Scotland, after the Glasgow Fair ended in July. They included the Woods, Betty Strain, a few of the Windsor's. It drew the boys from all quarters. Betty Strain of Glasgow married Michael Doherty.

"They kept coming back for maybe 15 years for holidays before the War. The McMullan's came - Bunty, Margaret and Kathleen. They all congregated at The Turn and Dunurgan. Dan McIlhatton and Tessie kept a very open house. As someone remarked, Dunurgan was the centre of the universe then. It was hiving. Alex McIlhatton played a wee melodeon. There was a Hostel there. They came from all over."

Dunurgan, of course, attracted all sorts, including an eccentric watchmaker named Fred Muir. "Muir was a War Veteran," added Kevin, "Nobody knows where he came from or where he went to. I think he may have ended up in Coleraine. He just came out of nowhere, and after a short spell living at Castlegreen, he settled for a time in Dunurgan. He was mending one watch out of another, because of the War he couldn't get parts for clocks. We once had a seven-day clock that my father wound up once a week. After Fred 'fixed it' it finished up a three-day clock, because he cut away half of the main spring to repair another clock.

"Alex 'The Sod' O'Mullan served his time with Fred at Dunurgan. We heard this story about a conversation between Alex and Mary 'Heery' McAuley, who had this famous clock. The mother had it, and so forth. It was handed down, a family heirloom. Mary took it to Alex for repair. 'Do you think you can fix it?' enquired Mary. 'I don't know," replied Alex. 'It is very precious, very important to the family," added Mary. 'I hope you can fix the clock. Can you?' Alex thinks for a moment or three, and slowly replied: "I'll tell you one thing - if I can't fix it, I'll leave it that nobody else will fix it."

# A SAD TURN

OCTOBER 2010 witnessed the once famous 'Turn' pub reduced to rubble. The sentimental demise of the old meeting place on the corner of the main Cushendun-Cushendall highway and the side road leading a few yards away to Dunurgan conjured up many memories.

The public house, part of the McKay family enterprise, featured a small cosy bar so popular once with not only the locals of the area but travellers from far and wide. My first abiding memory of the hostelry was during a balmy August early afternoon sitting in a public transport bus hired to take the hurlers of Cushendun Emmets to a Sunday game in Glenarm. Someone decided, during the stop to pick up some hurlers, to nip into 'The Turn' for a quick liquid refreshment, and also bring some spiritual additives onto the bus.

Unfortunately for the hurlers, passing RUC officers nabbed some of our thirsty boys, caught napping during closing time when it was illegal to be in a public house purchasing and drinking alcoholic beverages. It seemed a bit of a parochial scandal at the time, an episode in niggardly inflexibility, but really much ado about very little in today's terms.

The last survivor of that McKay family generation took me down memory lane. On November 1, 2010, Hugh McKay generously provided not only a feeling for the old pub but also folk in Dunurgan and the parish of Cushendun. Born in 1923, he recalled many great nights in 'The Turn' pub, where his older brother Patrick was generally mine host. Also there was another brother, Arthur. Hugh didn't bother much with the running of the public house, but stayed closer to farming business. His retired schoolteacher sister Kathleen lived in the home house, and eventually did not wish to have a pub facility continue.

Hugh said: "I can recall hearing of the O'Hara's delivering the crates of beer and whiskey from the railway at Parkmore to 'The Turn'. The pub was there long before I was born, and was shut down a long time ago. I didn't drink alcohol. Neither did my bother Arthur nor sister Kathleen. Patrick took an occasional drink. I remember many great characters arriving into the pub. Hugh McGavock came over from nearby, a few yards down the road from Dunurgan, from time to time.

"I remember old Alex and Mrs McGavock. Both were hard workers. She was a very strong woman, always feeding things. She worked steady, always busy. That was the way of things in those days, to survive. The lint pulling and saving it was very hard work. The job pulled the arms out of you, when having to pull it out of the ground, lying it up, and putting it into the dub. Hugh McGavock had a row of dubs. He made new dubs, I think five in all. He gave one to Hugh Murray. I think Hugh Murray made a dub in front of his own house, in a garden. This one was not used. We had one dub, up near our sheep dip. The Martin family also had one dub. That was it for the Dunurgan area.

"The lint was kept in the dub from eight to ten nights, and then you brought in one of the older wiser people to test it, if it was ready. The tester would catch the lint by the end, and if it broke in the middle it was ready. You let it go, the dub water. It was released into the nearby River Dun. Once the dub was cleared you went to the river to pick out dead fish. The lint water killed them, because the fish couldn't breathe, no air. We ate them. It did us no harm.

"Once the lint was saved it went to the nearby mill. I was at Sharkey's Mill to see the scutching in progress. The one thing I really remember was all the dust in the air. You could pick up a fever if you didn't watch out. When the lint saving was at McGavock's everybody helped. When it was at our dub everybody came along and helped. There was a good spirit then. That was a great thing in those days, but all that fizzled out when the lint business petered out at the end of the Second World War.

"Hugh McGavock also had a good milk supply business. He did well at that, providing milk all the way down to Cushendun. At first he went in a pony and trap on the milk round, with the milk inside a special can that had a tap attached to it. He would pour and measure the milk for the customers. I recall hearing about Hugh McGavock and Alex McKay crashing into a hedge at Dunurgan in a motorbike and sidecar. The story also had it that a hurling stick flew out of the sidecar and into the nearby River Dun, was washed away, and never to be seen again.

"On the subject of hurling, always an important part of life in the Glens, I attended the two matches between Cushendun Emmets and O'Connell's of Belfast to decide the Antrim Senior Championship of 1931. In the replay, the late David Macauley of Ballybrack was involved in the winning goal that Cushendun got because the ball came off his knee. He was behind the goalmouth, and told me the ball struck his knee and came back into play, but a goal was claimed and given. David had a sore knee for days afterwards. Following the final, Hugh McGavock and Denis McKeegan were selected in Antrim hurling teams. Hugh was a well-made man, powerful, very strong. He was very fond of sport."

Hugh McKay knew Minnie well, and added: "When I went to Knocknacarry Primary School, where Mrs Doherty was the teacher, there were occasions when Minnie McGavock did relief teaching for Mrs Doherty. Minnie was a wonderful woman. I recall reading an article she wrote about some people from Carey, walking all the way to Carnlough and back - and fasting. It was during Mission Week at Ballyvoy (Culfeitrim)."

One of my reasons for a chinwag with Hugh McKay was to try and trace the name of a man pictured during a corn-cutting day on the Brogan farm at Agolagh. He said: "The person concerned is John Cunningham. There was John and his brother Hugh Cunningham from Coiscib, near Tieveragh, Cushendall. John worked a good deal of the time for Eddie Brogan. He pleased Mr Brogan, because he was a first-rate worker. He also worked, later on, for your father, Alex O'Hara. The Cunningham's were farm labourers. Their father Hugh was good at paling. He put up all the Government fences on Carey Mountain, near Loughareema. All the iron palings and fences at the Lough were erected by old Hugh Cunningham and his sons.

"Talking about the 'Mountain' brings to mind many happy days during turf cutting there. We had a turf bank near the McGarry's. Alex O'Hara, Minnie's husband, was also nearby. He had banks beside the McKay's of Ranaghan, on the left side overlooking Loughareema. There was the spring well for ice-cold water to make the tea. Alex O'Hara liked the craic. We were farming neighbours for many years. I believe he used to sit on James 'The Barrister' McSparran's railings in Knocknacarry, or on the old steps outside the gate. Also there, usually, would be Jim 'Bach' McMullan.

"They would talk until well past midnight on a dry warm summer's evening, probably about hurling. Once, I was told, 'The Barrister' hopped down, and 'lit on' Alex and Bach for keeping him out of bed. He was, he said, losing valuable sleep because of all the chit chat, and couldn't get up in the mornings. Bach's reply, I believe, was: 'We never gave you a thought.'

"There were many great characters in those times, and probably none stronger than Jim O'Neill of Knocknacarry. He was a very powerful man. Once, during his young days, I believe he excelled himself. A donkey was beat to try and pull an overfilled cartload of potatoes up a slope and onto the main road from Kennedy's Field at Knocknacarry. Old Mr McSparran, Archie's father, apparently bet 50 shillings Jim O'Neill could do what the donkey was unable to. So they took the donkey from the cart, put Jim between the shafts and even down on his knees at times Jim managed to pull the heavy load onto the road. Jim O'Neill was amazing, probably the strongest man ever to come out of Cushendun Parish."

# FISHY SCALES

JIM O'Neill was involved in many scrapes. He was also a cute customer when it came to illegally 'gaffing' a salmon from the River Dun. Once I recall as a youngster being sent into Mrs McKay's shop a message, after Sunday morning Mass, just as Jim O'Neill, trousers dripping wet from the knees down from wading into the river, was having a very appealing salmon weighed on the shop scales before walking to Cushendun to barter and sell the catch to one of the local hotel owners.

In later years I realised the bold O'Neill not only knew exactly where the single salmon was lurking in some darkened pool, probably for a few days, but also he picked the perfect time to gaff the fish.

A Sabbath snatch, when it was more likely the river bailiff would be at church with his family saying prayers and not on river-bank patrol. I must admit I admired the subtle craft, a study in patience and the nerveless bravado of the poacher. He was on the same alert level as the moonshiner.

O'Neill was not the only 'observer' of the ebb and flow of salmon movements in the River Dun, and how to avoid the bailiffs. Bill and Paddy O'Mullan were also among the experts of this once thriving clandestine cottage industry.

From that gloriously interesting time after the Lint era I seemed absorbed in to the corn threshing and potato picking processes that also brought great community spirit. Tillage was everything. Farming families were self-sufficient, many growing crops of potatoes, cabbage, and turnips. Gathering the corn stalks into stooks at Straid led eventually to a day of corn threshing and baling, with neighbouring farmers all wading in to help. Paddy and Randal 'The Rock' McNeill provided my first recall of a threshing day.

I have good reason to remember. As a nosey kid in short trousers, and sporting new sandals, I went with Minnie when she brought a basketful of eats for the workers' lunch. The tea was brewed to pitch black in a large can hanging over Lizzie Martin's open fire. The Martin house, where Lizzie, Charlie and Jimmy lived, is the site 'wee' Barney McKay resides in. I think the helping hands that day included Jamie Martin - shortly afterwards to emigrate to New York where he worked as a gravedigger, Dan McAfee, Jamie McKendry and Charlie Leavey.

I brought along my little terrier dog 'Bruce', to suss out the mice as they scurried from the cornstack before sheafs were tossed into the machine. I was mesmerised how the corn came pouring out the other end, and directly into bags hooked onto the machine. Then I decided to give a helping hand and lifted a pitchfork. I went to raise a cornstalk from the ground but instead plunged one fork not only into the stalk but also through my left sandal and the nail of my big toe.

Around that period, Paddy McNeill sustained a serious injury to a hand, the damage caused in an accident with the jagged circular cutting blade of an engine-powered table saw. His nephew Sean McNeill remembered the dreadful day: "The shed beside the flat-roofed house, just across the way from our home, held the saw. My uncle Paddy, who lived with his brother Randal and sister Rosetta up the hill a little bit, was apparently making hurley sticks when the accident happened. He lost three middle fingers above the first joint of his left hand. It was about lunch time when the incident happened, and I'd guess it was in 1946. That ended the saw business. He made good hurls, indeed he was overly particular about the grain in the ash.

"I would think his life was probably saved that day by Danny McKay, 'wee' John's father, who was working at that time for Walsh's next door at Rockport. When the disaster happened Danny came on the scene fairly quickly, and stemmed and stopped the bleeding in uncle Paddy's arm. Then John O'Hara's taxi took him to Hospital in Ballymena. Uncle Paddy continued to do threshing after the setback, until he retired."

Paddy 'The Rock's' fascinating threshing machine was later purchased by the McCormick ('Tommy') brothers Joe and Hugh, from nearby Brablagh. It was a 'Leader Boyd' thresher, a buff colour with a red fascia board. Also, there was a red-coloured Jones baler. Before the McNeill enterprise, there were other operatives, including a threshing service supplied by freelance contractor Douggie Kenny. He would work late into the night for finish, and move on to the next customer the following morning. His cavalcade featured not only the thresher and baler but also two very interesting tractors, One was the first produced broad-tyred green painted Fordson 'Oliver', with fly-wheel to drive the thresher, and a fast moving McCormick-Deering tractor to power the baler.

Danny McQuillan, whose family was also heavily involved in providing a threshing and ploughing service, recalled those heady post-War days of hectic high tillage in the Glens: "Bell from Ballycastle threshed in the Cushendun area during 1943, '44. Douggie Kenny, who was from Ballygarvey, between Rathkenny and Ballymena, also came in around that time. He stayed in Annie Ball's house in Knocknacarry, and also did a lot of work in the Torr area.

"He first arrived with a big Fordson 'Oliver 80' tractor, and then an 'Oliver 90'. He also had an International Farmall, made by McCormick-Deering. Both tractors were of American origin. His other tractor man was Sammy Law. Douggie (Kenny) later gave up the business and emigrated to Canada. My older brothers, John and Jamie went into the threshing business in 1945, and stayed at it right up to the early 1950's. My mother bought the Boyd thresher in the Moneyglass direction, after it was sold on by Lynn's Mill in Cushendall. It was an original Boyd made at Bendooragh, outside Ballymoney,

"We also had a Boyd baler, two Fordson tractors, and also a Ferguson that was purchased new in February 1948. I was involved in ploughing, with the Ferguson tractor, while my brother John ploughed with a Fordson tractor. For a time I would have help from John McCrudden of Omerban,

Cloughmills. He lost an arm during an accident with a threshing machine. John and his sister Margaret came to stay on holiday with their aunt, Polly (Horley) McAllister, at Tyban. He helped me open and close potato drills, working the tractor and plough even with his one arm. Tragically, John was killed in a motorbike accident at a crossroads between Clough and Glarryford."

Potato picking, a long-forgotten enterprise that contributed to good community spirit in the country, was another period that brought a flurry of activity in the valley. I used to help out in the back-breaking job of collecting the 'spuds' behind a tractor opening the perfectly arrowed potato drills, then placing the fresh crop into a basket before carrying and emptying them in a mound known as a pit. This was later covered in patted down soil and sods. It was a period, after World War Two, when there was the transition in farm machinery. There was the move from the hypnotically spinning claw-like arms of the horse-drawn potato digger to the tractor-powered accoutrement. The tractor was generally a TVO (Tractor Vapourising Oil) driven lightweight Ferguson.

# CONNECTIONS

HOARDING a constant stream of cuttings and pictures from newspapers and magazines was a Minnie trait, forever seeking out fresh knowledge. Included was a very interesting Glens of Antrim Historical Society discussion on the iconic Irish poet and writer John Hewitt's *The Day of the Corncrake*. The introduction was by Ballymena solicitor Jack McCann.

He stated: "Long, long before the Glens of Antrim Historical Society was thought of, Mary Stone of Cushendall was gathering 'Glens-lore' which she gladly shared with all who cared to call. To me, she gave a Feis na nGleann programme, listing as winner of the premier award in 1929 for Celtic Design one Charles McAuley of Cushendall, with this whispered confidence: 'For Charlie, the real prize was his introduction to the Arts adjudicator - James Humbert Craig, no less.'

"He cherishes the moment and the medals, and still lives in Cushendall. Misty years ago, Miss Stone was all excitement when she announced to me that there was . . . 'a poet come to live above in Layd, the name of John Hewitt.' Not a Glens name, and one new to me. But, with the publication by Peadar O'Donnell in *The Bell* of the poem *Fame*, word got around that in this newcomer-poet the Glens had found their real bard: just as in Charles McAuley they had found their real painter. Sadly, John Hewitt had to leave his 'chosen ground'.

"When he returned to Ireland, he honoured our Society by permitting us, in 1969, to publish in paperback twenty-five of his poems of the Glens of Antrim under the title - *The Day of the Corncrake*. Now we are doubly honoured to present this up-dated elegant edition of that book, in which John Hewitt's evocative verses are matched with paintings by Charles McAuley, as our tribute to two men who have shown us the true meaning of love of one's native land. I know that Mary Stone would have approved. (Signed-Jack McCann)."

Minnie remembered the inaugural meeting of the Glens Historical Society. "It was held over two evenings in September, 1965. Guest speaker was a Father Webb from Campbeltown on the Mull of Kintyre. He highlighted the strong connection with the Antrim Coast. For centuries there was a brisk shipping lane between the two areas, and also, at times down the centuries, a corridor for warring tribes raiding across the Sea of Moyle between Scotland's Peninsula of Cantyre, featuring the Mull of Kintyre in Argyllshire."

The narrow neck of treacherous water, the North Channel of the Irish Sea, marginally over 13 miles 'as the crow flies' between Scotland's western reaches and the Torr Head/Culraney/Tournamona/Cushendun part of the Antrim coast, was awash with activity until the bristling trade ended shortly after the Antrim Coast road was carved out and opened to traffic in 1843.

Campbeltown Loch became famous in song, the area once regarded the 'Whisky Capital of the World.' The town in Argyll and Bute once featured 34 distilleries and held global acclaim for a significant flavour of single malt Scotch whisky. Merely three Distilleries survived after a decline in the export business from the U.S. Depression financial fall-out. Most of the activity between the Mull and the Glens involved Dunaverty and Cushendun.

It was the shortest sailing distance between two small ports. Dunaverty once paraded a fort for the Clan MacDonald. The Castle's remains lie on the rocky headland on the south east tip of Kintyre. It is also known as Blood Rock, because this is the site where 300 Clan MacDonald members were massacred in 1647 by supporters of Oliver Cromwell.

Fr Webb's lectures to the newly-formed Glens Historical Society illustrated that distant past vibrant trade between the Irish and the Scots. Minnie O'Hara diligently recorded the speaker's revelations. "Father Webb," she noted, "said he learned from Customs' records that the Ferry service from Cushendun to Dunaverty was in existence from 1739, with passengers and goods daily."

Here are some quotes from Custom records:

1745 - John McClarty, a Customs man authorised to investigate the 'integrity' of people travelling by the ferry.

1756 - Smuggled into Cantyre and seized were 66 casks of brandy, 42 casks of rum, 24 bottles of white wine, and one boat.

1772 - Commissioners in Edinburgh sent to Customs man in Campbeltown 2 muskets, 3 pistols, and a suite of colours. (Horses and wool brought into Ireland)

1773 - Seizure of shipment of wool to Ireland.

1780 - John Morrison intercepted on voyage from Cushendun by American privateer from Boston - the *Black Princess*. On her were mounted 18 carriage guns. Two Revenue cutters went out to intercept her. Hadn't much chance. (Apparently this schooner, built around 1774, was once used by Benjamin Franklin to capture British ships during the American War of 1776, and later, along with sister ship *Black Prince*, became part of the Atlantic smuggling scene).

1784 - Revenue cutters of Campbeltown seized 24.5 chest of black tea from Red Bay, in a long rowing boat.

1785 - 16 stone of wool seized. Salt smuggled to the fishing industry. Took it in barrels to the boats in fishing grounds, where fish gutted and salted on board. Boats also carried one or two coopers.

1786 - Sloop *James* - with its master, James O'Hara, seized off Campbeltown, landing 13 tons of Irish meal (there was a tax on meal and salt. O'Hara, apparently nicknamed 'The Pirate' and related to my family, was a well-known smuggler. A sloop was a sail boat with a fore-and-aft rig, and a single mast).

1787 - Seized 6,000 lbs of leaf tobacco from Rathlin. American privateers stored it in Rathlin Island - sugar too. Last ferry boat to Cushendun was in 1843.

# OCCUPATIONS

DURING the last quarter of the 19th century, and the first quarter of the 20th century, the area around and near Dunurgan was a hive of activity, and always involving good neighbours. Minnie made a habit of mentally filing all the happenings, and who did what, and what their nickname was, and why. Usually the answer to the latter developed through the occupation of the person concerned.

She wrote: "When I was very small there were two shoemakers and a tailor in Dunurgan. Two brothers, Donal and Jamie McKay were the shoemakers, while the tailor was named Magee. Robert Hyndman made nails in his forge. In Drumnasmear, at the Turn, lived another McKay man who was a shoemaker, who was married to Sarah Storey from the Randalstown or Toomebridge area, and whose brother was a priest. Another shoemaker was Archie Adrain in Cushendun.

"Down at Straid, James O'Connor was a carpenter. Also there lived Susanna McIlheran's father, Charles, who was a wheelwright. Susanna died in May, 1939. George O'Connor had a farm at Straid, now owned by the McNeill's of Park. He bought it from the Martins, who moved to Calishnaugh. His sister (unmarried) owned the home farm adjoining where Willie Gallagher now lives. George and his wife, big Sarah, had a shop. She was a sister of Alex John 'Bawn' McAlister, and her nephew Mick McKeown was reared in Straid with her. The shop window is still there, and the two-storey building beside it was called 'The Store'.

"George had many married sisters. He was an uncle of George McIlheran who inherited his place, and an uncle of Patrick Laverty of Ballyteerim. George's mother was a McAlister of Carnahaugh, who was a cousin of my grandmother's. He was also an uncle of Father George McKay, late P.P. of Carrickfergus. In the farm adjoining his lived his cousin James, who made those dormer windows in the house now owned by Hugh McKay of Layd. James was married to Catherine McKay of Dunurgan, whose mother was Rachel McAlister of Carnahaugh - an aunt of my father's.

"A sister, Rachel McKay, was married to Johnny McAteer of Glenaan, and they had a restaurant in Glasgow. The McAteer's bought the farm from James, who emigrated to Scotland - leaving a daughter Sadie to be brought up by the Granny in Dunurgan. Sadie later married Tommy Sharkey. Rose, a sister of James, was married to Neal O'Neill of Layd whose family made headstones from the sandstone rocks on Layd Shore. They owned the farm and fields leading to the shoreline. From their 'factory' they moved the heavy headstones by boat to Cushendun, and from thence they were 'sliped' by horse to the churchyard at Killavalla.

"He lived in Cushendun, in the Post Office. Their daughter, Madge was Postmistress after they died, and she married a Sean Rice from County Down. He had been a carpenter employed at the re-building of Glenmona House in 1923-'24. Madge, her husband and family left for Belfast, and later moved to Glasgow. She had a brother James, who emigrated to America, a sister Minnie - who married a Fyffe from Cargan, and they also went to Scotland. McAteer's house became the abode of our P.P. Fr McCann, when he left 'The Strand House'. The Curate lived in Cloney.

"Fr McCann left to be P.P. of Glenravel, and I remember after the First World War a family stayed in it (McAteer's). They were named Scott. Their mother was the widow of a clergyman. There was one son, Tom, just home from the War and studying for some profession. I think he was learning to be a Doctor. There was Laura and another sister, who was a teacher in France. There was also a sister who was married to a Queen's University lecturer named Ferguson, and was studying to be a doctor. They had a little girl of four named Rosemary Hope Scott Ferguson. She came to our school while they were in Straid.

"Then, in the early 1920's, Fr Blacker brought the Holbrook's from Belfast to put up a steel and concrete bridge across the River Dun behind the Church. They and their families stayed in McAteer's for months and months. Their sister Maggie was married to a little Welshman - and his younger brother was with them from Wales. Their home in Belfast was in a little street that led to the entrance of St Malachy's College on the Antrim Road, and on the night of the Blitz (1941) they were blown up and their bodies were never found. There were two brothers Holbrook - one was a widower with two children, and the other was married to one of the Beringers, the Jewellers.

"During the Spring, after they stayed in Straid, Lizzie, my sister, was up Jinny's Brae after cattle and found a lovely gold watch. 'From P. to J.' was on the back of it. Lizzie brought it to Fr Blacker, and he returned it to a very grateful Mr Holbrook, who sent Lizzie a grand silver watch as a reward. Lizzie lent me this watch when I went to St Mary's Training College in 1926, and some time during my two years there the watch stopped. I left it in Beringer's to be repaired. When I went to collect it Mr Beringer, Joe's brother, was very puzzled as to how I came to have a watch which was bought by his sister some years before. I think he suspected me of stealing it, but when I told him its story he was quite friendly."

Blacksmith's were understandably in high demand during the days before tractors were invented. As all farming was done by horses, there were several blacksmiths in the Cushendun valley to shoe them, make socks for the ploughs, harrows, and teeth for them, shoeing for cartwheels and heavy farmyard gates made of cart-shoeing bar.

"Charlie McAuley, and his son Charlie, had his forge in Knocknacarry," wrote Minnie, "Mickey Laverty had his at 'Mickey's Corner', where Pat Hamilton now lives, and John the Smith (McKillop) had his a field-length up the road where Margaret McMullan lives at Barmeen. Her garage was his forge. Across the road lived wee Archie McKillop, a relation, who was a carpenter. Also there lived another carpenter Johnny 'Putty' O'Hara. John Charles is his son.

"Mary Jane McGreer was a dressmaker in Knocknacarry. She lived with her sister Annie directly across the road from O'Hara's. They were related to my mother, because a McGreer married a Butler girl from Carey and their family included two daughters, Annie and Mary. There were other dressmakers such as Mary 'Horley' McAlister in Tyban, and Maggie Laverty in Ballyteerim.

"Dulse was gathered on the rocks, dried and taken to Ballymena where the inland people loved the smell and taste of the sea. Coarse sea wrack was dried all along the wall on the Strand Road, stacked in lumps, and in the month of May kilns were made in the gravel. The wrack was burned until it melted into a sticky brown mass called Kelp. This was also sold in Ballymena to merchants from factories, where it was made into iodine, and other medicinal products. They acrid smoke from the burning Kelp wasn't pleasant.

"In Glenaan, there were weavers to whom the wool from the sheep was brought to make blankets and quilts. At home the women of the house would spin the wool to knit gansies. They also would spin lint into linen thread for weaving into sheets. I remember many banks of linen thread in our house which had been spun by my Granny. The remains of the spinning wheel was there too."

# ON THE MOVE

TRAVELLING FOLK always caused arms-length interest when they filtered into the Glens. Following both the Great War and World War Two there was a constant stream of ever-shifting lost souls, some like ships that pass in the night. Others stayed longer. I recall a War victim who had both his legs amputated. He moved around at quite a brisk pace on a board with little wheels, and lived in an old ramshackle house at the top end of Craigagh Wood.

Minnie took an outside interest in the curious, but was especially attracted to the prolific literary output of the fabled 'Dusty Roads' - whose name was allegedly James Stoddard Moore. This latter claim by the transient poet was apparently in dispute by respected historian Mrs Stone of Shore Street, Cushendall. "Mrs Stone told me he was reared near Cushendall, and Moore was not his name at all," declared Minnie,

"When he went to register for something official he could not get his birth certificate, but 'found' one with 'James Stoddard Moore' on it, presented this to 'the powers that be' - and adopted that name ever after. It seems he was born on Christmas Day 1844, in what was known as 'The Ould Mill', a small house with a humpy slated roof a few yards on the Cushendall side of Mooney's cross at the bottom of Gault's Road. He was supposed to marry a lady named Butler from Dunurgan. The wallstead of the Butler home was in Murray's back garden. She worked in the rope mill at Cushendun."

Minnie named further 'characters' such as . . . "Dinny Buckley. It was claimed he was 'half-mad', and that he had been a clerical student when young, and 'operated' mostly in the Carey area - as did 'Dusty Roads', or 'Dusty Rhodes', who was accommodated in Clarke's of Murlough. There was also Harkin from Ballymena, and I think he was nicknamed 'Old Cousie'. Another character was Grace Anne from Ballycastle. She was not really a beggar. She was old and fat. She carried a bundle, out of which she sold things.

"Grace would get a 'lift' to the Glens in Boyd's bakery van every so often. She lived up a wee entry beside their shop in Castle Street. Another 'client' from Ballycastle was a small man in a long raincoat, who carried his wares in an attaché case. He also came to do his 'rounds' periodically by 'lift' in Boyd's van. He had a Jewish appearance. Another person to come round about once a month was Rose Mairs, who lived in a small slated cottage by the roadside not far from where sheep sales were once staged on this side of Cargan - and close to Parkmore Station."

On the light entertainment front, the Antrim Coast area was an attractive outlet for roving troubadours such as the legendary Irish balladeer Delia

Murphy, who was one of the massive music hall attractions. First famous for her rendering of *The Blackbird,* she made an appearance in Cushendall Parochial Hall. Born on February 16,1902, in Claremorris, County Mayo, her father Jack apparently made a fortune in the Klondike Gold Rush, and encouraged daughter Delia to maintain an interest in singing Irish ballads. In 1939 she recorded *Three Lovely Lassies, The Blackbird,* and *The Spinning Wheel* - and in 1961 recorded *The Queen of Connemara* while living in Ontario. Another favourite, and dear to brother Daniel's heart, was the lilting tale of 'broken-hearted farmer *Dan O'Hara*'. Delia died in Dublin on February 11, 1971.

I never met Miss Murphy, but recall a travelling troupe of a different sort, and one of seemingly limited resource, named Farrell's Famous Circus. It arrived from playing at Ballycastle amid great excitement among the youngsters of the Parish. It lasted one day in Mrs McKay's field on the fringe of Knocknacarry. There was another moveable feast of entertainment, named Farney's Circus. On top of all that we had 'Talent Contests' in Cushendun and in Cushendall Cinema, and in a 'Good Companions' tent at Legge Green on Cushendall Beach.

# WHAT's in a NAME

TWO or more families of the same surname in the Glens of Antrim meant a nickname was applied to distinguish one from another. However, as the decades rolled by some family nicknames were hard to distinguish from the real ones.

Minnie had a firm and often frivolous take on who was what during her early years, such as: "The 'Weavers' were the McKeegan's. The 'Baker's' and the 'Archie's' were McNeill's, as were the 'Rocks' and the 'Park's'. And as well as the 'Dear's' in Carnahaugh there were the 'Twins'. Three or four families in that townland above Cushendall were McAlister's - the same as old Daniel McAlister, whose descendants are distinguished by alling one cousin Danny Arthur and the other Danny Dan. The latter's father was Daniel's Dan - a brother of Arthur. Arthur and Dan were sons of old Daniel McAlister, who owned an establishment which kept everything from coal to coffins."

On November 11, 1974, Minnie added: "Where a few families of the same surname had a nickname to distinguish them I could understand, but I don't know why old John McMullan of Dirrah Tops was called 'The Ton', and why his second wife - who, as a widower, ended her days in Hyndman's house, Dunurgan, now owned by McPeake's, and was called 'The Crane'. I remember seeing John McMullan's picture in the waiting room of a railway station - either Ballymoney or Portrush - with an old horse and sidecar (slipe). I'm sure he's portrayed in the Folk Museum at Cultra - as a tourist attraction, and also on trains and in railway station waiting rooms, where these pictures were displayed of natives with ancient methods of farming.

"We seemed to be attracted to using the names of birds, such as Dan 'The Duck' (Hernon), Mary McKillop of Brablagh was called 'The Stork'- and her brother Archie known as 'Buller'. In the townland of Ardacoan, above the chapel were the 'Crows' (O'Hara), the 'Peacocks' (O'Connor), the 'Bears' (McDonnell's of The Tops and later Knocknacarry), the 'Mug' (O'Mullan, Glendun), and the 'Thrushes' (Whiteford).

There were so many McNeill's . . the 'Wheaties', the 'Andy's', the 'Jacks' in Cushleake, the 'Roes' at The Tops, the 'Fadgeys' of Tournamona, the 'Dan Roes' at Knocknacarry, 'Gantie' at Knocknacarry, and 'Nancy Bann' - who lived at what was to become known as Montreal Villa, and later The Villa. We had John 'Coal' (McAuley) of Tromra - and also a McAuley called 'Par Ghost', the 'Ned's' (O'Neill), the 'Coothies' (McCambridge, Glendun) and the 'Packer's' (McLaughlin). There was also 'Dan Nancy' (McKay) and 'Mary Nancy', after whom the steep brae above Tournamona is called. There were the 'Burns' (McKendry), the 'Duncan's' (McHenry), the

'Mullagh's' - one brother spelled his surname McKendry, and the other, McHenry.

"Up Glendun, there were many McCormick's - the 'Straws', the 'Far Ones' or 'Far Ups' - probably first named as 'Fir Eoin' - Owen's Men, the 'Casey's' and the 'Susan's'. A niece of the 'Straws' was Annie 'Ned' (O'Neill) who married 'The Mug' O'Mullan from Carey. His brother, 'The Sod' lived in Knocknacarry. William McKillop of Tyban, a grandfather of John, Gus, Charlie, Mary, Margaret, Alex and Annie McKay of Knocknacarry, was known as the 'Doctor'. The McKillop's of Gortacreggan were called the 'Navvie's'.

"Father George McKay's father was named 'Arthur Roe'. Jinnie Keenan's husband was Denis 'Ailie' McKay. 'Jinnie's Farm', behind Mrs White's, is named after her, and I remember her well. She walked with a waddle, and we used to say my youngest brother, Alex, walked like Jinnie. At Callishnaugh, there were the 'Tom's' (McCormick), and the 'Mick's' (McCormick). Jim McMullan of Knocknacarry had the nickname of Jim 'Bach'. The owner of the next farm, at Upper Agolagh, had the same name christian and surname, and was known as Jamie 'Scotland'.

"Alex McBride from Cushleake was called 'The Wedge', and there was a nephew of Charlie Murphy's called 'Wee Head' McKay, 'John-a-Kay', who would be a cousin of the great Commander Murray of Portmarnock Golf Club fame. The McKay's of Layd were the 'Holes' - and Denis McVeigh's father was nicknamed 'The Rabbit'. Two McKay brothers in Dunurgan were 'Donal Shoemaker' - married to my father's Aunt Rachel, and 'Jamie Shoemaker', who was a grandfather of Ned O'Neill. Paddy 'Ned' (O'Neill) was married to Sally McKay, and lived in Glendun. But, after Paddy died in 1911, aged 60, she came to live in Dunurgan, was known as 'Sally Ned', and inherited Jamie Shoemaker's house and farm. She was very funny. Sally died aged 79 in 1953. John 'Tailor' was McKay of Corrymeela, the 'Mor's' - McKillop of the Big Bridge, the 'Chips' of Tavanagh were McAllister's, and named thus because their father was a carpenter."

There was also sobering reflection on a period in harsh Irish life when the battle of survival, and always in poor circumstance despite being self-sufficient in this small-farmer community, was clinically illustrated when Minnie recalled a near neighbour's delight upon receiving the Government State Pension for a first time. Minnie related how great a boon the Old Age Pension was for so many folk during those difficult days. "I remember when I very young hearing this elderly lady, a neighbour of ours at Dunurgan, saying it was the first time in her entire life when she had money of her own in her hand."

State pensions paid to individuals in the United Kingdom have been in existence since the early 1900's. Lloyd George, then Chancellor of The Exchequer under the Liberal government led by Herbert Asquith, introduced the first State pension. He wanted to 'lift the shadow of the workhouse from the homes of the poor', and provide an income to people over 70 years of age and too old to work.

The Old Age Pensions Act provided between one shilling and five shillings a week, paid to citizens on incomes that were not over 12s.

(means tested). Lloyd George needed to find funds to pay for the pensions and raise Government revenue by an additional £16 million a year. In 1909 he launched the People's Budget, including increases in taxation. People on lower incomes were to pay nine pence in the pound, those on annual incomes of over £3,000 had to pay one shilling and two pence in the pound, and there was a new supertax of one shilling and six pence in the pound for those earning £5,000 a year. There was also an increase in death duties on the estates of the rich, and taxes on profits gained from the ownership and sale of property.

# TURNING PAGES

SCISSORS, a sturdy type fashioned mainly for cloth cutting and purchased in a shop at Clifden, during a holiday in Connemara, County Gaway, became a daily weapon in the hands of Minnie after she read her morning daily, the *Irish News*.

One of her many endearing qualities was her commitment to the almost daily routine of cutting little gems of news from the newspaper. She would pass on what was considered notable gems of high educational value to, first of all, her sons and then down the line her grandchildren.

This fastidious devotion to the written word, often culminating in some heavy underlining of bad grammar, checking the death notices in the *Irish News*, and the occasional urge to write of short poems, held a distinct fascination for her granddaughter Catherine O'Hara. On December 8, 1982, Catherine, then a 17-year-old student at Cross and Passion College, Ballycastle, County Antrim, penned *THOUGHTS* - a respectful and moving tribute to her Granny. A delighted Minnie picked on one line in the poem that she attached to her memoirs. It was *Pages of my Life*.

### THOUGHTS

*As the curtains of my life*
*draw slowly to a close*
*I sit and dwell of years gone by*
*those years have flown, God knows.*

*My thoughts turn back to Cushendun*
*the pages of my life,*
*the clippings tell a different tale*
*of joy, hard work and strife.*

*My life, I'd say, has been quite good*
*I've had my share of all*
*the tears I've shed of joy and grief*
*of those I can recall.*

*As I look upon my memoirs*
*the pictures I still see clear*
*I think of friends, they've come and gone*
*I wipe away a tear.*

*I hope you'll all remember me*
*when it's my turn to go*
*As I lie in rest, you'll say of me*
*'She wasn't bad, you know.'*

May 1980 provided one of many of Minnie's written recollections. Amazingly, despite suffering a stroke earlier that year, her little grey memory cells were not affected. Indeed, they seemed sharper than ever. However, even though she lived a further 16 years, she felt then the tide was running out on her, and there was the urgent need to place on record all her perceptions of the past.

"On this 12th of May, 1980, I am almost 76 and a half years. Having been at death's door from a stroke this Spring I must hurry with these memories - 'for time is running out.' My childhood in Dunurgan was very happy, for I was always occupied - herding cows, and working on a farm. I was the eldest of four, and as soon as I was any size I had to help my father drop potatoes, and carry buckets of corn to him when the sheet he was sowing from went empty. He would stand patiently waiting at the spot of his last cast, while I came 'sprakling' over the rough soil.

"Then came the weeding of the potato drills, and the thinning of turnips - both these occupations were carried out on one's knees in the middle of the summer - after school and on the Saturday. From May onwards, on good days, the mountain above Loughareema claimed all hands to work the turf - spreading, footing and rickling. In August, the lint had to be pulled when all the neighbours collected. For the 'lint-pulling' and, after finishing off the whole crop in one day, the young folk would take to the barn with a melodeon or fiddle and finish the day dancing.

"I remember James McFetridge bringing along two lovely daughters of Paddy Dinsmore's who were on holiday in Alex McGee's, Glendun. James and they treated us country folk to some delightful songs. One of them later became Mrs Watson, the mother of the very musical Father Noel Watson."

Among Minnie's first images of life were those of schoolchildren coming home from school. She wrote: "I remember the children going home from Knocknacarry School, and talking to me - when I was a four-year-old, through the bars of the big heavy iron gate at our house in Dunurgan. The gate was made from a cartshoeing bar by old Charlie McAuley, Mary's grandfather. It was attached to a rather weak post made of holly, and it trailed and made a furrowed arc when opened so that no child of my age could open it. Grown-ups could ease it round, to let in or let out cows or horses. The boys passing home, and noticing me, were my big heroes - Hugh McCormick of Callishnaugh, Alex McCormick ('Susan'), and a 'Casey' McCormick who spent their younger days at Glendun School. The senior girls talked to me, too. I remember two sisters named McDonnell, who lived with a relation in Knocknacraw."

She also held bright, happy recall of her own days at Primary School, from the moment she started out on the education route at four years of age. "Mary Jane Murray and I were like twins, and in 1908 we went to school together, about the age of four. We lived about a half-a-mile from the Knocknacarry School building, which had a sandstone notice on the outside front wall that read 'Knocknacarry National School 1850'. It was divided into two rooms - one for girls and one for boys. The rooms were separated by large folding doors, which were opened only about once a year for a children's concert. A makeshift stage was erected at the far end of the boys' room.

"Miss Mary 'Winnie' Wilde was the Principal teacher of the Girls' School section, with Annie Ball the assistant. Master Doherty and his wife, Mary, taught next door in the Boys' school. Mary and I thought Miss Wilde lived in the school. We asked one of the senior girls where Miss Wilde slept, and we were told that she slept on the window sill. As the sill had a very deep slope we doubted that. At first we wrote on slates with slate pencils, and did our sums on them during our whole school career.

"However, we were soon presented with a little grey-backed writing book with blue and red lines at a half penny, and a lead pencil at a half penny. We were allowed to bring the pencil home and, on the first night I was displaying mine, it fell into the big turf fire. It was all blackened and half burned before someone retrieved it with the tongs. I was mortified the next day when I had to use it in school. I can remember to this day the smell of that book and pencil.

"I progressed fairly quickly from making strokes to making the letter 'n', but when it came to the letter 'm' I couldn't manage the second leg. May Murray, a cousin of Mary's who came to school during her summer holidays from Glasgow and sat beside me, could make a perfect 'm'. Was I jealous! May was one of many visiting children who attended school here during the summer holidays just to boost the school's average attendance. Many of their mothers had been past pupils of Miss Wilde, who was a brilliant teacher. We didn't have holidays in the summer - just a fortnight for putting in the crop and a fortnight in the autumn to harvest it. Most children came to school in bare feet during the summer. As there was no tarmacadam on the roads then they were very rough, and our soles were sometimes blistered.

"Our Readers, in those days, had a list of difficult words and their meanings at the top of each lesson, and we had to learn these by heart. I remember in the Second Book at the top of the lesson, one of the words was 'drags' - meaning 'pulls'. One of the bigger girls was sent to ask us our spellings, and when Mary Murray was asked to spell 'drags' she answered, in a flash, 'rags', 'flitters'. She pretended she didn't hear the 'd' of 'drags'. Mary was a brilliant scholar, but neither her nor my writing pleased Miss Wilde. We both wrote in the same style which Miss Wilde attributed to the teaching of some old woman in Dunurgan.

"Still, we gained an excellent grinding in the 'three r's', and singing. Before we left school we had learned many of Shakespeare's plays - and studied Dickens, and couldn't be puzzled at grammar. Mary Jane was a brilliant essayist, and won each week the sixpence which Father Skeffington awarded for the best composition. He visited the school each day, and woe betide us if there were any papers lying about or anything out of place. Two of the 'big girls' each Friday donned meal-bag aprons, got down on their knees, and spent the whole afternoon scrubbing the wooden floor until it gleamed. Two different girls did it every week, and were delighted to escape lessons for the afternoon. The buckets of water had to be carried from the 'Spout' at the gable of O'Hara's house in Knocknacarry.

"A few of the girls were adjudged 'non singers' and I was one of these. We sat and 'carried on' on the back seat while the singers stood up in front of us for the singing lesson. Loveday Cochrane was one of the best singers, but one day she was tempted to stay with us at the back. We must have made a mighty racket for half way through the lesson Miss Wilde ordered her class to sit while she chastised the bold girls at the back. She went on and on scolding, and I cried and cried, but Loveday wasn't a bit perturbed. She just said: "Minnie, you're far too sensitive. That was the first time I had heard the word 'sensitive'.

"The desks held six pupils each. They had three ink wells with brass lids, and slits in which to stand the slates. There was one very long form in front of the fire. In those days there was no 11+, so we didn't leave school until about fifteen years of age - and with as much knowledge as many Secondary School pupils have at seventeen. As we grew older, Mary Murray's father Hugh took charge of the older member of both families on most wonderful excursions. Every Ascension Thursday (six weeks after Easter Sunday and in mid-May) he conducted us, armed with cans, aprons, flour bags and stumps of knives up Jinnie's Brae over the top of Layd, and down Jamie McKay's brae to the Layd Shores.

"Beforehand, he would find out when the ebb tide was - for that was the time for us to gather the dulse in our aprons and spread it on the warm rocks until home time. I don't remember a day that wasn't sunny. Then, as the tide began to come in and the limpets rose to meet it, we took our knives and filled our cans with these wonderful shellfish. The half-dried dulse was scooped into the flour bags, and each bag over the shoulder and can in the hand we started the long trek home.

"Hugh Murray was the most patient of men, but I think he enjoyed our company too. He brought me down to Ligadaghtan to see the three empty troop ships which ran into the cliffs on their way back to America, after bringing troops to Europe during the First World War. Troop ships ran aground below the cliffs on Dan Jack's farm. They should have passed north of Torr Head. We met officers in uniform on the road, but the sailors were coolies and not allowed on shore, and from the cliff top we watched dozens of them running around the decks."

There are sketchy reports in Belfast newspapers of a trawler *Greatful* that sank on March 25, 1916, close to Torr Head. Perhaps, tying in with Minnie's memory of that walk to Tournamona was the mid-summer 1916 incident when the liner *Laertes* ran aground - 'near Torr Head, but was refloated'.

Minnie also recalled the 1915 sinking of the King of Belgium's Yacht, *Clementina* in Cushendun Bay. A link to this tragedy is the burial record of one member of the crew of the stricken vessel in the Church of Ireland graveyard in Cushendall. The headstone has: 'Asst Engineer RNR. E.S. Manning. HMS *Clementina* 20th Sept 1915. The vessel was named after King Albert I's great aunt Clementine - the Princess Bonaparte. Albert I reigned from 1909, when 16, until his death in 1934. The steam yacht was in the service of the Royal Navy. The O'Hara house in Kocknacarry salvaged from that wreck a ship's carved wooden door, a stairway and banisters.

Minnie added: "I also remember we were making a Novena to beg that Ireland would escape Conscription, and we were returning home via Jinnie's Brae, when we heard the bell ringing for Benediction. Mary (Murray) and I didn't want to break the Novena, so off we ran from the old wallsteads, dumped the heavy bags of wet dulse at home, and ran down the loaning to the Church. I can't remember if we made it for Benediction. Still, Conscription was averted. Hugh Murray also always brought us to the October Devotions round by Sharkey's, as Dunurgan Loaning was too muddy. With a lighted 'Hurricane Lamp' he led the way. I'm sure he is reaping a great reward for all his acts of kindness."

# LINT PULLING

FLAX was widely grown in the Glens for a number of years following the 1914-'18 War, and to achieve a good crop it had to be grown on rich soil. Flax, grown both for its seeds and for its fibres, produces a vegetable oil known as flaxseed or linseed oil.

Minnie appreciated a time when lint was a key component to the small farmer's survival. She also related that flax fibre is among the oldest fibre in the world, and its use for the production of linen can be traced back to ancient Egyptian times. Farming flax, the emblem used by the Northern Ireland Assembly, requires little fertilizer or pesticides, and within eight weeks of sowing the plant will reach upwards of 15cm in height. Various parts of the plant have been used to make fabric, paper, dye, hair gels and soaps. Linen products included bags, towels, bed linen, tablecloths, chair covers, handkerchiefs.

Minnie knew all about this crucial cottage industry of the Glens, and wrote in great detail: "I stayed on at school until I was 15, and then revelled in the farm work until I was 17. Included in that time was a first-hand knowledge in the growing of flax. The holms along the River Dun were suitable for growing good flax. Most farmers would sow about an acre or less, as lint would not grow well in that patch for seven years. The seed came from Baltic lands, and, as it was very small, the sacks containing it were of very strong and thick material.

"The lint seed was bought by the peck not by the stone. About five pecks sufficed for a fair-sized plot. I remember making schoolbags and pencil cases from linseed bags. The seeds were so small that the clay had to be well harrowed and rolled before sowing in April. My father sowed it by hand, from a sheet attached to his neck - and the breadth of the cast had to be carefully marked by poles. If the casts overlapped there would be stripes of too closely-grown stalks, and stripes of too thinly grown stalks. The fields of blue-flowered 'lint' made a beautiful sight during the summer. Then, in August it began to ripen - the little leaves turned yellow and began to fall off, while pods of seeds formed where the flowers were. These pods had many spikes on each of them, and stalks would have about 10 pods. When ripe, the stalks were tough, with wood inside a surround of fibre.

"The harvesting began about the middle of August. From the beginning of August, the farmer would cut sprit - a kind of tough rushes, and leave it to dry. This sprit was then made into bands, and placed in bundles, to be taken to the fields on the morning of the lint pulling. On account of having the little short root, lint was pulled and not cut like corn. A special day was set aside for each farmer's lint pulling, and a dozen or more men and women, boys and girls, would pull all day, and finish that farmer's crop before night. Many girls made and carried food to the field, and at night there would be a 'Lint-pulling Dance' in the barn, with someone playing a melodeon or a fiddle.

"The next day the farmer and his sons would yoke a horse and cart and bring the lint to the dub. Before they left the field the previous day, the pullers would stook the beats (sheaves), root upwards for if they stooked them with the pods up - as I saw them do at Cultra on the TV, they would never get them separated. The bands of sprit were used to tie three or four handfuls of lint to make a beat.

"The outlet of the Dub was locked with sods early in the summer, so that by mid-August it was full of stagnant water into which the beats were forked - about two layers of them. Rushes were spread on top, in order to keep the light of the sun from reaching the lint. Sunlight during time in the Dub would result in the fibre being streaky in colour - and thus lowering its price at the market.

"Then, on top of the layer of rushes were heavy stones to keep it under water. Barefooted children would get tramping on these stones, to keep the lint down every day for over a week, and sometimes a fortnight. At the end of this time, the pods and the internal wood had become rotten in the putrid water, but the outside fibre was unharmed. Now the water was drained off the dub, and the stones and rushes removed. The dripping beats were then lifted by men, dressed in nothing but underpants, and placed on the bank of the Dub. A horse and cart then brought the heavy wet beats and distributed them over a grazing field to be opened - and the contents spread in rows by men and women in overalls of old sacks. The lint at this stage had a shocking smell, but it never did anyone any harm.

"In a few days it was dry and ready for lifting, and being tied in sheaves again, with the same sprit bands which were now dry. This was the time the farmer took a few beats to the Mill to be left as 'shall'. Each farmer took his turn to bring his lint to the Mill for scutching in the same rotation as the 'shalls' were left. Now the dry lint was stooked right-side up, for the pods were all gone - and after a few days made into windrows and then into stacks in the hazard.

"There were several lint mills around, but Sharkey's in Calishnaugh was near us. It was water driven, the water coming in a 'laid' or 'layde' all the way from the Big Bridge. They employed four scutchers, two strickers, while Hugh Sharkey worked the rollers. One of the strickers was Maggie O'Neill, who lived up Tromra Brae, and each morning all winter came across the top of Dunurgan brays and down to the Mill to reach it around 8.00am. The lint was carted to the Mill and placed in a corner behind the rollers. The sheaves were handed to Hugh, and he would take a handful and send it through to the stricker on the other side. The rollers crushed the wood inside the fibre.

"The stricker would give it a twist and lay it beside other stricks. Sometimes they would allow me to strick. Each of the two strickers supplied a scutcher nearest them. The scutcher then held one end to the blades which beat out the wood (shous), turned it, and had the other end beaten. These beaten stricks were then taken to the two finishers, who produced the beautiful silk bundles of fibre ready for the market in Ballymena on the next Saturday. Linen merchants attended these markets, and bought up all the fibre which the farmers brought in carts the night before. Fibre with the least streaks got the best price.

"The scutching also left heaps of shous, and many people carried them home in sacks to make a fire on the hearth. Among the shous would be some tow, and this enabled them to make a kiln by using two large bottles - one upright and one lying, to be removed when the 'shous' were firmly clapped around them . . . thus making a draught. A great glow of heat came from the kiln. Nothing was wasted in those frugal times. Incidentally, while the lint seed bags were converted to bags for school books and cases for pencils, so the flour bags, which were made of soft cotton, were converted to bed sheets and linings for quilts. Flour was bought by the bag, which contained 10 stones - and when empty and washed, four bags made one double-bed sheet.

"The bag was ripped, and the thick cotton thread then rolled in a ball for further use. Then it was washed, boiled, and bleached . . . and it took some boiling to eradicate the 'black crow' emblem from Morton's bags. The red lettering was much easier dealt with. A sheet made from these bags was as warm as your modern flannelette sheet."

*A stunning vista of Cushendun Bay from Rockport.*

*The Square, Cushendun.*

*Glenmona House, Cushendun.*

*Dunurgan, Cushendun, where Minnie was born.*

*Loughareema - the 'Vanishing Lake'.*

*Once the Custom House buildings at Rockport, with Liganergat - the Rigs hurling pitch, in background.*

*Minnie and grandaughter Orla O'Hara.*

*Minnie entertaining Mrs Elizabeth Gilligan of Garrison, County Fermanagh, and Marie McGuigan, sister of Elizabeth O'Hara.*

*June 5,1971. Proud Minnie at her eldest grandson Eamonn's First Communion in St Paul's Church, Cavendish Street, Belfast. Also pictured are Brother Leopold, Headmaster of St Gall's Primary School, Clonard, Eamonn's brother Sean and sister Catherine.*

*Minnie's Close, Knocknacarry.*

*The rhododendron bush at Craigagh.*

*August 5, 1969. Emily McGavock, daughter of Minnie's yougest brother Alex, weds Kevin McAfee of Ballycastle. They are pictured at Glenmona House gardens, Cushendun.*

Minnie's nephews Capt Alex Blaney and Dr Sean Blaney during Capt Alex's marriage to Margaret Black of Ballycastle.

The McGavock house at Libertyville, Lake Michigan.

Minnie celebrates her 80th birthday with her sister Lizzie Blaney.

Minnie, now retired from teaching.

St Patrick's Church, Craigagh, Cushendun.

# THE VIADUCT

THE MAGNIFICENTLY crafted bridge, which spans the beautiful valley of Glendun, lies about one and a half miles from Cushendun. It was one of Minnie's favourite sights. Adding to her interest in 'The Big Bridge' was the fact her father, when in his teens, carved his name at the base of one of the arches.

This graceful and imposing piece of masonry, with its tall central arch (84 feet) and two smaller arches, bears the Antrim Coast Road across a river and a road on the picturesque journey from Larne to Ballycastle. William Bald, the great Scottish engineer, planned the Road. In the face of much criticism he proposed to blast the coastal cliffs, and thus provide material with which to make the foundation for the Road close to the shore.

The work commenced at Larne in 1832. In this bold plan, gunpowder was used for blasting rocks. He was the first person to do so. The limestone rocks along the Antrim coast were easily blasted to form a road under the remainder of the cliffs. His project proved such a success that it has been dubbed 'the second finest Coast Road in Europe.' The date on Glendun Viaduct is 1839, seven years after the Coast Road was commenced. By this time William Bald was dead, and it was his young assistant engineer, Charles Lanyon - then 22 years of age, who supervised the work which must have been the completion of the Coast Road - as earlier dates on all the small bridges from Glendun to Ballycastle testify that his northern end of the road was made before the 'Big Bridge'.

A date was engraved on a big flat stone on each of the bridges that spanned streams in Carey mountain, and these dates are all earlier than 1839, which is the date on the Viaduct. It needed five years to build the Bridge, from 1834 to 1839. The river was paved by Mr McClarty of Layd, while the scaffolding was supported by ships' masts. Bald must have taken great trouble to design the Viaduct. The Viaduct is built of sandstone stones which were quarried and dressed near Ballycastle, and taken from there by horse and cart at two shillings and sixpence a load - the carting of one load taking a whole day. Stonemasons were paid 1 shilling and 2 pence a day, labourers 10 pence a day, and barrowmen and cartmen a shilling a day. The weekly wages bill was £3 and 18 shillings. The road over the Bridge was called 'The Line'. It begins at Castlegreen, and goes over the mountain with a fine wall built round the top of Craigagh Wood. The Antrim Coast Road, a splendid piece of engineering, cost was £37,140, and was £12,000 over budget!

In 1965, Antrim County Council gave the bridge a well deserved 'face-lift'. Workmen pumped cement between the stones (grouting), and re-pointed the whole structure, to replace the original sand and lime which was deteriorating. Their wage per hour was twice as much as the stone mason received in a week at the time of the original construction. This work was skilfully carried out by Cementation Company Limited of Belfast.

After the making of the Coast Road the ferry service between north Antrim and Scotland was no longer necessary. Before that, it was easier 'to go to market' by sea than to try and get to Ballymena over the bad mountain roads. Before the Ballycastle Line was made as part of the Coast Road project, there were two Coach roads from Cushendall to Ballycastle. One went up High Street, then continued on the Middle Road, across Dunurgan Road, up Craigagh, and straight past Gortin.

In 2010, it was still possible to see the outline of the course taken, as it is grass-covered with a little heather. The other Coach Road came over Layd and across Knocknacarry Bridge, then up Tyban, and past McClintock's. It can also be plainly seen climbing the heather-covered mountain. The Ballycastle Line is sited mid-way between these two roads.

# BACK to SCHOOL

DIVINE intervention probably played an acute role in Minnie taking a new direction, one away from the farm that would eventually lead to her becoming a schoolteacher. She looked back with justifiable pride at her persistence in overcoming so many hardships and obstacles to achieve her goal.

"A relation of my father, Father George McKay of Carrickfergus used to visit us, and insisted that I be sent to study for the King's Scholarship. I joined The National Correspondence Course, but soon found that I needed the help of a good teacher. So - on the next page of my life it was off to 'Cullen's Academy, Ballycastle'. I don't know who suggested Master John Henry Cullen, probably my mother's brother, Uncle Johnny. My mother, Lizzie McCambridge, was a native of Carey, and she and Uncle Johnny had been pupils of Cullen's when he taught in Ballyucan. He was a brilliant historian and mathematician. He was a B.A. who came from 'the banks of the Blackwater' (to quote himself), at Portadown.

"While in Ballyucan, he prepared two McKinley boys in their studies for the priesthood, Pat McHenry of Torr for teaching, my aunts Rosetta and Mary McNeill - who was reared with the Darragh's on the next farm to Crook, for the teaching training college. The children of the McNeill's (Jacks) were reared by relatives - Mrs Reay of Carnlough was one of them. Rosetta and Mary McNeill became teachers, Rosetta in England, and Mary in the south of Ireland at Ferns, County Wicklow, where she married. Rosetta died after teaching a few years in Lancashire.

"Master Cullen became Principal of the Boys' School in Ballycastle, and went to live there. After retiring, he started teaching boys privately in the billiard room behind the Dalriada Hall in Ann Street - above Ramsey's chemist shop. He coached young boys who were about to go to St Malachy's College - John McDonnell, Davy Morgan, Edmund Black, Eamonn McCambridge, Joe Casseley - to name but a few. When I went here I was his first girl pupil, and he took me in because of his friendship with my mother's people. I was isolated from his boys at a special table at the back of the class, and in winter the only one-burner oil heater was placed near me. His blackboard was the billiard table with the baize removed. It leaned against the wall.

"He always addressed me as 'Madam'. I'm sure he was in his seventies then, but he always took two steps at a time up the stairs at the school. He had a very keen eye set in a football-shaped head, with white closely cropped hair and a nice white beard. He always wore a black swallow-tailed suit, the tails of the coat being knee-length for he was very small. In the evenings, and well into the night, he coached young men who had done a stint at sea and were preparing to sit for their 'tickets'. Keevers Douglas, who later married a near neighbour Greta McFetridge of Castlegreen, and many more became sea captains, doctors and so forth with the help of Master Cullen.

"It was Mary Butler of Doon, my mother's cousin, who came with me to look for 'digs' - and she had me installed with a second cousin of theirs, Ms Annie McAuley (nee Annie McCaughan of Glenshesk). She had a delph shop in Ann Street, where her nephew Frank now has the chemist's shop, so I hadn't far to go to school. I started there in May 1921, when I was 17. Mary Clarke of Murlough and Joe Casseley were the boarders in 'The Mug Shop' - as Mrs McAuley's emporium was jokingly called, and Mary Clarke and I were called 'The Mary Mugs'. Mary had been a pupil at the Cross and Passion Convent, and also at Orange's Academy, Belfast. The nuns lived in a house in Market Street, and their school was upstairs in a building in the back yard. I think there were just two nuns teaching there.

"They prepared girls for English training colleges, so that's why I didn't think of going there. Afterwards, Canon Murphy bought the field on the hill behind their house, and a real convent was built - and finished around 1928. Tom O'Neill was the architect. During the autumn of 1921, Mary Clarke had complete control of the 'Mug Shop', for Mrs McAuley had to have an operation for appendicitis. I'm not sure if Dr Boylan performed it, but she was taken to a room in the old Workhouse where the inmates were looked after by Nurse Whelan and Nurse Wallace.

"A Mr Keenan from Glenshesk was the Master. Mary Clarke and I carried, at night, a mattress and blankets for the patient. She remained there for a month, at the end of which she was taken to Glenview to recuperate. Her cousin, Denis McBride had a taxi - and he drove Mrs McAuley, Mary Clarke and me up to 'The Magistrates'. Her brother was not long married to Mary Devlin of Armoy, and she had a delicious tea ready for us in a lovely dining room.

"Not many houses in those days had a separate dining room. Afterwards, the two Marys rode in state back to Ann Street. Mrs McAuley had a long convalescence for, when she stood up, a thick scab over the sole of her foot burst to reveal a festered sore. A hot water bottle had burned her during the operation and she was months treating it with boracic pads. So, Mary Clarke had a full-time occupation, and her sister Charity came to stay.

"At weekends, I sometimes went with them to Murlough, but I mostly either cycled home over the mountain, or stayed with Aunt Catherine or Aunt Kate and Uncle Daniel McKendry, who had no family and reared Maggie Gore.

"Cullen always had lessons for the half day on Saturday, so it would be pretty late by the time I reached Dunurgan. For the King's Scholarship one needed to learn tonic sol-fa, so I had lessons from Mrs Lamont, Bishop Lamont's mother. Her husband, Dan was great craic. He never missed Morning Mass, and always ate an apple as he waddled down the hill afterwards."

# PINS and NEEDLES

NEEDLEWORK was then on the syllabus. Master Cullen couldn't teach that, so he proposed that I go to Fullerton's Academy in Ballymena. He wrote on my behalf to Bob Fullerton, who had a Scholarship Class, and his sister, Miss Fullerton - who taught in a Primary School somewhere in the country, but then taught me needlework each Saturday forenoon.

"It was October, 1922, when my father came with me to look for digs in Ballymena. We were in Mick McAuley's van, for he took boxes of eggs and passengers on a Saturday. Charles MacCormack and his mother Bella were with us, and she came with me for the Academy interview. Afterwards, Charles insisted on my going with him to have our photos taken in Young's of Wellington Street. We later went to Mrs McIlwee's 'eating house' for a meal. She did a roaring trade on a Saturday, making 'meat teas' for hungry country folk. It was there I had a bed for the next five months. She charged me three shillings a week, at first.

"I fed myself, and Mick McAuley brought me butter and soda bread from home. Baker's bread was not wrapped nor sliced when I came back from morning lessons on a Saturday, so I sliced away at loaves of bread for the customers. To compensate me for this she reduced my weekly tariff to two shillings and six pence. I shared a small room with Jeanie and Lily McIlwee, her stepdaughters; they slept in a double bed on one side of a small back window, and I in a bed in the other corner. Under the window, between the two beds, was a dressing table at which I did my homework.

"I would be hours there, doing essays etc; and it was very cold. Jamie McIlwee, her husband, worked in Paddy Murphy's, and he was so concerned for my welfare that he brought home an old battered rectangular petrol can. I filled it with boiling water, placed it under the dressing table, and sat all night in comparative comfort with my feet on the petrol can. No central heating in those days. How did we survive!

"Every Sunday night, Jeanie Boyle took possession of me, and brought me on long walks out the Broughshane Road. Jeanie was a 'do-gooder', and kept me from harm. I forget the name of the teacher of the King's Scholarship class in the Academy, but he was great at English and Maths. A Miss Boyle taught me Botany most efficiently. Many pupils came from Glenravel on the old narrow gauge railway, Nora Healy and Jean McKeever among them. An uncle of Eileen Brogan's, Danny McQuillan, and Charlie Dowling were in the class. The McQuillan boy, the son of a publican, became a famous athlete, and Charlie, another publican's son, became a cattle dealer whose wife had a repository in Broughshane Street. They both died young.

"As I had never learned to play the piano, and thinking that I wouldn't be allowed into St Mary's Training College without it, I didn't apply for training. I just put down my name for a certificate to teach as a Junior Assistant Mistress. The examination was held during Easter Week, and one day in March I met Father Blacker, our P.P. in Cushendun. He asked me if I had applied to St Mary's, and I said that I hadn't Music. He said: 'Well, couldn't you learn it.' - that was about three weeks before the Exam.

"During that Spring, measles were rife in Ballymena. Jeanie and Lily McIlwee contracted them, and as I never had the disease I contracted it from them. I was feeling miserable on Easter Saturday and Sunday. On Easter Monday my head was splitting, as the Orangemen paraded up and down Broughshane Street beating the big drum. On Tuesday and Wednesday, I managed to walk to the Model School for the Examination. Mary MacCormick, Caroline McCormick, Annie Gore and Cissie McCollam were there too - and I sat in a desk beside Jeanie McKendry of Ballintoy. These girls were in digs for the week in Market Road, I think.

"There was a very cold wind blowing, and as I must have had a high temperature I was just shivering and miserable. On the Wednesday evening, when I came home to the warmer air and looked at my face in the mirror you may imagine my consternation to find it all out in spots - and with two more days of the Examination to do! But Mary Jane solved the problem by sending me in a taxi on Thursday morning. The invigilator (the Exam supervisor) placed me at a desk at the back of the room, well away from the other candidates, and allowed me to sit at an open fire in a wee room while the other candidates went home for lunch. But how cold my feet were! Mary Jane sent me a lunch with the Cushendun girls, and a wee bottle of whiskey to warm me.

"After the evening session, the taxi brought me home. Next morning it drew up at the door for me, but I couldn't go. When I tried to get out of bed my nose started to bleed - and I think I filled a wash-hand basin. So, I missed Friday, and I thought all my studies over two years were in vain. Mary Jane kept me in bed until the fever died down. Meantime, she was telling Mrs Fyffe of the shoe shop about me, and she sent word to me to get a doctor's certificate, and give it to the Fullerton's of the Academy to send the Ministry. No doctor attended me for the measles, but Mary Jane was friendly with old Dr Kennedy of Wellington Street.

"He was a cousin of Miss Kennedy of the Post Office in Knocknacarry, and she brought me to him. He had no hesitation in giving a certificate which I took to the Academy. Some weeks after I returned to Dunurgan, I received a letter from Mr Fullerton to state the Ministry would mark my Writing Ability from the papers I had done, and if I passed in the other subjects they would send for me to sit my Needlework exam in Belfast. The two subjects I missed on the Friday were Penmanship and Needlework.

"After I came back to Dunurgan I felt quite shaky, but had to knuckle down to helping in the fields. After a week or two Hugh, Lizzie, and Alex were down with measles. I had brought the germ home. Hugh was 17 at the time, and on the evening of Cushendun June Fair he stood at the gate talking to Glendun men about the prices etc; It was a cold, dewy evening, and he with a high temperature developed ear ache which turned into a mastoid. He was miserable for a few weeks, until Dr O'Kane sent him to the Mater Hospital for an operation performed by Dr Mulholland.

"About that time the results of the King's Scholarship appeared (just numbers), and Annie Gore's was the only one to appear. I remember Annie Ball saying: 'I'm surprised at you, Minnie'. However, before the week was out I had a letter from the Academy that I had passed in all subjects for which I sat, and that I'd have the Needlework exam later. So, early in July (Hugh was in the Mater by now - he was there for a month) I was notified to appear at Stormont Buildings on the 10th. When I got that letter, I was thinning turnips in the field below the Line, and my hands were not in a fit state to do fine needlework. However, I put on my Sunday best - a heavy Donegal tweed costume that Dickson the tailor had made for me during my sojourn in Ballycastle, and headed on a very sunny afternoon on the bicycle to get the train at Parkmore. I had to wheel the bicycle most of the way up Gault's Road, and the heat and weight of my suit were oppressive on that uphill stretch."

Reaching Belfast for a first time, and all on her own, was quite an ordeal. Minnie wrote: "I managed to make it to Belfast somehow. I had never been further south than Ballymena before, and made for a house in the Corporation Street area where Mrs Cavanagh, nee Ellen McKillop of the Big Bridge, had an 'eating house' and kept boarders. Patsy Connolly, Rosie Emerson's father was there - staying, while waiting for a vacant job on a ship."

Ellen Cavanagh's niece, Dan McKillop of The Viaduct said: "My aunts, Ellen and Kate once operated a B & B in the docks area of Belfast, above the Sunflower Bar on Garmoyle Street. It was mainly for seamen. Ellen (who died in 1930) married a Carnlough seaman James Cavanagh. The other aunt, Kate also married a seaman from Carnlough named Regan."

Minnie added: "Mrs Cavanagh brought me to the Mater Hospital to visit Hugh, and next day I started on my own for Parliament Buildings. Stormont wasn't built then, and Parliament was held in a wooden structure in the grounds of Queen's University. The trams were running then, and one could travel long distances very cheaply. They travelled very slowly, but at last I reached my destination."

When the Parliament Buildings Stormont were completed they proved an excellent example of Georgian architecture in Belfast. Stormont Castle was the main building in the Estate. Around the end of the 18th century, the Rev. John Cleland was Rector of Newtownards from 1789 to 1809. It was at Storm Mount, as it was then known, that about 1830 Cleland created 'a plain house'. It was a mid or late Georgian house in the shape of a plain rectangle. On the southerly facing side was a projection, presumably for the entrance.

Later on in the 1800's, the Cleland family commissioned local architect, Thomas Turner, to convert the house into a Baronial style castle. The time of origin of certain drawings held at the Public Record Office in Belfast, suggest that Turner may have taken his inspiration from them when designing the modifications to Stormont House, believed by some to be the work of Edinburgh architect William Burn, who had designed several buildings such as Ballywalter church and Castlewellan. In 1921, the Estate became vacant, and in the absence of any purchasers it became available later that year. It was acquired for the erection of Parliament Buildings for the new Northern Ireland Parliament.

The grounds of Stormont Estate covered 224 acres at the time of purchase, and cost approximately £20,000. The cost of constructing Parliament Buildings came close to £1.7 million. The Prince of Wales, later King Edward VIII, declared the Buildings open on November 16, 1932, on behalf of King George V. The building is designed in Greek Classical tradition, constructed by Stewart Partners Ltd under the guidance of architect Arnold Thornley, from Liverpool. He was a man who paid great attention to detail with many of the features in Parliament Buildings having symbolic reference. One example of this detail can be illustrated by the length of the building for it measures exactly 365 feet wide, representative of one foot for each day of the year. Arnold Thornley later received a Knighthood from George V in recognition of his architectural work.

Minnie's first trek through Belfast proved a pleasant one. She recalled her test: "There in the sunshine outside one of the buildings at Queen's sat two lady inspectors in beautiful light summer frocks. One of them was Miss Jackson, who was later drowned in the *Princess Victoria* disaster. I felt completely 'out of it' in my heavy tweed costume. Inside, I was set some work to do, and managed a pass. Miss Jackson drew a sketch of how I was to reach Fountain Street, to buy from the Educational Company a manual of needlework.

"After many stops, and enquiries from policemen, I reached Fountain Street, and then Corporation Street. Next day, I returned home - and it must have been the morning of July 12, for the train from Belfast to Ballymena was filled with men in regalia. My King's Scholarship pass didn't help me to get a school, and the certificate was to last only three years. The only job I got was a three-month substitute's job for Miss Healy in Knocknacarry School.

"I returned to Cullen's 'Academy' in September of 1925, and by then he had a mixed class including Lena Gillan of Armoy and Mary Molloy. I remained with him until after Christmas, and then headed again for Ballymena. The St Louis Convent was opened a year or so before, so I became enrolled there. Mairead McLaughlin, Cassie Geddis and myself were the only pupils doing the King's Scholarship. Besides two or three nuns, there were just three lay teachers. I felt it strange moving from room to room to the different teacher after sitting in the one room with Cullen at the 'Academy'.

"During that Spring, I boarded with Nurse Devlin in Suffolk Street. Mrs McIlwee couldn't take me, as she had full boarders, one of whom was Jim Gillen of Armoy. During the exam week Maggie Scullion of Portglenone stayed with us in Suffolk Street. She took 2nd place in the exam, and was

*Minnie, with son Daniel (left), at the Mass Rock Procession.*

*Old time Cushendun hurlers assemble at Knocknacarry Hall in 2009 during a special night in honour of long serving official Malachy McSparran. BACK-Danny McQuillan, Terry O'Hara, Mick Quinn, Denis O'Hara. FRONT-Raymond McHugh, John McKay, Malachy McSparran, Alex McKay, Johnny White.*

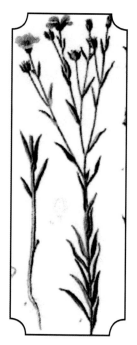

*Minnie with daughter-in-law Maura O'Hara, wife of her eldest son Alex, and grandsons Peter O'Hara, front, and Michael (in pram). Also facing the camera are her sons Daniel (back) and Hugh.*

*The Lint flower*

*Cushendun Harbour*

The late Paddy Hamilton, skipper of Cushendun Emmets, proudly holds the Antrim Junior Hurling Championship trophy after beating Belfast St John's at Loughguile in 1963.

Harry McGavock, a nephew of Minnie and son of Hugh McGavock.

Mary Gilligan, eldest daughter of Minnie's brother Hugh McGavock. Mary, who lives in Lisnaskea, was born in Dunurgan.

The new generation. In July 2010, Megan Morrow, the 12-year-old neice of Emily McGavock from Ballycastle County Antrim, made history as the youngest capped international in an Ireland Under-25 outdoor bowls team.

*Minnie's celebrates her 90th birthday with her sister Mrs Lizzie Blaney.*

## From Railroads to Lumber:
## The McGavocks in Beloit

### by Scott Reichard

From Adams to Warner, many names are associated with the history of business in Beloit, and not least among these is the name McGavock. From the 1860s to the 1950s, whether the talk was about railroads, groceries or lumber, the McGavock name was sure to come up.

The McGavock's association with Beloit began with the arrival of Hugh Sr. Born in 1828 in County Antrim, Ireland, he immigrated to the United States in 1847 with his parents, three brothers, and two sisters. An enterprising young man, Hugh became a grading contractor for the old Galena Railroad which eventually became the Chicago Northwestern. When the line reached the Wisconsin state line at Beloit in 1852 and construction stalled for a time, Hugh decided to purchase land in the area and start farming. He stayed here for the rest of his life.

Hugh married Catherine Buckley in 1857, and together they raised ten children to adulthood: Alex, John, Hugh Jr., Patrick, Thomas, James, William, Edward, Charlotte, and Mary. Some well known Beloit businesses were developed by their children. Alex and John, and later Hugh Jr., went into the grocery business in Beloit in 1882 and continued for over 30 years, eventually building the McGavock block on 4th Street (still standing.) Hugh Jr. and John went into the coal delivery business and eventually expanded into lumber and building supplies, known as McGavock Bros. and later as McGavock Lumber. They were located at Cross Street and St. Lawrence until the late 1930s, and then moved to Porter Avenue. They sold the business in the early 1950s. They also had a construction company, and many quality homes were built in Beloit by the McGavocks; the author's house was built as a wedding present by the family for sister Charlotte and her husband in 1906. Most of the family was involved in these businesses in one way or another.

The land that Hugh Sr. and his family farmed eventually became important additions to Beloit's west side. The area bounded by Hackett, Portland, Eighth, and St. Lawrence was know as "McGavock's Forty," and here he grew tobacco and dried it in sheds that were located at 10th and Roosevelt. Mr. McGavock's house still stands at the corner of 9th and Roosevelt. The land on which St. Jude's Catholic Church stands was a donation from Hugh McGavock, a devout Catholic. The current offices of the Beloit Historical Society are located in McGavock's 3rd Addition, and in all there are 6 McGavock additions on Beloit's west side.

The McGavocks were well known for non-business endeavors also. John and Edward were city aldermen at different times during the first two decades of this century, and various members of the family were very active in the affairs of St. Jude in the days of father Hanz. There was a time when everywhere you turned you encountered the McGavocks.

Even though the McGavock name isn't as familiar today, their descendants still live in the area, including Finnegans who are descended from Hugh Jr. When talk turns to the history of Beloit 100 years ago, whether it be about farming, railroads, retail, or politics, the McGavocks are sure to figure prominently.

Contents

*The website chartered history of the McGavock's of Beloit, U.S.A.*

called to St Mary's. Instead she joined the Cross & Passion nuns, went to England, and was the recipient of many degrees there. Another boarder in Nurse Devlin's was Maggie Reid of Cloughmills, whose sister Mary later married Jim Richmond. Loughguile and Antrim hurler and top violinist Seamus Richmond is their son. Maggie Reid died young. The Parochial Hall, Ballymena, had just been built, and to raise funds there was a concert or play every night during Easter Week, and we attended a few despite examination fever. I sat the King's Scholarship examination during Easter 1926. Mairead (McLaughlin) and I were called to Training.

"I entered St Mary's Training College early in September, 1926, getting a lift with Alex Scally of The Villa, and staying on that Sunday night in his digs in Mulholland Terrace beside the College. Next day, I entered College and met my companions for the next two years - 33 of us - and 85 or so second-year students. Mairead was there, and so too was Father Blacker's niece, Anna McArdle. In Cushendun, I would feel it presumptuous to associate with the Parish Priest's niece, but in College we were all equal, and became life-long friends."

By the way, St Mary's, opened in 1900 on the Falls Road in west Belfast, was the first teacher-training college in Belfast. In 1999, St Mary's became a College of Queen's University, Belfast.

Minnie loved every moment of her term at St Mary's: "Those two years were the happiest of my life. When we went back, after the summer holidays of 1927, each girl's name was stuck on the inside of the desk she was allocated in the big study hall. And where do you think mine was? - under the lid of the first desk. I had been appointed President by Mother Francis on her last year as Reverend Mother and Principal. Eileen Keville of Lurgan was Vice-President, and Anna was the Third Prefect.

"I think they chose me because I was a good deal older and staider for this job at which my heart failed. I had to remember to ring bells for the different classes, and I nearly always forgot to ring the bell for Miss Murphy's Art class. She complained to the nuns that I had no respect for her. Even with these onerous duties I did enjoy myself. We danced every night in the Recreation Hall. Over 80 first-year students came in that year, and Kitty Kelly - Cushendall Mrs Stone's niece, was one of them, as was also Dolly McWilliams of Ballymoney - an aunt of the eye specialist."

# SOUTH ARMAGH

THERE were few teaching vacancies in the Autumn of 1928, but Minnie remained patient. Her great friend, Anna McArdle was appointed to Cullyhanna School almost immediately.

"I answered an advertisement for a substitute for Alicia Lavelle in Ballynacloshe School in the Crossmaglen Parish. Her husband, Denis said that he picked me for the job because he couldn't find Knocknacarry on the map. 'She'll do for this country school, for she's from the back of beyond.'

"We corresponded at how and where we should meet in Newry. I told him that he would recognise me because I would wear a Donegal tweed coat and a black hat which mercifully hid my very red hair. I didn't read over what I wrote and what he received was 'hair' instead of 'hat'. The flippant letter he sent informed me that I shouldn't be difficult to recognise as he didn't think there were many piebalds about. And he said that he had red hair too, but didn't hide it under a hat and that he would be sporting real gold Fainne.

"He brought me by bus to Silverbridge, where he and his wife lived - and then by pony and trap to his mother's house a few miles away near the Border with Louth and just across the 'loanin' from the School. Old Denis Lavelle had been his son's predecessor, and built this very big house and shop to which there was only a vegetable garden attached. The old man was ill, but his wife was quite active. Their daughter Rosie was in charge of the shop, and Nan and a servant girl named Alice did the housework.

"Their oldest son John was the accountant with 'Quinn's of the Milestone' in Newry, and he came home every Saturday night. I think that he really owned the shop. Tom was a carpenter in Dublin. Peter, the youngest, delivered groceries in a horse and cart round the countryside. He and Rose had served their time in Quinn's branch in Newcastle. A daughter, Brigid was married to a Customs Officer Hayes (before I went the Customs men, who were not married lodged in Lavelle's big house - for their 'Post' was only about 200 yards away), and lived a few miles down the road beside Kilcurry Church. It is in this Parish that Faughan is situated up the hill from Kilcurry, a couple of miles from Dundalk.

"I didn't have too much to spend, for out of my £2 and 10 shillings a week I paid £1 for board, and sent £1 home every week. But Rosie and I had a wonderful time, and during the long Hallowe'en week-end she brought me by train to Dublin to stay with Tom, who took us to the Abbey Theatre to see *The Plough and the Stars*. The Abbey opened on December 27, 1904, and in 1925 it became the first State-subsidised theatre in the English speaking world. The original building was destroyed by fire in 1951. In the early days the Abbey witnessed the launch of works by playwrights such as William Butler Years, Sean O'Casey and John Millington Synge. O'Casey's first play to be staged there was *The Shadow of a Gunman* in 1923, then *Juno and the Paycock*, followed by *The Plough and the Stars* in 1926.

"One week-end, I cycled up to Anna's place, and one week-end she came and stayed with me in Lavelle's. Anna's father, James McArdle, was living then. Louis worked the big farm and Dora, the youngest girl of a big family, kept house. Gene was the youngest, then a boy in shorts. Their mother, Fr.Blacker's sister, was a lovely person, and played cards with the family every night - until the 'wee' small hours. We also sang and danced to the music of a fiddle played by an old neighbour. Rosie and I cycled to Kilcurry for Mass on a Sunday, yet once or twice we must have gone to Mass in the old church in Glassdrummond, where the Crossmaglen P.P. Canon Sheerin, or his curate, Fr Ward, said Mass.

"Canon Sheerin was the manager of Ballynacloshe School and of Glassdrummond and of Crossmaglen Schools. I don't know how many teachers taught in that large parish. Beside Glassdrummond's old church was a three-teacher school. A man and his wife taught there, and lived miles away from the school, like the Lavelle's. During the summer of 1928 there was a vacancy there for the third teacher. The Canon contacted Sister Augustine, Principal of St Mary's who had succeeded Mother Francis that year, to find a suitable applicant from her past students. She wrote to me, probably because I had been president, and because I came from the country, but the new teacher would have to be able to play the organ in the new Church he was going to build at Glassdrummond.

"As Sister Raymond, who taught singing, was on 'Retreat', she couldn't find out if I would suit, she said 'Of course', I had to reply that I had no instrumental music, and let go a good permanent job when jobs were scarce. Then in the Autumn, in the very same Parish, I had this substitute job, and met the new teacher, Molly Grant, from Buncrana, who had a Degree in Music. She invited me to visit her where she boarded, with the Principal and his wife. She was miserable in this lonely country place, and she was not required to play the organ until the opening of the new church, two or three years after she married a doctor.

"Years later, when I was back in McArdle's during the summer holidays, Anna and I visited that church - the most impressive I ever saw. It is situated on a hill with the dark hills of Louth and Dundalk and the sea in the distance. Above the front door is a row of white statues, and inside the ceiling is made of of saucer-shaped domes along the same lines as a famous church in Dublin. Mrs Conlon's brother lived in a big house nearby. There must be a very big population in south Armagh. But I don't think I was once in Crossmaglen, which was about five miles away. It was awkward getting home before Christmas.

"They got me a lift to Newry, in a bread van, and I stayed overnight in John Lavelle's digs. Another of Quinn's men lodged there too. He was Mr O'Donnell, who later married a Belfast girl named McAlister, and started up on his own. This McAlister girl was a cousin of Mrs McHugh, as her mother was a Delargy from Glenravel. Turlough O'Donnell, the judge, is their son, as is journalist Donall, once a colleague of Denis in the *Irish News*.

"Old Mr Lavelle died after I left, but I kept in touch with Rosie and Nan. Rosie married a man named Toal, and lived in Dundalk. Anna and I visited her when she had two lovely sons, but Nan wrote to tell me the sad news that she died at the birth of her third child. Nan married a shopkeeper in Cullyhanna, while John married a relation of James F. Fitzpatrick, the solicitor. They said that he about owned Quinn's business. When he died a few years ago they said one of his sons was going to be a priest. Peter runs the shop."

# DOWN to DROMARA

ARLY in 1929 Minnie received word of a possible teaching post high in the Mountains of Mourne. "I was spending a holiday in Ballypatrick with Aunt Kate and Uncle Daniel McKendry - who were my Godparents, and Maggie Gore, when my brother Hugh arrived on a motorbike with a letter from Mairead McLaughlin to inform me that a teacher in Muninabane, Dromara, County Down, required a substitute for March and April.

"This teacher, a Mrs O'Hare, was friendly with the teacher in Crebilly, County Antrim, and asked her to help search for the substitute. The teacher near Slemish contacted Mairead, who had already got a permanent job in Randalstown, and wrote to me to come to Ballymena so that the Crebilly teacher could interview me. I don't remember how I managed to safely reach Ballycastle Station, with a good depth of snow on the ground. Hugh brought me on the back of his motorbike, and I reached Mairead's house that evening. Her father, who was the kindest of men and a real gentleman, walked with me by moonlight through deep snow to Crebilly, some four miles away, to be interviewed by the teacher there. In turn, the Crebilly lady teacher, whose husband taught there also, then communicated with Mrs O'Hare, and I got the job.

"I travelled to Dromara on a Saturday evening, and the bus from Belfast was packed with teachers returning from a day's shopping. The fare was one shilling. I assumed that Dromara must be very near Belfast. After stopping and starting, and being in the bus what I thought was a considerable length of time, I asked a man in the seat opposite, if we were near Dromara. He laughed, and said we were still in Belfast - just on the Lisburn Road. He asked where I came from, and told me he came from Ballycastle, and was a brother of Mr Craig the Auctioneer. He taught somewhere between Belfast and Dromara. He told me Dromara was over twenty miles away, and the fare was so cheap because there was a rival bus company.

"I was to stay with a Mrs McKay and a Mrs Morrow - two widows who lived together in a little thatched cottage about a mile from the School. They were relatives of Mr O'Hare. Mrs McKay hired a taxi to meet me at Dromara, and we travelled for a mile through rich level country, until we reached Finnis at one end of a road which stretched round the hip of Slieve Croob, about half-way up this mountain where the River Lagan rises. Along this road were dotted small thatched farmhouses with enormous two-storey slated outhouses adjoining. The farms were small, and the land poor on the mountain side - not like the rich farming country around Dromara.

"At the corner near the Dromara-Rathfriland road were the Church, the School and the Parochial House of Finnis, while a few miles along was Muninabane School. Across the road from Mrs McKay's were three houses. One was owned by a farmer named Peter McKinney. He was a young married man who knew Pat 'Casey' McCormick of Cushendun, as he had spent some time on the prison ship SS *Argenta* with him."

The SS *Argenta* was the prison ship when internment began in May, 1922. Dawson Bates, the Northern Ireland Minister of Home Affairs, imposed Martial Law on the nationalist community of Northern Ireland. Under British Partition, and the formation of the Northern Ireland Government there were 300 'Sinn Fein' men arrested within a 24-hour period starting close to midnight on May 22, 1922. Most prisoners were allegedly Nationalists and Pro-Treaty. On the orders left by James Craig, the Prime Minster of Northern Ireland, over 900 people were arrested under the Special Powers Act, and held on the SS *Argenta*. In late 1939, following a mutiny in Derry Jail, the Prison Ship penal system was again adopted with some 200 suspected IRA men detained by the Northern Ireland government transferred to a specially-adapted prison ship in Strangford Lough. The ship was the 4,000 ton steamer and one-time troop ship, the *Al Rawdah* - charted from the Ministry of Shipping and fitted with 300 cells. In the 1970's, and mainly following arrest without charge or trial, there was a further round-up, with prisoners incarcerated on board the HMS *Maidstone*.

Minnie added: "Peter's unmarried young brother and sister lived close by in a newly-built big two-storey house. They had been orphans, and an uncle who was a Parish Priest nearby regulated their lives. Maggie McKinney and I became great friends. She was very industrious, and had umpteen hens set on eggs, and had a turkey too. She attended needlework classes in Dromara Technical College, and brought me with her. One night we were at a function in Ballynahinch Technical College, at which Lord Charlemont was the principal speaker."

Born in 1880, the 8th Viscount Charlemont was the Northern Ireland Minister for Education from 1926 to 1937. He was elected to the House of Lords as a Representative Peer, and to the Northern Ireland Parliament as a Senator - sitting there from 1925 to 1937. He died on August 20, 1949. The Charlemont named emerged from Sir Toby Caulfeild, born 1565 in Oxfordshire. Caulfeild was given lands in Ireland, and created the Barony of Charlemont from the name of a forest along the River Blackwater. The first Lord Charlemont created an empire. He was the biggest landowner in County Armagh and County Tyrone. The 8th Viscount inherited the Viscouncy of Charlemont and Barony of Caulfeild from his uncle in 1913, and after Charlemont Fort in County Armagh was burnt in 1922 by the IRA, he resided mainly at Drumcairne, Stewartstown, in County Tyrone.

Minnie resumed her memory rewind: "Mrs McKay's thatched house was built on an incline, and the kitchen floor sloped as the foundation had not been levelled in the long ago. Mrs Morrow taught me to sew on her treadle machine, and when I would start to move the treadle with my feet the machine would move down the floor! It was a big kitchen, and in a corner near the 'Modern Mistress' stove was a big table at which the game of Poker was played every Sunday night, and many week nights. The keenest, most punctual, player was the old Parish Priest, Fr McAvoy - a chain smoker, who had the top of a finger missing, just like Dave Allen on TV. He was a great character, much loved by his Curate, Father MacCartan, who once did relief for Father Blacker and knew Cushendun and Cushleake well.

"They said that the old P.P. had been educated at the University of Salamanca, in western Spain - some 200 km west of Madrid, and close to the Portuguese border. Salamanca's seat of specialist learning was founded in 1218. It is the oldest university in Spain, and once was regarded one of the four great universities of the western World, alongside Oxford, Paris and Bologna. Because of his training in Spain, Fr McAvoy was used to early rising, would be walking in the garden reading his breviary at 7 o'clock in the morning. He used to say that the number of hours in bed were 'six for a woman, seven for a man, and eight for a pig'.

"I don't think either of the widows played. I 'ceilied' with McKinney's, but around that table would be six or eight people, some from far away, and one woman from across the road. Once they held a sweep for the Grand National and my name was pulled out of the hat for outsider *Gregalach,* which won at 100-1. That was the 1929 Grand National. The jockey was a Robert Everett, the trainer Tom Reader, and the owner a Mrs M.A. Gemmell. The first prize from our sweep was a big turnip of a man's watch, which Hugh got when I came home."

The path down from the rarefied air in the Mountains of Mourne led Minnie from what she regarded an enchanting time to a job closer to home, merely 14 miles up the County Antrim Coast Road in the holiday seaside town of Carnlough. It was a short-haul exercise, as a substitute teacher for a Miss Grant. Her sister Lizzie alerted her to an advertisement for the job.

"While I was in Dromara, there was an advertisement in the paper for a substitute for Mrs Grant in Carnlough. My sister Lizzie secured this job for me, from Father James Clenaghan P.P. He had previously been President of St Malachy's College, and was very interested in the welfare of the youth of the parish. He had classes on a Saturday for the senior boys and girls - and taught them Irish and Mathematics. I was assistant to a grand old lady named Miss Kennedy, who was a brilliant teacher. Her class in the singing section of the Glens Feis won every year.

"Fr Clenaghan didn't allow me home at week-ends, although Cissie McCollam, who taught in Ballyvaddy, never missed a week-end home to Cushendall. He told me that the parents of the Carnlough children would expect me to stay, and teach something extra to the children. I can't remember ever teaching anything at the week-ends, but Miss O'Hare and I and Miss Kennedy had lovely walks - and I remember visiting Miss Bertha Hamill and her mother in a delightful house with a large garden in Stoneyhill - the first house on the left of the Ballymena Road. Miss Hamill was a Music Teacher, and travelled each week to give private lessons in Cushendall.

"Miss Ellie McKay and she became great friends, and many pupils of Miss McKay's did her Music Exam in Miss Hamill's parlour where the examiner came each year. Miss O'Hare was assistant in the Boys' School. She was from Killough, County Down, and we both lodged with two Belfast sisters, who occupied the renovated stables at the back of the house now owned by Quality Supplies McAlister's. It was next to the Church and graveyard, and most convenient to the School, which was situated behind the Church and between the two old garages. There is a new graveyard up Drumorne loaning."

# WINDOW GAIN

**F**ATHER George McKay must have been not only a bit eccentric but also a very impatient parson. Minnie's tale of a fun trip to Carrickfergus in 1929 witnessed the premature promotion to Sainthood of Irish martyr Oliver Plunkett. She also quietly slips in a subtle mention of meeting her future husband, Alex O'Hara, during what proved a unique occasion.

"For St Patrick's week-end of 1929, I was invited to Carrickfergus to stay with Mary McCorry in Father George McKay's, the P.P's house. He was her uncle, and also a second cousin of my father. The occasion was a bit of a do, as Master and Mrs Doherty were coming from Cushendun with their troupe to perform and raise money for Father George's Renovation Fund. That was the year when he erected a new window dedicated to Saint Oliver Plunkett, who at that time was Blessed Oliver and was not canonised for many years after Fr George had died. But he thought in 1929, "it was time he was canonised, as he'd been Blessed long enough."

Incidentally, Fr George was 46 years ahead of his time regarding the elevation of Oliver Plunkett to Saint Oliver. Born on November 1, 1629, in Loughcrew, County Meath, Oliver Plunkett became Archbishop of Armagh and Primate of All-Ireland. He was arrested during the English persecution of Roman Catholics, and was accused of treason at a kangaroo-style court, despite a lawful court failing to convict him. In a shameful episode, Oliver Plunkett was hanged, drawn and quartered at Tyburn, London, on July 1, 1681. He was 51, and the last Roman Catholic martyr to die in England. On May 23, 1920, he was beatified in Rome by Pope Benedict XV. On October 1, 1975, he was canonized in Rome by Pope Paul VI - the first new Irish Saint for close on 700 years.

In 2010, I checked on the whereabouts of 'The Window' through detective work by Glenarm-born Canon Alex McMullan. He discussed the uniquely special pane of glass with Cushendun-reared Fr Dermot McKay. It was discovered the window was saved after a new church was erected, and the uniquely special pane was placed in the Confessional Room.

Minnie added: "Also there, for the Fr George week-end, were Maura O'Clery-Clarke, who was trained with me, and a Miss Ryan, who taught with Maura - and stayed with her in a rented bungalow somewhere in County Down. They stayed in Carrickfergus with Miss Ryan's sister, a Mrs Savage whose husband and she taught in the School. The Ryan's came from the west of Ireland. Some years afterwards, both Miss Ryan and Miss O'Clery-Clarke were burned to death in their bungalow when a Tilly lamp fell and set it alight. .

"That was a memorable night for the Renovation Fund. As well as the Doherty's and the actors, there was a 'following' from Cushendun, and Alex O'Hara was among them. Mr and Mrs Doherty taught in the Boys' School in Knocknacarry - and at first trained their pupils to act, but later brought in past pupils to perform in the more advanced plays. These plays were famous at that time, and after being performed in Cushendun they would be asked to help raise money in such parishes as Toomebridge and Carrickfergus. It was an all-male cast; some dressed as ladies - and very funny they looked. 'Wee' Hugh Murray was always cast as the flippant young female, with Jack ('Bill') McCormick and my young brother Alex McGavock as the elderly women.

"Although they felt embarrassed they always obeyed their old teachers, and loyally went to the school for practices every other winter night. When the locals saw it in the School, on a stage erected in the Master's end and the folding doors drawn open, they had great fun picking out who was which lady! Alex McGavock always flicked a big white handkerchief across his face, and blew his nose about a hundred times to try and conceal his identity. Just once, in Father Joseph Boylan's time (1917), did the Doherty's invite any of Miss Wilde's pupils to perform with their boys. They put on a play entitled *The Wishing Princess of the Glens.* I was the princess. Mary McBride was the witch. Maggie McCormick and James O'Neill were King and Queen. Charles MacCormick was a government official.

"Miss Wilde produced many action songs with her pupils that night, among them being *Eight Little Mothers.* My sister Lizzie and Mary Margaret McKay (later to be Mrs John O'Hara, my sister-in-law) being two of them. Fr Boylan had priests from Belfast singing, and that famous man who composed songs of Belfast in the vernacular sang one of his famous compositions - *My Aunt Jane.*" Miss Wilde remains an iconic figure in the history of education in Cushendun Parish. In 1893, she arrived in the Glens from Laurencetown, County Down, when appointed the Principal of Knocknacarry Primary Girls' School. She retired in 1936, and died in July 1948.

"Fr Boylan had a cinematograph show during his short stay in Cushendun, about a year and a half until he died in November 1917, and I saw Charlie Chaplin for the first time, and also a play called *The Shanughram.* Fr Boylan succeeded Fr Henry Skeffington as P.P. Neither had any curate, nor had Father Tom Blacker of Dorsey, County Armagh, who succeeded Fr Boylan. But the predecessor, Father McCann had several. Father McCann christened me, yet never entered my baptism in the Parish Register, but Father Tom Keenan, the curate in Fr Fred Burns' time, rectified that at the time of my marriage. Kathleen McBride's name was also omitted. I think all baptisms in 1904 were not entered.

"Father John Small was the curate at the beginning of the century. He lodged with Mrs Stewart, where Rosemary McKay now lives in Knocknacarry. Then there was Fr MacConnelogue (later P.P. of Bellaghy) who lived in Cloney. After him came Fr McDonald to Cloney, while Fr Rhodes lived in Innispollen. As there was no Parochial House, Fr Bernard

McCann first occupied the Strand House, but was later evicted for non payment of rent - and then moved up to Martin's house in Straid. He came over Dunurgan Road for a walk every day, and on the way bought a quarter of cinnamon lozenges from Anne at the Turn's shop. I was usually at the gate waiting for him, and he always shared his sweets with me, and then when he went past Dunurgan gave one to Johnny McAteer's dog, Spring.

"He was later appointed P.P. of Glenravel, where he died many years later. Fr Skeffington (and no curate) was next. He lived in the old Coastguard Station (now the Maud Cottages). His first baptism was my younger brother Alex, who was born on 11th February, 1912. Fr. Skeffington had a housekeeper and two maids when he hob-nobbed with influential people who came to stay in the 'Big Houses' like Glendun Lodge and Cushendun House. His housekeeper was a widow named Mrs Carr. Her maiden name was Flora McDonnell. Her husband had been a native of Portrush. She was highly educated, and held evening classes to teach French and Music. Greta McFetridge was one of her famous pupils. I was too busy in the fields to think of going to her.

"Fr George McKay held a Sports Day in Cushendun on 15th August, 1916. I think Fr Joseph Boylan was here at the time, because it was his friendship with the Riordan's which caused them to holiday in Cushendun. There were two girls, Eileen and Elsie, and three boys, I think. Mrs Riordan was a widow - a sister of Maurice Maguire, the famous Belfast dentist, and also a sister of a Dominican nun in Portstewart. In later years, a dentist son practised in Larne, and he and a Larne chemist took Michael McKillop's house in Drumfasky as a holiday home. During the Second World War, my husband's brother John would sell them meat at the weekend, although they were not rationed with him. I remember the chemist bringing a present of sugar to Granny O'Hara in acknowledgement of this concession.

"On a day before the 15th, Miss Wilde sent me with a live duck to Mary Adrain in Cushendun to ask her to kill, pluck and prepare it for Fr George's fete. I remember the Riordan boys riding round me on bicycles and snatching the duck from me. I think they later delivered it to Mary Adrain. Everyone in the country was expected to support Fr George's big day at which tea would be served by the young ladies of the parish. My mother said afterwards that Annie Ball was the best looking girl there - dressed in a green frock. Father Boylan succeeded Fr Skeffington, who was appointed P.P. of Portrush and later became the P.P. of St Brigid's, Belfast, where he died.

"After Fr Boylan died, Fr Tom Blacker came and stayed until the mid 30's, when he then became P.P. of Holywood. Next came Fr Burns, and Fr Keenan as curates. Fr Burns was in ill health, and died in December 1943, and then the Parish Priest appointed was Fr John Matthew Lynch from Roscommon. He had several curates - Fr Padraig Murphy, Fr Charles Vallely, Fr Henry, Fr Courtney, Fr Tom McKillop, Fr Frank McCorry, Fr Fred McSorley and Fr Patrick McVeigh.

"Fr Lynch made many changes in the parish. He had the Parochial Hall built and completed by 1947, the old school renovated, both churches renovated, and the Woodwork (Youth) centre built. Night class in woodwork, cookery and needlework were held by teachers from the Technical colleges. Master Fullerton of Ballymena supervised the woodwork classes, and also later at Garron Tower. Then, in 1958, when there was nothing else here to renovate, Fr Lynch went as P.P. to Ballycastle to build schools."

# CAUSEWAY CALLS

AFTER the spell in Carnlough, Minnie heard, in August 1929, of a job vacancy in Portstewart. The post was at St Colum's, a Primary outlet opened in 1912. Headmaster was Mr McHugh.

"Mairead McLaughlin notified me of a vacancy in Portstewart Primary School," recalled Minnie, "She said if I got the post I could stop with her Aunt Kate in Belmont, Atlantic Circle. A Miss Matthews, a relation of Mairead's, had been the school's first Junior Assistant Mistress at St Colum's P.S. She suffered a bad chill in the Spring, and died at the end of the Summer. Portstewart was then a curacy of Coleraine.

"I went to Father Blacker for a recommendation, and he told me he'd meet with the manager, Fr MacLaverty P.P. Coleraine, at the installation the next week of Dr Mageean as Bishop of Down and Connor and he'd put in a word for me. That night, Fr MacLaverty and he slept in the same room in St Patrick's Presbytery in Belfast, and it was the middle of the night when Fr Blacker remembered to mention me to Fr MacLaverty. That was in the middle of August, and Fr MacLaverty said he was going on holiday and the appointment could wait, until he returned.

"But, a day or so later, Fr Blacker received a phone call from Fr MacLaverty, asking him to send me over for an interview immediately as the Principal, Mr McHugh, insisted on having a teacher when the school re-opened before the end of August. Anna McArdle was on holiday with her uncle Fr Blacker - and he sent her with me on the bus to Coleraine. We went via Ballymena. Fr MacLaverty treated us right royally with a lovely lunch, and then accompanied us in a taxi (he never owned a car) to Portstewart to visit the School. It was an old corrugated church that had been converted to a two-room school after the new Star of the Sea church was built.

"The Junior room had a stage which occupied the place of the Sanctuary, and on this stage I observed a piano. I was in terror, lest he asked me to play, which I couldn't. Luckily he didn't, and I was appointed the school's first trainee assistant - but on probation for two years. Because there was a dance at home on the last Friday night of August I didn't start in the school until Monday the 2nd of September. There were some visitors in Belmont, but I got a lovely room to myself. I thought I was in heaven that September, soaking up the Autumn sunshine in such congenial surroundings. Master McHugh was very helpful, and I had a class of the best children I ever met. I often wonder what happened to them all. I know Dan McLaughlin is an R.M. His cousin Danny Taylor is head of a university in Tasmania, and Biddy Taylor became a specialist dentist in Belfast.

"I often wonder what happened to the soft-spoken McGarry's, and the 'regal' Heustons. They were born in Africa, where their mother had been a nurse. Their father, the son of a Portstewart clergyman, developed Polio. They were converts to Catholicism. The family comprised of Peggy, Denis, Eric, Sheila and Dodo. Portstewart's Star of the Sea Church was built with money left in the Will of a Coleraine publican, Mr Glenn, and there was as much money left over to build the new St Colum's School - which was built in a big field donated by Mr Montague, the landlord. I was in the new school only three months when I came to Knocknacarry on 'All Fools' Day 1936. But, in Coleraine they had a beautiful Parochial House at the top of a very large field, but the old St Malachy's Church was a dilapidated affair surrounded by distilleries and public houses. The first time I visited it, a drunk man was singing outside the pub next door.

"In the yard was the sacristan's little house, and between it and the church was attached a clothes line on which hung the children's nappies. Most of the windows were broken too. Bishop Mageean insisted on Fr MacLaverty making an effort to collect money for a new church, but he hated begging. Anyhow, he asked the parishioners of both Coleraine and Portstewart to contribute a weekly subscription for the new St Malachy's. Two girls in Portstewart and four in Coleraine were to visit the houses each Sunday to collect the shilling or sixpence a week offered.

"I was one of the Portstewart collectors, and made many friends among the old retired teachers, policemen etc who comprised the majority of the parishioners. Each Spring the collectors enjoyed a party in the Coleraine Parochial House and one Sunday, after the party, I went to old Miss Diamond for her shilling and she said: 'I'll give you nothing for I hear you were in Coleraine eating the Collection.' Father Paddy Fullerton, our Curate, ran a Whist Drive every Sunday night in the little clubroom behind the Star of the Sea Parochial. At most there would be six tables. I think the entrance charge was a shilling, and it was the same people who came - just to oblige Fr Fullerton each week. The person who won a box of handkerchiefs or a tablecloth usually returned it - and in this way the prize lasted over the winter being won in turn by each of the participants.

"Father Gerard MacNamara, the Convent Chaplain, was a regular and quite witty. There was a Bazaar in Coleraine one Spring organised by Mrs Dillon and Mrs Mullan, and we had a function in Portstewart on the Big Sunday - the last Sunday in September - with fortune telling in the school during the day, and a dance in the evening. We sold buttonholes to the hundreds of people coming out from the many morning Masses. Mrs Harvey was in charge, and she was a great organiser. She was manager of Miss Woods' bookshop in Coleraine, and she and her husband, John, and her niece travelled on the 7.30 bus to work each morning. John was a whisky traveller. She was in the choir too, and had a powerful contralto voice. When I would buy books from her in the shop she always gave me a few marker pencils as discount. When Miss Woods died she left Mrs Harvey £100, and for each of her three assistants £50. Mrs Harvey's niece was one of these. Mrs Harvey was a convert to Catholicism. Her niece was not.

"After I left Portstewart, Fr MacLaverty had enough money to build the shell of the new church in the field in front of the Parochial House, but it had to wait some time for the seating. When I was in the parish an energetic curate named Fr Scott got some boys to build a corrugated-iron Hall in a corner of the field, and in it he had money-making functions. It is still there, but has wooden panelling inside now. Fr Scott had been an Altar boy in Glenarm, when Fr MacLaverty was P.P. there. Fr Mac told me that many of his Glenarm altar boys came to Coleraine as curates. Fr Joe Maloney being among them. He told me that when in College his name was twisted to - 'Moe Joloney'".

# PLANE SAILING

LIZZIE McGavock, Minnie's sister, was married at 22 years of age to John Blaney on Monday August 11, 1930. It turned out a momentous occasion. The wedding breakfast was in the family home at Dunurgan, and the lunch in Portstewart. The day out on the Causeway Coast caused quite a stir in more ways than one, with some members of the wedding party making unwanted headlines after dicing with death.

Minnie wrote of the events leading to and during the happy day: "Mary Scally, dressed in light green, was Lizzie's bridesmaid. Lizzie had to have a white outfit, but as John was not going to wear a dress suit she had to have a specially-made white picture hat, and not a white veil. I accompanied her to Belfast that summer to have the frock and hat made in the Bank Buildings. Willie Blaney was best man.

"We had the wedding breakfast in Dunurgan, where the meal was supervised by Catherine 'Kathleen' McBride, a second cousin, of Cushendun Hotel. Then we all went to the Belmont Hotel, Portstewart, for lunch. Before the summer holidays I heard of a small aircraft stationed in a big field on the Coleraine Road, which was used to give people joy rides, or flights. I told my brother Hugh about this, and after the meal Kathleen McBride, Willie, Hugh and I headed down the Promenade and up the Coleraine Road, where Hugh and Kathleen said they would love to have a flight. On the way we called in at the Star of the Sea Church, made a visit, and lit candles. When Hugh saw the small craft he took 'cold feet', and said he wouldn't risk going. Kathleen was furious, and then dared Willie to go. He complied, and after a lot of snorting and pushing by a mechanic the plane took off with the pilot and two passengers, Kathleen waving a white handkerchief as they revved up across the field and became airborne.

"They disappeared over the hill towards the harbour, and then the mechanic took to his heels over hedges and fields shouting, 'They've crashed'. Hugh followed him, and I could trail only slowly after them. I met people coming down and as I was carrying Kathleen's camera, they said, 'You'll be in good time for a snap.' No one knew who was in the plane when it struck a whin fence, and was wrecked. When I got the length of Joe Bradley's house there was Willie Blaney washing blood from his lips at a pump in the yard. Kathleen hadn't a mark on her. So we walked down the loaning pretending that we had just returned from viewing the wreck - and answering many enquiries, as to who crashed, in the negative.

"That evening, before we left Portstewart, Kathleen foolishly gave the show away by going to the police barracks to demand their money back from the pilot (10 shillings each). That night we had a dance in Dunurgan, and Kathleen sat in a corner moaning that every bone in her body was aching. In the meantime, the *Belfast Telegraph* reached Cushendun, and as Kathleen had not returned home her mother was nearly out of her mind with worry on reading her daughter's name as being one of the victims of a plane crash in Portstewart."

## PORTSTEWART THRILL WHEN 'PLANE CRASHED.
### 'SAFETY' DIVE TO FIELD
### OCCUPANTS' LUCKY ESCAPE.
### CUSHENDALL FOLK PASSENGERS.

Holiday-makers at Portstewart had a thrill last evening when an aeroplane which had been giving passenger flights crashed in a field just at the rear of the town.

The aeroplane it is understood is the property of the North British Aviation Company, of Hooton Park Aerodrome, Cheshire, and for some weeks has been giving passenger flights from a field at Burnside, on the Coleraine Road, just outside the town. This was the first mishap of any kind.

The pilot on this occasion was Mr. Leslie A. Lewis, and with him in the two-seater Avro aeroplane were Miss Catherine M'Bride, of Cushendun Hotel, and Mr. Wm. Blaney, Cloughs, Cushendall.

The '*Tele's*' single column story, on page eight, featured one main heading and three sub headings. Flagged up was 'Portstewart thrill when plane crashed'. Then it was - 'Safety dive to flight'- 'Occupants lucky escape' - and 'Cushendall folk passengers'. The report of the incident was . . . . "Holiday makers at Portstewart had a thrill last evening when an aeroplane which had been giving passengers flights crashed in a field just at the rear of the town. The aeroplane, it is understood, is the property of North British Aviation Company of Hooton Park Aerodrome, Cheshire, and for some weeks had been giving passengers flights from a field at Burnside, on the Coleraine Road just outside the town. This was the first mishap of any kind.

"The pilot on this occasion was Mr Leslie A. Lewis, and with him in the two-seater AVRO aeroplane were Miss Catherine McBride of Cushendun Hotel and Mr William Blaney, Cloughs, Cushendall. The flights generally last about three minutes, and the aeroplane had been up a couple of minutes and was at a height of about 100 feet when the engine suddenly stopped. The pilot rose to the occasion, and turned the machine into a glide towards a field at the back of the town. The machine came down in the corner of the field about 15 yards from a thorn fence, and then jumped the fence, the end carriage being damaged as it came into contact with the embankment. The rapid descent of the plane was watched by hundreds of people, who rushed to the scene fearing the worst, but fortunately it was found that the occupants had escaped with a shaking and very slight injuries.

"The pilot's left wrist and left leg were slightly hurt. Miss McBride's left arm was bruised, and Mr Blaney had his forehead slightly cut when he was thrown against the seat in front of him. Both Miss McBride and Mr Blaney seemed to regard the accident as quite the best thrill of their lives, and appeared to be nothing the worse of their exciting experience, and were quite unperturbed. The accident was attributed to Magneto trouble, and the pilot was warmly complimented on the skill with which he dealt with the sudden situation."

Incidentally, this nerve-wracking brush with serious injury did not dissuade Kathleen McBride from taking to the air in later years, on commercial flights. Her nephew Randal McDonnell revealed a special junket when not only Kathleen but also her sister Mary McBride went to Paris. He said: "I went on the trip, also my cousin Maire Kelleher. Aunt Kathleen won a prize for four people with her entry to a Smithwicks contest to promote a new beer then invented named *Time*. Her slogan entry was *Time always Time* - and the prize meant two weeks in Paris for the four of us."

# CONGRESS CAVALCADE

**M**AKING tracks for Dublin, to attend the 1932 Eucharistic Congress, proved to be a mixture of tension, trauma and ecclesiastical enlightenment for Minnie. The long jaunt from Portstewart to Phoenix Park began with Midnight Mass in the Dominican Convent. There was great excitement in the air as Minnie, Miss McLaughlin and Miss Condon joined a group of travellers.

She penned: "In June, 1932, we linked up with others for Midnight Mass, on the last Saturday of the Eucharistic Congress. After Mass we walked the two miles to Cromore Station, and then joined the train for Dublin at Coleraine. The 31st World Eucharistic Congress was held during the week of June 21-26, and the historic occasion was reported as the largest public spectacle in 20th century Ireland. It commemorated the death of St Patrick, patron saint of Ireland. The Papal Legate, (Pope's envoy) was Cardinal Lorenzo Lauri, who arrived at Dun Laoghaire Harbour on Monday, June 20. Six days later, in front of 100,000 people, he said Papal Mass in the open air at Phoenix Park, where there was the exceptional singing by Papal Count John McCormack - with his rendering of Panis Angelicus (Bread of Angels). There was also a live Papal broadcast from Rome.

"At Coleraine, many bus loads joined the train and, as we started off singing hymns, we heard crack, crack, crack. Someone said well-wishers were setting off fireworks, but when the train stopped at Ballymoney it was discovered that the paintwork was damaged by stone throwers. Luckily no windows were broken, and no one was injured. The Carey contingent joined us at Ballymoney. They had travelled from Ballycastle on the Narrow Gauge. At Ballymena, another contingent joined us. We expected to reach Dublin before dawn, but there was a great traffic jam in the County Down, and we sat outside the back of a street of houses in Scarva for hours.

"Young men were rising there, and many a wry face and spit was aimed at us. The Orangemen didn't like to see so many Catholics going South to the Congress, and the pilgrims going in the specially chartered boat from Larne were severely beaten and battered on their way from the Church to the Harbour. Many pilgrims in the Down and Connor section of the procession from Phoenix Park had bandaged heads. We didn't arrive in Dublin 'till after 11 o'clock, too late to join the Down and Connor group. We got on a tram, and reached the outskirts of the immense crowd in time for 12 o'clock mass. It was a hot day, and we were tired - but we each had a stool.

"We heard the Pope give his blessing from Rome, when he called Our Lady 'Queen of Ireland'. In the afternoon the immense congregation, with each Diocese headed by its bishop and clergy, headed for the O'Connell Bridge for Benediction. The Rosary was recited on the way. Many of the foreigners wore national costume. A Canadian Bishop, a Red Indian, wore his feathered headdress, and a Dutch group of girls were in flowing silk shawls of golden colour.

"Instead of going to Benediction, we followed a couple of priests to an hotel beside the markets, where we enjoyed a lovely meal after our long fast. But, we missed our train North, and had to remain in the Station all night - getting to Belfast on the first train on Monday morning, and then on to Portstewart. Although I was very, very tired I boarded the Catherwood bus for Cushendun, as we had a few days off school, to recuperate."

During summer holidays from teaching duties, Minnie often went to Cullyhanna to stay with Anna McArdle. They took off on cycle raids to visit friends and relatives. This was a wondrous time. Minnie loved to meet people. She never forgot a face, a name, a place, and especially the many kindnesses showered on her.

She related many of the magical moments: "From near Cullyhanna, Anna and I would cycle all over the place, going to visit the Lavelle's in Ballynacloshe, and Rosie, now Mrs Toal, in Dundalk. James Conlon of Belfast was her cousin (Mrs Toal's mother was McArdle), and his wife was Connolly from Glassdrummond, Crossmaglen. The Conlon's were from there too, and I was introduced to James's brother on his big farm. While I was in St Mary's Training College, Anna brought me many a Saturday to Conlon's in Victoria Square.

"Anna was married to Archie McSparran of Cloney, Cushendun, in September 1933, and I spent a good while with her when she was getting her trousseau ready. We went to Castleblayney, where she bought a big trunk in which to store her purchases. Then we went to Newry where she bought 'rings round her'. We had a great time. She invited me to her wedding in Rostrevor, but I was afraid of offending the Master (McHugh) at Portstewart, and I didn't accept. Later, Anna visited me in Dunurgan, and I visited her in Cloney after she became installed there. We kept up the warm friendship all our lives."

However, there was a sad chapter to this part of Minnie's 1933 vacation in south Armagh. "One day we went to Rostrevor to book the wedding breakfast in the Northern Counties Hotel. On our way to the Hotel we passed a few men leaning against the sea wall, and Anna asked them if any of them remembered the night of the disaster when the Connemara and a coal boat, Retriever, collided in fog and were wrecked. Bodies were washed ashore at Rostrevor. Yes, they remembered it well. It was November the 3rd, 1916, when Anna's eldest sister Mary was on her way to Liverpool to embark for America. They said she was still alive when washed ashore. She was holding a baby in her arms, trying to save it, when they found her - but both died of exposure.

"Her father and brother Louis had seen her aboard the boat at Greenore, where they stayed overnight. They were amazed at the concerned whisperings at the Railway Station next morning, and then heard of the disaster when Mary's boat collided with the coal boat coming in. As was the custom, neighbours came to the McArdle house in Mulladuff for the Convoy, and stayed on to console the family on the emigration of one of their daughters. The night became very stormy, and every lamp was blown out by a gust of wind."

The 1916 collision between two boats at the neck of Carlingford Lough, beside the County Down coast line and that of County Louth, was the second biggest peacetime maritime loss of life along the County Down coast.

The next cruel sea tragedy along the northern coastal line was that of the Larne-Stranraer ferry, the *Princess Victoria* sinking at two o'clock on the afternoon of Saturday, January 31, 1953, with the loss of 135 lives. Only 44 men were rescued. No women or children survived.

The accident happened during hurricane force winds, mountainous waves, and dark conditions. Mary McArdle was one of 97 lives to perish on that dreadful night. Mary travelled from Dundalk to Greenore for what was the intended first part of her journey to Chicago, where she planned to join her brothers, Ted and Tom. Earlier that week she missed a planned Wednesday passage on the Dundalk and Newry's Steam Packet Company's boat from Dundalk to Liverpool. She apparently waited over in Dundalk until the Friday, and caught the evening train to join the SS *Connemara* at Greenore, the boat lifting anchor at 8.00 pm.

The sole survivor from the horrific incident was ironically a non-swimmer, James Boyle. He was listed a 21-year-old fireman on the *Retriever*, who clung to an upturned boat. Boyle lived for a further 50 years. He died in April, 1967. The *Connemara* was a twin screw steamer, launched by Denny Brothers in 1897 at Dumbarton, Scotland. It was 272 feet long, 35 feet broad, and 14 feet deep. The skipper was 50-year-old Captain G.H. Doig. All crew of 30 came from Holyhead in Anglesey, north Wales. On that fateful occasion, when struck amidships, the cargo included 51 passengers and livestock. The *Connemara's* lucrative trade route was from Greenore to Holyhead.

The Captain of the coal ship *Retriever*, a 168-feet long three-mast coal-fired steamer built by the Ailsa Shipbuilding Company in 1899, was Patrick O'Neill from Kilkeel, County Down. His son Joseph O'Neill was the Second Mate. The crew of nine came from nearby Newry, except James Boyle, who was from the more immediate area of Summerhill, Warrenpoint. The atrocious conditions caused the cargo of coal to list, and near the Haulbowline Lighthouse

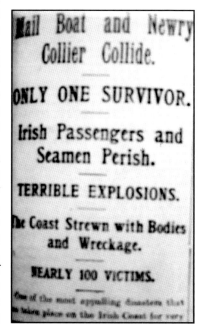

Mail Boat and Newry Collier Collide.

ONLY ONE SURVIVOR.

Irish Passengers and Seamen Perish.

TERRIBLE EXPLOSIONS.

The Coast Strewn with Bodies and Wreckage.

NEARLY 100 VICTIMS.

the *Retriever* ripped in the port side of the *Connemara*. Holed below the waterline, from bow to amidships, the *Connemara* sank in a matter of minutes. The *Retriever* sank after 20 minutes. Her boiler also exploded on contact with the icy water.

The *Irish News* edition of Monday November 6, 1916, reported: "One of the most appalling disasters that has taken place on the Irish coast for many years occurred near Cranfield Point, Carlingford Bar, on Friday night. The London and North-Western Railway Company's steamer *Connemara* which was just after leaving Greenore, came into collision with the steam collier *Retriever* - homeward bound from Garston to Newry. A fierce gale was raging at the time, which was between 8 and 9 o'clock." The report added: "Over 50 bodies have been washed ashore from Cranfield Point to Kilkeel."

Another story headline on the tragedy was: "County Armagh Families Bereaved" . . . and, the report revealed: "Among those who have been bereaved are Mr Charles Kearney N.T. Drumnacheon, Balleer, Co Armagh, and Mr James McArdle, who resides near Cullyhanna, Co Armagh. The former lost his son and daughter, both teachers, who were going to Liverpool to meet their sister, who was coming home from America, while Mr McArdle's daughter, a girl of about 18 years, was going to America."

Elsewhere, there was further article, stating that . . . "Mary McArdle, Crossmaglen, County Armagh, who travelled from Dundalk to Greenore, was bound for New York. "She had, it is stated, intended travelling to Liverpool by the Dundalk and Newry Steam Packet Company's boat on Wednesday, but missed the sailing. She waited over in the town until Friday, and left by the evening train." Another passenger to perish was a Lizzie Collins of Ballycastle, County Antrim.

# WEDDING BELLS

L IFE with her back to a classroom blackboard was about to end for Minnie McGavock, as she agreed on a change of surname. During the Autumn of 1935, Alex O'Hara and Minnie decided to marry before the end of the year.

She recalled: "I met him (Alex) in Ballymena where, in McBride's Jewellers, Bridge Street, he bought a wedding ring for £2. Then I went to the White House in Portrush, and chose a nice green pattern of woollen cloth to make a long coat and skirt. They had to send away for it. I have the bill yet - £5, and I recall the tailor always called me 'Miss McGaffickin'. Greta McFetridge, then Mrs Douglas, came to stay with me in Belmont for a few days, and when she saw my green outfit, she said, 'Green is unlucky. You can't get married in that'.

"So, off I went to Coleraine to buy a long brown dress with a yoke of coffee coloured lace and a big brown felt hat with coffee coloured spots. Annie Gore was my bridesmaid. Alex and I were married on the 30th of December, 1935, by Fr Terence Keenan, CC. Agnes McMullan (nee Brogan) - a cousin of Alex's, came specially from Glasgow for the wedding. Alex's sister Auntie (Mary O'Hara) bought a new fur coat for the occasion. There were 14 at the reception in the Cushendun Hotel. Nora McBride made the 14th, as 13 was considered unlucky. Nelson Brogan and his son Maurice Noel were at it, as they were on holiday in Agolagh.

"Incidentally, Greta McFetridge was married some time before me, to a Captain Keevers Douglas of Ballycastle. At that time she taught in Ballintoy, and when she saw the array of wedding presents she exclaimed I taught in a better locality than she did. I received a multitude from old and young in Portstewart. Father MacLaverty gave me a lovely cut crystal jug, Fr Dick O'Neill a silver and glass cake stand, Fr Paddy Fullerton - erstwhile curate, but then in Ballymacarrett, a canteen of cutlery, and Convent Chaplain Fr Haughey offered a Mass for us.

"The schoolchildren gave us a salad bowl and tray, and Master McHugh a lovely sandwich tray. I also got several half tea sets and aluminium saucepans. Anna and Archie (McSparran) gave me a lovely tea set and dinner set to match, and Annie Gore gave me a lovely tea set. A Miss Cameron gave me a fruit set, Greta a large glass dish, Daisy McBride a clock, Miss McLaughlin an eiderdown, Kathleen McGavock blankets, the Brogan's blankets, Annie McLaughlin gave Old Bleach pillow covers, Mairead a beautiful Old Bleach tablecloth with a circle of roses to fit over our big circular table.

"A sister of Brigid Darragh from Cushleake was a secretary in Hughes Bakery in Belfast, and someone contacted her for the wedding cake - one tier - for 25 shillings I still have the receipt of the bill for the wedding breakfast. On that day, and in from Dublin on holiday, in the Cushendun Hotel were Mr and Mrs McCann (cousins of Daisy McBride's), and Mrs McCann recommended we spend our honeymoon in the George Hotel in Parnell Square.

"So, we travelled by car, with cars following, and boarded the bus for Belfast in Ballymena, and thence by train to Dublin. Alex knew Dublin well, for he studied for his Mate's Ticket there, stopping with Nelson Brogan and Johnny McVeigh at Brogan's butcher shop in Parnell Street. We visited Gertie, Nelson's wife, and then went back for an evening when Nelson and Maurice returned from Cushendun. We also visited Nick and Mary Bohan (nee Redmond) more than once, and on New Year's Day Nick accompanied us on a bus tour around south Dublin, and then back to a big party in their house. We returned home on the Friday. Uncle John (Alex's brother) met us in Larne, and also with Auntie and Nurse Quinn. We went to the 'Pictures' there. The film being shown was *Ben Hur* - a talkie then, but I had seen it in Belfast years before as a silent film - and liked it much better. John and Alex left me back to Portstewart on the Sunday, to work my three months' notice."

Married life, however, meant a cruel dictat by the Catholic hierarchy in the Diocese of Down and Connor forced her to give up the post of teacher in Portstewart. "Dr Mageean was very insistent all female teachers who married in his Diocese should give up teaching at the end of three months after marriage," stated Minnie,

"In the Derry diocese they were allowed to stay on. That January (1936), we moved into the new St Colum's School, and I left it at the end of March. So, I came to live in Knocknacarry on the 1st of April 1936. Unfortunately, I never got a chance to visit Portstewart even for a day, until a Sunday in early summer 1953 - 17 years later - when Mrs McHugh of Cushendun and her group had a rally there to raise money for Cushendun Parish.

147, VICTORIA STREET,
S.W.1.
TEL. VICTORIA 2853.

With all good wishes
to Alex O'Hara on
his wedding.
Jan 1936
from Lady Cushendun.

"Cushendun P.P. Fr Lynch divided the parish into groups - each to raise £100. Our group had two concerts to raise our £100. Mrs Archie McSparran raised it with one concert, at which my second son Denis recited *Me and Me Da* which Anna taught him. That was the year (1953) when Alex had an unsuccessful operation from which he recovered for two more years - but died on 11th September, 1955. R.I.P."

Minnie maintained her close alliance with and respect for her great friend Anna McArdle, now Mrs McSparran. There was always time for lively banter, and prayer. It was the latter devotion that inspired Anna on January 24, 1961, to pen her witty poem . . .

### THE LOSS OF 15 MINUTES

*Trotting up the st...air*
*in the dusk of d...awn*
*To say an extra prayer*
*All upon my o...wn*
*I never shall forget*
*I sure was in a fret*
*When I found the inner door*
*Had been locked the night before*
*And there was I alone*
*And almost turned to stone*

*So, I sat upon the stair and waited*
*It was just a bit frustrating*
*When one had trouble waking*
*After being late the night before*
*My spirits did arise*
*When there, before my eyes*
*Eddie entered through the door*
*And very nearly swore*
*When he saw me on that cold and frosty morning*

*So, he soon did try the door*
*but found he'd need do more*
*And straightaway to parochial house he went*
*Then from door to window*
*And thought 'twas time well spent*
*When he managed to arouse the sleeping Rose*
*Who gave him a key*
*with which he released me*
*from my cold and draughty prison*

*Now all you would-be saints*
*pray learn from my complaints*
*that the way to get to heaven*
*is to stay in bed past seven*
*And you'll never have to sojourn on the stairs.*

# OCEAN ADVENTURES

WRITING on December 26, 1982, Minnie gave further insight to the O'Hara family background. She explained her husband was the second child of Alex and Katie, nee Catherine Brogan - born October 8, 1869, at Hutchesontown, Glasgow. Alex was born on the 17th of October, 1897. His sister Mary arrived on this earth on the 12th of October, 1895, and his brother John was born on the 12th of July, 1899. Alex was given Anthony at Confirmation.

She scribbled: "After John's birth, their mother stayed in some house in Ballycastle to receive treatment from old Doctor McIlroy. There was no hospital there then, just the Workhouse. I think she was there for months, during which time the other two children were cared for by Mary MacCormack's mother and father, Bella and Charles. Bella and Charles were also Alex's Godparents, and all his life he was very fond of them.

"During his school days he used to deliver the telegram for the Kennedy's of the Post Office next door. As many men from the district went to sea there were regular messages from them to their homes. Often, during school hours, Alex O'Hara had to run bare-footed up Glendun to deliver a telegram. In later years Mary McAllister ('Chip') delivered them on Miss Kennedy's bicycle. I remember I was learning to ride an old bike when accompanying her along Dunurgan road. I wasn't too steady. My bike gave a wobble, hit her back wheel - and both of us fell on the road!

"Alex O'Hara was 14 when he left school. His daddy and his uncle Dan had the only transport business in this part of the Glens. Drays, Jaunting Cars and Traps, which were two-wheeled carriages, were all drawn by horses - an occupation dear to the heart of any boy. The O'Hara's owned big horses, which his mother's people, the Brogan's, sent over from Glasgow.

"When I would be going to school in the morning from Dunurgan I would meet two drays going to *Retreat* Station, and long after school time in the evening they'd rumble down delivering boxes of bottles to McKay's Pub at 'The Turn', boxes of groceries to O'Connor's shop in Straid, and provisions to all pubs and shops along the way. I can still hear the rumble of the iron-shod wheels under their heavy loads. John McGowan from Tromra Cottages usually drove one of the drays.

"The Jaunting Car was used to bring people to and from Parkmore Railway Station. So, Granny O'Hara was familiar with Miss Ada McNeill, a cousin of Lord Cushendun, and all their distinguished guests coming to order transport. There were no hotels in Cushendun then, and no motor cars. The guests stayed in the 'Big Houses'. In the early years of the First World War, Alex O'Hara was in charge of a Jaunting Car which was engaged to bring three McLarnon uncles of Mary MacCormack to and from the Lammas Fair.

"Pretty late in the evening he drove very fast up Knocknacarry street, pulled up with a jerk, and dumped his passengers over the wall into the yard below. There was no paling (fence) in front of Mary MacCormack's then. He (Alex) must have been severely reprimanded, for he then left for Glasgow - and through his uncle, John Brogan, got a job on a ship. That was the beginning of his sea-faring career."

The date of Alex O'Hara's entry into National Health and Insurance is October 4, 1915. On the 13th of October, 1915 - four days light of his 19th birthday, he had his maiden voyage, working as an assistant steward for the SS *Verdala* of Glasgow. The ship's business is listed as 'trooping', and in this hazardous war-time period his third voyage with the same vessel was to the United States, leaving Barry on September 7, 1916, and returning to the Welsh sanctuary on December 1, 1916.

Minnie added: "During the 1914-'18 War much tillage was ordered, and when Alex would be at home for a month or two at a time he would work for Father McKay and his sister Mrs McKinley, and as he loved horses he did a lot of ploughing in the Dromore and Knocknacarry farms. Then he'd get a telegram to join some ship, and he'd have to leave all and go.

"After the Great War, he was on a ship which had been taken from the defeated Germans, and was ship-wrecked off the coast of Cornwall. Himself, Charlie McLarnon, Dan Hernon and Pat McKendry (an uncle of the present Pat) were rescued by Breeches Buoy. This was a rope-based device, including leg harness, attached to a line, used to rescue people from wrecked vessels and generally deployed to complete single person evacuation from ship to ship, or ship to shore. He told me that all the ships taken from the Germans suffered a similar fate."

Minnie also referred to a book by Lionel Fleming, one that mentions Tom Casement, brother of Sir Roger. The tenuous connection relates to her husband undergoing studies in Dublin. She wrote: "The Fleming book is *Head or Harp* - and it is a reminder of a time when Alex did a course in Dublin, to try and advance his position as a merchant seaman. Alex sat a course in Dublin in the early 1920's, to get an examination for Mate. He was examined in 'something' by Tom Casement.

"A Ship's Mate Certificate was awarded to become the deck officer who was second in charge to the Captain. Alex stayed with Nelson Brogan, then a bachelor who had a butcher's shop in Parnell Street. Johnny McVeigh, another cousin, was a butcher for him. They used to hire horses on a Saturday, and ride in Phoenix Park. Alex's course lasted three months. He got the certificate, but never used it!"

An avid reader, with an exceptional command of the English language, Minnie also mentioned and recommended a book by Frank O'Connor, *The Backward Look,* which she described as 'a delightfully written history of Irish Literature.' Following the First World War, Alex O'Hara was recommended, in 1919, for British War and Mercantile Marine War

Medals, although these were not processed until October 1925. Here is the data involving the awards.

BOARD of TRADE. Marine Department (War Medals Branch), Cornwall House, Stamford Street, S.E.1: 'Sir, I am directed by the Board of Trade to forward herewith the British War Medal and the Mercantile Marine War Medal, which have been awarded to you in respect of your services in the Mercantile Marine during hostilities, and to request that the enclosed form of receipt may be completed and signed by you and returned to this Department. The form of authority (W.M.2) to wear the Medals and Ribands is also enclosed. I am Sir, Your obedient Servant. (signed by C.Hipwood). On the left bottom in handwriting is Mr A. O'Hara. Knocknacarry.Co Antrim.

'W.M.5 APPLICATION for British War Medal and Mercantile Marine War Medal. by O'Hara. Alexander. Born at Co Antrim in the year of 1897. FORM OF AUTHORITY (W.M.2) MUST ACCOMPANY THIS APPLICATION. W.M.2. AUTHORITY to Wear WAR MEDALS FOR THE MERCANTILE MARINE. Awarded by H.M. The King through the Board of Trade. Alexander O'Hara (handwritten). (Dis A` No.842895 R.S. 2 No.376784) is authorised to wear the undermentioned medals and ribbons against which the signature of a Board of Trade Officer and an official stamp have been affixed. Marine Dept. Board of Trade C. HIPWOOD, Assistant Secretary.

'Medal details - British War Medal ribbon Authorised 18-10-19 Signature of J.W. Stewart - Superintendent of issuing M.M.O with office stamp. The stamp is H.M Office dated 18 Oct 1919. Glasgow. Mercantile Marine Medal ribbon - also 18-10-19, and same signature British War Medal (and clasp) and Mercantile Marine Medal - dated 27-10-25. Signed - Wm. Callaghan Board of Trade stamp Authorised 27 Oct 1925. Below it all is signature of holder - Alex O'Hara.'

On the back of the card is . . . 'NOTE to the holder of this Authority. When public notice is given that the medals are ready for issue, you should hand in this Authority at a Mercantile Marine office and should ask for the issue to you of one or both the medals. This authority will then be completed overleaf by the Board of Trade official, and returned to you. It is important that this Authority should not be lost. It should be kept in your Dis. A.'

Included were two tiny cardboard holders for the medals. On the front is printed: 'This medal should be worn on the left breast with the King's head showing. The red strip of the riband should be nearest the left arm. When worn with Mercantile Marine War Medal it must be worn on the green strip. that is : the Mercantile Marine War Medal must be nearer to the left arm'.

# PAIN in PANAMA

A LEX O'Hara was fortunate to survive a serious health calamity during one of his numerous deep-sea trips to Central and South America. He was given up for dead by his parents. Minnie heard the story of great hardship from her husband. He was abandoned by the ship he was with, after he took seriously ill in Panama.

He joined the SS *Volga* on October 18, 1919, leaving Glasgow, and then discharged on the 29th of November. The British Consular office in Panama appears to have provided some help when he took so seriously ill at Colon, Panama. On release from hospital, he worked passage home with the SS *Trident*, departing Colon on December 31, 1919. He was discharged from that ship at Newcastle-on-Tyne on February 2, 1920.

Minnie remarked: "In those days most sailors arranged for their parents or relatives to receive half of their pay. Just before Christmas 1919, his parents received a telegram saying 'No more half pay.' Until this crisis, his money was sent home. Now alarm bells were ringing. There was no explanation as to the reason for no contact, and naturally they (his father and mother) thought he was dead. "It was first feared he suffered the yellow fever. But, after a month or so they learned that he was in hospital in Panama. He had severe dysentery on the way out to the Pacific, and was just left off there. He managed to return home early in 1920, very frail after having to work his passage home on another ship. He was very weak, yet returned to sea with the SS *Ansgir* near the end of 1920."

Alex followed with spells on vessels such as the SS *Hindu Warrior*, the SS *British Light*, the SS *Barra Ailsa,* the SS *Atalanta*, the SS *Voreda* - on return from the U.S.A. he was discharged in Hamburg. "He was on merchant ships and oil tankers," added Minnie, "And during the Coal strike of 1926, he was on a ship which brought coal from the port of Galveston. This city in Texas, on the Gulf of Mexico, was also famous for the great boxer Jack Johnson, the first black Heavyweight Champion of the World. Alex told me it was frightening when crossing the Atlantic from England light, being tossed about like a cork. During two such journeys he was ship's bo'sun (boatswain) or petty officer."

The 1926 General Strike in the United Kingdom lasted ten days, from May 3, 1926 to May 13, 1926. The Strike was called by the General Council of the Trades Union Congress (TUC). It proved an unsuccessful effort to force the British Government to act to prevent wage reduction and deteriorating conditions for coal miners. Productivity in the mines was low after the First World War. The strike created extremely tense times, during which *The Flying Scotsman* was derailed by strikers outside Newcastle-upon-Tyne. His closing days on the waves was as bo'sun of the

SS *Vestalia,* making two trips during late 1926 and most of 1927 to the U.S.A. and Brazil.

Minnie stated: "At the end of the 1920's, he finally gave up the sea, rented McIlreavey's farm - and kept cows and two horses. By now, the motor car and the bus and lorries were on the road. The only relic of earlier days was the trap which brought Father Blacker from Craigagh Church to Culraney for Mass on a Sunday. The little bell attached to the harness let the priest know that transport had arrived, and also probably summoned the Faithful to Mass as the horse plodded along the miles of rough road from one place of worship to the next.

"I believe his brother John had the first motor car here. He continued to transport people in it, but the Cushleake road was too rough then for motor traffic. Alex's father died mid-20's, and in the early 1930's they built a butcher's shop with dwelling attached where the drays etc used to be housed. As the Brogan's were butchers in Glasgow. Granny O'Hara knew all about the trade."

During a more detailed background on the O'Hara-Brogan link she added: "I am writing this on the 8th of September, 1981, and being our Blessed Lady's birthday I am filled with thoughts of Granny O'Hara (nee Katie Brogan), whose birthday it was. In the late 1930's and early '40's we had no birthday cakes for grown-ups, but I remember putting a plain bun with one candle in the middle of the table for her birthday.

"She was born in Glasgow on the 8th of September, 1869. My mother was slightly younger, being born on the 12th January 1870. Lizzie McCambridge was 69 on the day my second son Denis John was born. Granny O'Hara's father was Denis Brogan from Donegal, and her mother was Mary McCormick from Innispollan, Cushendun. A sister was married to a McSparran. Donal McCormick, who left Innispollan to the McSparran's, was her brother.

"Denis Brogan was in the old RIC as a young man, and was stationed in Cushendun, at Agolagh. I think Denis McKay's house, later to serve as the Parish Priest's house, was occupied by the RIC in the last century (19th) - as was later the house in Knocknacarry owned by the late James McSparran. Also used as an RIC station was the old Coastguard Station - now the Maud Cottages, right on Cushendun Beach. It was also occupied by both B-Specials and new RUC men in the early 20's.

"The Sergeant was named McGovern from Cavan. There was also a fine looking constable from Galway named Killelagh - from the same parish as Miss McDonagh, a teacher in Coleraine with whom I was friendly during my sojourn in Portstewart. I think that after the 'Troubles' Constable Killelagh resigned from the Force, and went home to farm in Galway. In May of 1922, the RUC replaced the pre-partition All-Ireland force, the RIC. Around that period the back-up force generally known as the B Specials was formed.

"To continue the Brogan saga. Denis Brogan and his wife lived in Glasgow, and I'm not sure if they were always butchers, but I know Granny O'Hara taught her son John how to cut meat when he opened the shop in Knocknacarry, for she had done it in the Brogan shop in Glasgow, in her youth. I don't know when her mother died, but Denis Brogan married a girl from Glenariffe named Delargy for his second wife. They had no children.

"The children of the first family were John, Dan, Mary and Catherine (Kate). John and Dan went to sea, and Dan died in India. John spent some years in Australia, came home to Glasgow, married and had a thriving business as a butcher and supplier of ships. They provided all kinds of food for a voyage. Mary married Dan McVeigh in 1893, and lived in Brablagh, Cushendun. One of their sons, Denis McVeigh is called after his grandfather, as is my son Denis, for his great grandfather.

"Kate came on holiday to Innispollan, and she and Margaret McSparran - later Mrs McCart of the Bay, Glenariffe, had great times. Margaret married James McCart on February 6, 1894, with Daniel McCart and Anne McSparran the witnesses. Then John Brogan bought Agolagh house and farm. There had been Delargy's there some time previously - as Master Delargy heard this from the famous Hamilton Delargy, and one of them was called Turlough.

"On February 25, 1895, Kate married Alex O'Hara. Witnesses were Charles MacCormack and Catherine Dinsmore. Alex's father was also Alex - and whose mother was McNeill - a relation of the 'Fadies'. His grandfather was Daniel O'Harra, the surname using two r's. This name is on the headstone at Craigagh. Granny O'Hara told me the first of these O'Harra's (2r's), probably the one named Daniel, came from Crebilly, Ballymena, with a horse and springcart to collect eggs, and settled here.

"I was also told by Kate that her aunt, Biddy Brogan from Donegal visited them in Glasgow, and the children were frustrated when her father and Aunt Biddy conversed in Gaelic. They couldn't understand a word. It all seemed very secret. Granny O'Hara, who died on 13th August, 1947, recalled the little ditty to advertise Brogan's shop wares in Glasgow. It went like this . . .

*Brogan's beef goes near and far*
*By ship, by rail, by motor car.*
*No Sunday dinner is complete*
*Without a joint of Brogan's meat.*

"With this background in the beef trade, Granny Catherine O'Hara set up the butcher's shop in Knocknacarry. John learned the trade from his mother. In Knocknacarry at that time, and until War-time rationing commenced, John went each week to Ballymena to buy choice sides of beef from a butcher in Ballymoney Street. Granny O'Hara also helped 'Uncle' John become a carman. Alex and John used to go by car to Glenravel to buy lambs. Dan McGonnell came then and killed them in the garage, where they would hang for a day before being hung in the shop."

McGonnell was one of many quirky characters of the Glens, a poet, wit, butcher. Perhaps his epitaph should be for penning *Dan Hyman's Grey- hound* and *The Courtin' of Henry Pat.* Daniel O'Hara recalled his mother's fascination for this strange man who would arrive in the backyard at Knocknacarry to kill and prepare spring lambs for sale in the butcher's shop. "Minnie found it hard to believe McGonnell was going to work dressed in a black claw-hammer suit and white dickey false shirt-front," Daniel said, "Into the heat of the work he would take off his coat, and reveal how eccentric he really was. McGonnell kept the trousers up with galluses, but his back was bare. He had no shirt . . . just the bow-tie fixture around his neck."

For the shop trade John O'Hara took weekly orders, and delivered to customers on a Friday and Saturday. Minnie added; "The orders were laid in lovely wicker baskets, covered with immaculate white linen towels. Alex's sister Mary, better known later as 'Auntie', became a nurse. She trained in the Mater Hospital, Belfast. Her first appointment was as a District Nurse. Lady Cushendun, Miss Ada McNeill and Mrs Parry - a cousin of Roger Casement, took it upon themselves to provide and pay for a nurse in the district."

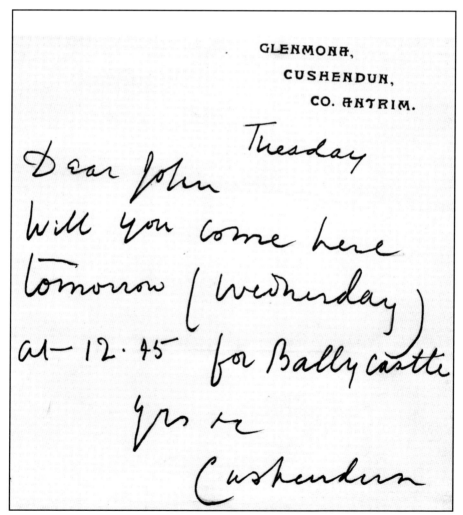

GLENMONA,
CUSHENDUN,
CO. ANTRIM.

*Tuesday*

*Dear John*

*Will you come here tomorrow (Wednesday) at — 12.45 for Ballycastle*

*yrs re*

*Cushendun*

*Lord Cushendun calls for a cab, seeking the services of John O'Hara's Taxi*

Lady Cushendun was formerly Elizabeth Maud Bolitho, and married to Ronald John McNeill - the first and last Baron Cushendun, who was born on 30th April 1861. Lord Cushendun, a former Member of Parliament for Kent, and once the Under-Secretary of State for Foreign Affairs and Chancellor of the Duchy of Lancaster, was created 1st Baron Cushendun on November 7, 1927. He died on October 12, 1934. The family of Lord and Lady Cushendun were the Hon. Ester Rose McNeill, the Hon. Loveday Violet McNeill, and the Hon. Mary Morvenna Bolitho McNeill.

Minnie added: "Auntie was the second nurse to be appointed. The first stayed in Miss Wilde's house at Innispollan, and then left to marry a doctor who was a surgeon in the Mater Hospital, Belfast. I think the post folded when Auntie was about a year in it - that was during the 'Black and Tan' period. After that, she was appointed to Larne, but spent two or three years in the Braid Valley Hospital, Ballymena, while the Larne Workhouse was being converted. Nurse Quinn came from County Tyrone to help in Ballymena, and thus began a life-long friendship with Auntie.

"Incidentally, the Braid Valley began as Ballymena Workhouse when opened in 1843. This system ended in July 1948, when it became known as a Hospital. When I came to Knocknacarry in 1936, Granny and Uncle John lived there, and Auntie came on her days off. I learned to bake and churn at Dunurgan. So, with one thing and another, I was kept pretty busy."

Minnie's loss of her beloved husband Alex, on September 11, 1955, through cancer, aged 57 and a few months short of the 20th anniversary of their wedding, was borne and accepted with a quiet dignity. "It is God's will," she would say. Later, she had to bear another shattering setback, when her devoted youngest son Hugh, he of the flaming 'McGavock' red hair, tragically died aged 40 in Dublin, in December 1983, following cancer. No matter how bleak things appeared she would bear the cross and say: "It is all for the better."

# FAMILY VALUES

A LEX and MINNIE O'Hara reared a family of four boys at Knocknacarry, the first being born in Ballycastle Hospital on the 26th of June, 1937. There was a mix-up in his name. He was to be known as Alexander Paul, but later in school and public life was Peter Alexander.

Minnie explained: "The nurses there were very friendly, but a very special one was Nurse Sefton. She asked me what I was going to call the child, and I said that he would have to be Alex, with either Peter or Paul added as it was near their feast on the 29th. I intimated that I was very fond of St Peter, but made no final decision. Alex was born on a Saturday, and on the Sunday week after that he was christened.

"My husband's brother and sister, Uncle John and Auntie Mary, were his God parents, and Mrs Agnes McMullan (nee Brogan) came with them to Ballycastle. She said he should be christened Alexander Paul, because he was born on the feast of St John and Paul (26th). So that was his name, and for years his Granny O'Hara called him Paul. When Alex O'Hara Jnr had to undergo obligatory vaccinations as a baby it was then discovered the errors in his christian names.

"When he was three months old, we had a letter from the 'powers that be' to have Alexander Paul vaccinated against Smallpox, forthwith. That was the first indication that Nurse Sefton had him registered as Peter Alexander on the Wednesday after he was born - four days before he was christened Alexander Paul. This mix-up didn't worry us a bit, and at Confirmation he took Paul, but in later years it did matter with Peter Alexander being on all his examination papers - and the priest who married him and Maura (Wilson) in St Brigid's, Belfast, having to deal with an 'alias'.

"Denis John was born on the 12th of January, 1939, also in Ballycastle, while Granny's brother John Brogan lay dying in Agolagh. 'Pa' Brogan expired two days later. My brother and sister, Hugh McGavock and Lizzie Blaney were Denis's sponsors, and there was no confusion about his names, although Uncle John always called him 'Johnny'.

"Daniel Vincent was born on the 16th of November, 1941. He was baptised in St Patrick's Church, Cushendun, on the way home from Ballycastle - about two weeks later. Annie Gore and Eddie Brogan were his sponsors. Eddie was head of St Vincent DePaul in Cushendun at the time, and insisted on him being named Vincent. Daniel felt the real influence in this secondary name selection was Granny O'Hara, with the Vincent emanating from the Brogan butcher's shop at 303, St Vincent's Street, Glasgow. Granny accepted the 'Alex' line of succession for our eldest boy, and then Hugh to link with the favoured McGavock name.

"Hugh was born on the 5th of September, 1943. It was the first Sunday of September, and a very wet day on which Antrim played and lost in the All-Ireland Hurling Final. I listened on Radio in Hospital, and heard of Bishop Mageean throwing in the ball. I don't remember the name of the opposing team (Cork), but they proved superior to poor Antrim. Hugh was the only red-head in the family. He was christened Hugh Joseph on the following Sunday. Dan McKinley and Maggie (Gore) were his Godparents. I gave Hugh the name of Patrick at Confirmation, Daniel was given Oliver, and Denis got Benedict."

Incidentally, those faithful friends and supporters of Alex and Minnie O'Hara, Agnes Brogan and her husband Alex McMullan, were married on May 20, 1909. Daniel McAlister and Catherine Brogan were the witnesses. Alex McMullan survived some scary moments on the high seas during World War Two. A ship's engineer, he was torpedoed three times. Born in Glendun, Alex moved at four years of age with his family to Belfast where he attended a Technical college and qualified in Engineering. He joined the Royal Engineers as a Lieutenant in the First World War, and served in Mesopotania (now Iraq). In World War Two he was a Chief Engineer, and served at sea in Convoys.

A nephew, John Brogan had insight to some fascinating drama, that later led to a best-selling book: "Uncle Alex told me three ships were sunk under him in the North Sea. Once, during heavy fog, they were sunk by a torpedo. While they were taking to the lifeboats a U-Boat surfaced and the U-Boat Commander threw them down a bottle of brandy into their lifeboat, and also gave them bearings for land. Such incidents were recalled in a very special book called *The Golden Horseshoe* about the exploits of a German U-Boat Commander called Kressmer.

"In the Kressmer story it mentioned he would always do that . . . throw a bottle of brandy and give bearings to a lifeboat crew. Kressmer was eventually captured and imprisoned near Liverpool, on Aintree Race track. Alex McMullan was able to verify it was the same Commander who sank his boat off the north east coast of England. I also believe one Commander was ordered, during an internal German prison camp Court Martial, to escape and sink his captured U-Boat in Liverpool docks - but was shot dead while trying to escape.

"Many of the German prisoners were then sent to camps in Canada. After World War Two, Alex McMullan returned to normal life as an engineer at sea, and retired around 1950. The McMullan's first lived in Kennedy's Row, Knocknacarry, when they came in during the summer months from Glasgow - before purchasing the house at Barmean."

Mary 'Auntie' O'Hara spent most of her working life in Larne, where she became Assistant Matron at the Moyle Hospital. Auntie was a close personal friend of the ever-welcoming McCambride family, who lived a few doors down from the bottom entrance to the Moyle Hospital on the Old Glenarm Road. A daughter of the McCambride's lived around the corner on Victoria Road. She was the wife of famous Belfast Celtic, Irish international, and Great Britain Olympic soccer team member Robert 'Bertie' Fulton. The McCambride clan was also steeped in soccer folklore, as 'Hootie' McCambridge was an ex-Ballymena United and Irish international player.

"Auntie, who retired in 1961, came home most weeks for her day off, and arrived laden with goodies for us all, and clothes for the children," added Minnie, "Nurse Quinn came with her on the odd holiday. She was like a sister to Auntie, who was her bridesmaid when she married John Joe Quinn of Crocanroe, near Ardboe and close to the west shore of Lough Neagh. Nurse Quinn left Larne. Auntie and I went to visit the Quinn's, while Nurse Quinn comes with her cousins, the McQuaid's of Armagh, to visit me nearly every summer.

"I made many other great friends, and none more surprisingly than folk from England. One week-end in May, 1935, two fishermen from Liverpool came on a fishing holiday to an hotel in Ballymena. They were directed to the River Dun, and Uncle John drove them up the Glen. That evening they asked to be put up here in Knocknacarry, rather than travel up and down from Ballymena. They came back in September. The May after I came to Knocknacarry they returned, and in September too. This twice-yearly visit continued, until War broke out in 1939.

"After the War, they brought their wives to the Cushendun Hotel. I remember they bought webs of beautiful tweed Dan Brogan wove on a loom in a specially fitted house with double doors at Innispollan. Jim O'Neill lived in it after his own house was burned in Knocknacarry. One of the Liverpool gentlemen was a dentist named Frazer Bell, and the other was an undertaker named Evans. His daughter is the famous singer, Nancy Evans. Mrs Frazer Bell sent many presents to our children, and for years afterwards she sent them valuable books for Christmas. They had three sons.

"Mr Frazer Bell later had heart trouble, retired, and he and his wife lived in a nice house with a garden in the Wirral of Cheshire, their sons being married. His wife told me of how he loved gardening, and one day he was in the garden he had a heart attack and died. She didn't live many years after him, for a card that I sent her one Christmas was returned to me with 'deceased' written on the envelope. I don't know what happened to Mr Evans."

Life away from the schoolrooms meant Minnie had to revert to her farming roots. Her husband was also back to his beginnings, giving up a life at sea, and returning to his beloved horses. "Alex rented Jamie (McMullan) Scotland's farm, and also the McIlreavey's farm which adjoined," recalled Minnie, "He kept cows, their calves, and a couple of horses - and, of course, dogs. In his younger days his favourite sporting pastime was to play hurling when he was home on a break from his sea adventures. But, he had to quit after sustaining a nasty patella injury, in his left kneecap.

"We had milk pans in the kitchen of the unoccupied house next door. I churned butter in a plunge churn, and later in a small milk house erected beside the entrance gate at the edge of the building, where we moved to a barrel churn that had a tiny window to let you know when the butter was ready. John's butcher shop was in the lower house too, but had a separate door and a big front window. On a Saturday, he delivered meat to people who had ordered it - in Cushendun, mostly."

Minnie, who adapted to help and do meat cuts in the shop, reared pigs for a spell in what was known as 'The Pig Crew' - later to become a coal store. The pigs were slaughtered on the premises then, usually by Johnny 'Archie' McNeill and Jim Magee. The carcases were 'hung' - and then sold in the shop. This was a time before strict Ministry regulations were instigated.

The year of the big snow, 1947, ignited memories of hedge-high snowdrifts that began with persistent snowfalls from late January to mid-March. It was a memorable winter of a testing survival time that reached epic proportions. It was one of the most difficult winter weather conditions experienced in the 20th century. New Year's Day was a Wednesday, and by now there probably was a strong hint of things to come when a ferocious blizzard bombarded parts of Canada. From January 30, to February 8 all townships from Calgary, Ontario, to Winnepeg, Manitoba, were buried under snowdrifts. The icy grip moved swiftly across the Atlantic.

1947, the year that also marked the launch of the International Monetary Fund and the deaths of fabled gangster Al Capone and car making tycoon Henry Ford, proved a great hardship for the farmers of the Glens. While feeding of stock bordered the impossible, the first sample of a picture postcard 'ice-age' provided unexpected bliss for youngsters. Schools were shut for an eternity.

The snow was heaven-sent as far as I was concerned. It was a dream time. I recall the same field behind the old Primary School used for a bit of toboggan fun. We improvised by using flat and corrugated tin sheets from the roofs of old outhouses to race down the hill and zip across the obliterated main road and into Kennedy's Field, all the farmland owned by Archie McSparran of nearby Cloney House.

Other inclines were sampled. The snowdrifts were so high they covered the roadside hedges so much so there was a guaranteed soft landing. There was a more professional approach when Terry and David Walsh arrived with a special steerable sledge, named the *Yankee Clipper*. It was a rare treat to gain a sail on the *Clipper*, which the Walsh brothers used to take to Cushendall for some 'derring do' down High Street, from near Cairns. The slick machine had waxed runners, and sometimes didn't stop until it reached Dalriada Avenue. There was also the story of someone on the *Clipper* getting angles wrong and careering through a window of what was Pat McCambridge's corner shop.

The snowstorms of 1947 also bring to mind the first UTA 'Utility' bus to reach the marooned folk at the Cushendun outpost. My Aunt Mary usually made frequent trips back home from Larne, where she was the Assistant Matron of the Moyle Hospital, but was unable to do so during the snowfalls because roads were impassable. She had to wait until the cold snap eased. Affectionately known as 'Auntie' she was on board the first bus to make it down the Coast Road from Larne to Cushendun. The roads remained covered in packed snow, some melting but ice underneath. Vehicles, mainly tractors, were now able to carefully negotiate the roads, inching over the treacherous surfaces.

It was a dramatic return for the very brave Auntie. I remember sitting in the kitchen at Knocknacarry when the front of the house shook ever so slightly, the light from the front window suddenly blocked out by the front of a bus. The driver lost control when trying to halt the bus in an attempt to let Auntie off. She was the lone passenger remaining in the bus, when the vehicle with the folding doors lurched sideways and crablike. Auntie was shaken but not stirred, thankfully unhurt as she gingerly made her way down the steps of the bus and almost straight in our front door.

Auntie likely had an influence in the wedding reception destination for her brother John's marriage to Mary Margaret McKay of the Milltown, in April, 1947. I remember that exciting occasion. It meant as an eight-year-old my first long trip outside of Cushendun, to attend the reception in the King's Arms Hotel on Larne's Main Street. The hotel manageress was the delightfully charming Miss Mary McKillop of Glendun, Auntie's close friend. She supervised a super feast. Sadly, granny Catherine O'Hara died later that year, on the 13th of August, 1947. The *Irish News* of Belfast published her obituary on Saturday, August 16, 1947.

The 'Death of well known Cushendun Lady' item stated: "She was renowned in the district for her piety and benevolence. Her husband, the late Mr Alexander O'Hara, who predeceased her over twenty years ago, belonged to a family who were the pioneers of posting and haulage in north Antrim, their tradition going back well over 100 years to the days when their vehicles were the main means of passenger and goods conveyance from and to Cushendun."

1947 was also to prove hugely important to the masses of Primary School students, as it was countdown to the 1948 complete overhaul to the education system in Northern Ireland. There was the fresh news of a mysterious new system that was to revolutionise education. It was the coming of the 11+ Examination, scheduled to be launched in 1948.

Minnie wrote: "This caused a great flurry of excitement, and hard swotting. "As my eldest son Alex would be eleven that summer of 1948, Master Delargy worked his class - with his nephew Kevin McHugh in it, to the utmost of their ability. He secured test papers and books of tests from Glasgow, and other places where exams like it were in force for some time. So, each night our kitchen table was pulled out and homework which lasted for hours, undertaken. English Composition, English Appreciation and Maths all had to be conquered.

"He (Master Delargy) put specimen descriptions on the blackboard, and also had them copied. He was brilliant at English, Maths and Gardening - and worked himself and his pupils to the limit. His results were phenomenal. When Alex and Kevin went to St Colman's College, Newry, the President there asked for the name of their teacher, because they knew so much more than the other boys in their class, and he had them promoted to a higher class after Christmas.

"At that time there were three divisions in the Knocknacarry School. Miss Healy, a Junior Assistant Mistress, although untrained, was a dedicated teacher, and could predict after three months in her babies' class which child would eventually pass the 11+. Then, there was a middle group - taught first by Mrs Doherty. This was after Mr Doherty retired, and the Boys' and the Girls' Schools were amalgamated under Peter Paul Delargy.

"After that, it was by Miss McGaughey, then by Miss Kathleen McNeill, newly trained about 1950. In 1951, Frances Murphy, who had married Charlie McHenry, was expecting her first baby and was retiring from Culraney Primary School. So, Father Lynch saw fit to give the School to Kathleen (McNeill), who had a bicycle, and lived in Ballycleagh - this leaving a vacancy in Knocknacarry. He insisted on my taking it, in September 1951. So after 15.5 years from the job of teaching I returned, and about a month after that Alex complained of pains in his side.

"He blamed lifting bags of turf onto the cart, when in the mountain overlooking Loughareema, but he did not go near a doctor until 1953, when he had his operation, and died in 1955. So, God saw to it that after his death I earned enough to keep the boys at Secondary School. Alex came from Violet Hill to St Malachy's College, Belfast, in 1951, and Denis went to Garron Tower, which opened that September. He was, accidentally - as I placed his application in the month of May, accepted the first registered student at St MacNissi's College. Daniel and Hugh also went to 'The Tower', and all stayed as boarders.

"In 1954, St Aloysius' Secondary School was opened in Cushendall, and Master Delargy B.Sc. became Principal. It meant I now had the senior classes of P4, P5, P6 and P7. It was tough work preparing for the 11+, but we did all right. Then, when Miss Healy retired, I became Principal, with Mrs Gus McKay the Assistant. In 1968, the McAlister's of Drumfasky got a Council house behind the Hall, thus taking three pupils from the small Glendun school, which was then closed.

"Mrs Elizabeth 'Betty' Lynn (widow of George Lynn of Cushendall and Chicago) and her pupils were accommodated in a Mobile Classroom in the Hall yard. When I retired, in 1969, Mrs Lynn became Principal, and when she retired Mrs McKay became Principal. With new Council houses, and many young families moving in, there was about twice as many on the roll as when Miss Healy was Principal. They enjoy all the amenities of a beautiful new school - St Ciaran's - about 100 yards up Layd Road from the old school."

# DIAMOND DELIGHTS

KNOCKNACARRY's 'Diamond' was a magnetic piece of no man's land, where young and old often congregated to hold talks, or for a bit of hurling practice on the main highway. It was also the setting for an occasional fist fight that inevitably followed a day at the Fair in nearby Cushendall.

I remember some rough and tumble action in the 1940's, watching wide-eyed as some over-imbibing clients of the then McCann pub were ejected onto the street. The hostelry was then owned by Charlie and Rose McCann, grandparents of prominent Glenariffe hurlers Randal and Charlie McDonnell. Charlie McCann was born in Buffalo, New York, where his Glenariffe-reared parents emigrated to. According to Charlie McDonnell, the McCann's once paid a visit to the Glens. Charlie McCann was due to return to the USA, but changed his mind and stayed.

Rose McCann was formerly Miss Kelly from Glenarm. I was led to believe she generally supervised the traditional background warning in the cosy if claustrophobic pub. Mrs McCann turned up the volume in a radio that blared out the strident chimes of 'Big Ben' as BBC *Home Service* news programme tolled out the deadly 9 o'clock 'shutters-down' signal that the premises must be cleared. There followed a back-up call from behind the pub counter of 'Drink Up'. No access to further alcohol was hard to swallow when the summer sundown was nowhere near complete over Glendun.

The punters shuffled out into daylight, and often had to shield their eyes from the sun. The untimely ejection seemed to infuriate some of the cranky customers, now spoiling for a fight. A row was inevitable, with lots of wrestling and invective - but precious little blood count on the Diamond. More often than not, when the loud and untidy hostilities petered out, the protagonists adjourned to either McKay's or McGreer's shop to purchase a McLarnon's plain loaf, a key-attached tin of spam, and a bottle of HP brown sauce. In the early 1950's, of that gloriously idyllic era, closing time advanced by one hour, to 10 o'clock.

The firmly managed yet cosy sanctuary of McCann's changed hands, and became known throughout North Antrim, and beyond, as the magnetic watering hole - 'Pat's Bar'. The infectious atmosphere of the fabled oasis inspired my brother Daniel to try his hand at poetry. He produced mischievous verse to suit the recurring angst when the curt query, from either Tournamona-born Pat Hamilton or his wife Lily (nee Delargy of Glenravel), of 'Have you no homes to go to. Drink Up.' echoed from the low-roofed compact room that was the 'ordinary' bar in Pat's. Daniel modelled his song on the Australian hit - *THE PUB WITH NO BEER*, made famous by singer Slim Dusty.

*It's happy we are, and it's long after nine*
*And Pat he shouts: 'Boys, it's damn near the time'*
*But Bill he says: 'Right, but I'm not atall well.*
*If I miss you in Pat's sure I'll see you in Hell'*

*Paddy the Burns says: 'Now Boys, stop your laughin*
*'We've not got much time for another wee haffin*
*Same again, Pat. It makes me feel swell*
*Sure if I'm not here in Pat's you'll find me in Hell.'*

*An ould man from the home says: 'A Guinness, I'm poor"*
*Ah. No more,' retorts Lilly, 'You've already had four.*
*"Och Aye,' says he, 'I understand well*
*If I miss you in Pat's sure I'll find you in Hell.'*

*Now Henry's just passing, on his way to the Club*
*And it's a custom of his to drop into the Pub*
*'Just time for a McEwan's, and a wee Bush as well*
*Well I'm damned if it kills me I'll not be in Hell.'*

*John Leech he comes in - 'A carton for Jack*
*And put me up a Larne Guinness, I'll be soon back.'*
*"Hurry up John,' shouts Pat, 'You'll have to run from the bell*
*For when that clock strikes ten it's out into Hell.'*

*It's ten minutes to ten, a car pulls into the yard*
*'Ouch,' Alex Ned says, 'Pat you have it damned hard'*
*To the Lounge came a party, and McGaffin as well*
*'Aye, Alex', says Pat, 'Sometimes it's like Hell.'*

Those were the 'halcyon' days, when men were mad and women wisely stayed indoors. It was also an unmatchable time-frame of goodwill and caring neighbours when Knocknacarry village, now Minnie's home, boasted two full-time shops . . . McKay's and McGreer's. Annie Ball's occasional part-time wooden structured sweetie shop opened at weekends for 'big nights' in the new Parochial Hall. The close-knit community also boasted a blacksmith's forge, a butcher's shop, a shoemaker, a barber, a public house, a petrol pump, a taxi rank, and a Post Office.

My one-time next-door farming neighbour, Alex 'Stoots' McKay, one of the stellar hurlers of the Parish, was of a similar mind, suffering a sense of sadness that the old days of a vibrant Knocknacarry so suddenly vanished. Alex, who was originally nicknamed 'Scoots' because of his quicksilver feet and evasive speed as a kid, said: "There was always something going on. When I was young Fair Days usually caused quite a stir. I used to be scared stiff when I heard very loud shouting by men in our backyard, on their way home after spending too long at a Fair Day in Cushendall. Such a Fair often meant three days away from home, for some. Then a few of them would try to prove how strong they were.

"There was always plenty of talk about how our hurling team was doing. I recall the 'Bears', great hurlers James and Dan McDonnell, coming to reside in Knocknacarry. At one time they lived way above Brablagh, Cushendun, and then up the 'Corkscrew' on the way to Ballycastle, in the second of the two 'cottages' - before coming down to Knocknacarry. When James became a married man he lived in the top house on Kennedy's Row, were Tommy Ross used to live. His mother and brother Dan lived in the bottom one, towards McGreer's, and beside the village water pump. I can also vaguely remember a veterinarian who lived in Eddie Brogan's wee house, at Knocknacarry 'Diamond'. His name was McKillen. I don't know where he came from. He was nearly retired at that time, and rented the house from Eddie.

"Yes, Knocknacarry was THE place. Everything was here. I remember Dr Alex McSparran having a chat with me in his surgery in Cushendall. I was in for a Medical Card in the Dispensary, as I had to go to the dentist. He saw me, called me into his room, and talked about happenings in the Parish of Cushendun. He asked about different things, and then said: 'Knocknacarry is just like one big happy family, and Cushendun is the very opposite.'

"I also used to get involved in Lint spreading for Hugh McGavock. He arrived in Knocknacarry with his blue vehicle doing his milk delivery, using small cans. Youngsters like me used to hop on the back for a lift. Hugh would invite all the schoolboys he could muster to help during the Lint-saving season. We lifted the Lint. That was around 1942. At the end of the day Hugh held races for us, around the field, and then took us to the pictures.

"John McSparran (later Dr John) and me won most of the races. We'd receive a money prize. John was a good sprinter. It was great fun. Also in the races would be Paddy O'Mullan and Jim McSparran. He gave them something, too. Hugh McGavock was very generous, a great sporting man, and would take us to the pictures in Cushendall. The films were still on there, despite the War. The cinema showed silent movies. There was a 'Blackout' at the time, with no street lighting.

"I have vague idea of Alex McGavock, Minnie's father, but I knew the mother well. She was a good woman, very hard working, and knew everything about farming. I particularly remember when I was asked to help during the time of the lint saving, because many men cleared off to Dublin, to watch the All-Ireland hurling final of 1943. Hugh McGavock, our Gus (Patrick McKay), Harry McKendry and Alex McKay of the Milltown all skedaddled to Croke Park. They left me with two men, known as 'Danagher' and 'Gantie', to put out the dubs of lint. I was about 15 at the time. Mrs McGavock knew when the lint was ready. She would come out of the house, and test the lint, to make sure it was right.

"There were other very kind folk who took the young people of the area to see film shows in Cushendall. The Walsh family came down from Belfast, and first rented McGreer's end house in Knocknacarry. I remember being taken to Cushendall in a brilliant V-8 car to see the films then staged by Mrs Whan. The Walsh's moved to Rockport House, before buying McIlreavey's farm near Knocknacarry. Mrs Kay Walsh was a very generous lady, a lovely woman, and always a very active person who organised parties for the school children of the Parish. Another very decent lady was Lord Cushendun's second wife. She also ran parties and great occasions for the kids."

# SCREEN GEMS

KAY Walsh was a very special lady. She performed countless works of charity, and I hold warm affection for that very special day she brought film fun for the first time to the kids of Cushendun Parish, during the closing years of the Second World War.

Retained is a flickering memory of watching open-mouthed at a new phenomenon, a little show of silent films featuring that funniest of screen comics, Charlie Chaplin. The little man became my instant hero. He was mesmeric. During fancy dress parades at Parish Sports on Glenmona Lawn, I tried to copy the little man's quirky walk. Who can forget the quivering moustache, the oversized well-worn boots, and the swinging walking cane that was always in synchronised swirl with his distinctive waddle?

Mrs Walsh not only supplied the picture parade, and my first brush with the escapism of the celluloid screen, but also copious amounts of lemonade, sweets and sticky buns. It was a heavenly day at Rockport House, where the Walsh family was then living. Handling the technical end of things for that glorious occasion was Mrs Walsh's son Robin.

He recalled the outing for the kids, and the equipment used for the party: "The Charlie Chaplin film show was just clips, black and white. We used a hand-cranked machine, a Kodascope film projector. I worked the handle. For the power needed to show the film, we used a 12-volt car battery - for the light. My mother used to have sales on the 8th of December, some in aid of the Lifeboats."

It was a defining occasion, one that has never left me. In modern times it would have no appeal. But, in the harsh era of the 'War Years' this was a magnificent milestone. I had to wait a few years before being able to attend the 'pictures' in Cushendall and Ballycastle. Sadly, the great lady, Mrs Walsh, was to suddenly die at 5 o'clock on the afternoon of the 5th of the 5th (May) in 1955, and spookily when she was 55 years of age.

Before her marriage to the highly successful businessman and world renowned 'Ham' radio operator, Mr R.V.E. Walsh, she was a prominent Rally driver mainly during the mid-1930's. The enterprising Katherine Mann and her three sisters became known in pre-War Irish motor racing circles as *The Four Graces*. Kay was also Lady Captain at Bangor (1939) and Cushendall (1947) Golf Clubs.

Robin followed her into Rally racing, and also Hill Climbing events. Another son, Terry, was an active racer in Northern Ireland Karting tournaments and also played hurling for the local Emmets' teams. The youngest son, David, was also close to local motor racing, model aeroplanes, and historic motorbikes. All members of the Walsh family vigorously involved themselves in many passages of the idyllic antics in Cushendun.

Robin disclosed how the family came to love Cushendun, of his first sighting of the Bay and the valley: "I was out with some pals one Sunday, on a drive from Bangor, and coming around Torr, from Ballycastle, we reached Tournamona for a first time. Looking across from the top of Dan Nancy's Brae I couldn't believe the scene in front of me. Gazing down on Cushendun, I just couldn't believe there was a place like it. It was so lovely. We came down before the Second World War. We lived at McGreer's in Knocknacarry for a time. At one stage we had a Ford V8 'Pilot' car that I drove in a Rally. We moved to live at Rockport, for some 14 years, before going to McIlreavey's farm at Agolagh."

The Walsh family also had a tenuous connection with the weekly film shows in Cushendun Parish. My introduction to the fantasy world of the silver screen increased my curiosity, later to be satisfied when the Parochial Hall at Knocknacarry came into full throttle in 1947. I believe Mr Walsh and his Supreme Cinemas helped Parish Priest John Matthew Lynch launch the cinema shows at Knocknacarry, and on how to book and secure the hire of films. On top of that, Walsh employee Danny McKay became the first projectionist. The flat circular tin cans, protective covering for the film reels, arrived at Knocknacarry Post Office every week, along with large-sized colour posters to depict coming attractions.

Robin Walsh added: "Danny (McKay) was the operator. He picked it up on his own, how to work the projector. He was a very gifted person. Long before he joined us, he was chauffeur to Mrs Parry, and was taken with the Parry family to London for a spell. There, he drove famous people such as George Bernard Shaw."

Denis McVeigh succeeded Danny McKay as film projectionist. It was a marvellous time, the film shows including 'shorts', and also *Pathe News*, to provide an Aladdin's Cave that included make-believe journeys throughout the world. For the record, the first full-length film to be shown through smoke haze from a little porthole at the back of the Parochial Hall was a Western or 'Horse Opera'. The Wild West show featured the weather-beaten, chiselled face of Wallace Beery, in the black and white 1937 release - *Bad Man of Brimstone*.

Alex 'Stoots' McKay added: "Danny McKay also chauffeured for 'The Barrister'. The time James McSparran was the Nationalist MP for Mourne. I was one of a few folk from the Glens who helped out during the Election involving 'The Barrister'. We went to Annalong. We were in different parts of the south Down country, with a fella from there along with me who knew where to go, where I had to pick up voters, and bring them to the Polling Station. I had to drive Arthur's (McAlister's) grocery van, which was adapted for the situation. David Macaulay also went along to help drive people to the voting booths."

The Glens of Antrim has a high percentage of Tartan family background. The Caledonian connection, just like the arrival of the McGavock's and McSparran's to the north Antrim coastal areas, is particularly prevalent in the case of Clan McKay. 'Stoots' highlighted his own strong family links to Scotland: "There was a time we (the McKay's) were Presbyterians, coming over from Scotland around 1620. Four fellas arrived at Ballintoy, County Antrim, from Blantyre, and went to the Hiring Fair in Ballycastle. Two of them went to Carey to work, and the other two went in the opposite direction - probably to the Mosside area. The ones that came up to Carey eventually married into Catholic families, and that is how we became Catholics.

"Wee Jamie McKay, a mill owner in Mosside - and a Presbyterian - once told me, when I would be in there chatting to him, that we are probably related. He had a Meal Mill, and bought in the grain. Jamie supplied meal for the farm animals, and also maize - yellow meal. He came round the Glens with meal for the farmers. I would be over at Mosside, paying for meal. One day we were coming out from his office, and he said: 'You know we are the same McKay's.'

"Brian, the son, lives in Ballycastle. I believe he is an engineer. Jamie had another brother. I think he was named Willie, and his family worked in the Mill. When Jamie died suddenly, Brian took over, and then his young ones had no interest, I believe, so there is no Mill any more. It was interesting to find out the way things worked out in olden times. Also, the reason why so many people are related to one another in the Glens, as Minnie O'Hara relates, is because there was not too much travel done in olden times. Road conditions were pretty poor. Three of my grandparents came from Glendun, and the other from Cushleake - all in the Parish of Cushendun."

# VILLAGE PEOPLE

THE BRUTAL dismantling of Knocknacarry's special charm and the exceptional family-friendly and good neighbourly aura, perfected over decades, was a crying shame. It remains one of great sadness, as far as I am concerned. In the interest of 'progress', alongside the changing face of the harsh business world, the 'convenience' facilities were wiped out. By the end of the 20th century the landscape drastically changed.

Extensive building of new houses was completed, but others stalled due to the world 'recession' of 2009. Long before the vulgarities of global financial greed plunged the planet to disarray, a special way of life in this small part of the Glens was over. Alarmingly, every facility vanished in Knocknacarry. It became the 'deserted' village. The old neighbourly ways were sadly air-brushed, and replaced by soulless 'modern' electronic living - the charm of an easy-going era wiped out, and with the community spirit reduced to selective necessity.

Minnie helped to trace the make-up of the 'real' Knocknacarry from the beginning of the 20th century: "Old Jamie McGreer and his brother Denis obtained from publican Mrs McKinley a small triangular corner on which to build the house where the shop is. The house they let is of a much later date. I remember a wee house in which an old lady lived in that garden beside Mrs Lynn's house. McGreer must have got it when she died - and then clapped that long slim house onto his own.

"Before McGreer's house, and shop, there was a cottage on the site of their small garden. There was also a house where the quarry was, and Dan Laverty lived there. Dan's mother had a shop. I just remember the wallstead of the shop. Dan Laverty then lived in The Square, Cushendun, and he had two beautiful sisters who came from somewhere to visit him, now and then. Dan's mother was a sister of Neal O'Neill, who owned the Post Office in Cushendun. Neal's wife was Rose O'Connor of Straid. She was the boss, a most efficient Post Mistress. They had one son, James - and he went to America. Minnie was married to one of the Fyffe's of Glenravel, and went to Scotland.

"Madge, the youngest, lived on as Post Mistress after her mother's death. In 1923, when Glenmona was being re-built after being burned down in 'The Troubles', a young carpenter named Rice worked at it and lodged in O'Neill's. He married Madge, left for Belfast, and ultimately Glasgow. Last year (1973) I was speaking to their daughter coming out from Mass. She and a Mrs Cassidy had McGreer's house rented for July. I thought Madge was dead, but she told me that both her father and mother were living."

Minnie added: "The row of four small slated houses, with their diamond pane windows, were situated where Mrs Lynn, John Brogan and John McAuley now live. Each of these small houses consisted of just a small kitchen and a small bedroom. Known as Kennedy's Row, originally they had no back doors. Granny O'Hara told me that a family of the widow O'Brien lived in the end house, next to McGreer's. She had two sons. Pat was a carpenter, and made a nice wooden seat with a back and arms on it which adorned our kitchen until lately. I'm not sure if he made the settle-bed too. I always had to scrub them, the chairs, and the kitchen table every Saturday, so I should remember them.

"The O'Brien's died off, and when I was at school it was Daniel 'the Scutcher' Doherty, who lived there and was later found dead in it. When I was a child in Dunurgan, old Daniel passed up to Sharkey's Mill carrying an empty hessian bag. He walked to the Mill every morning, the empty bag to bring back 'skows' for his fire at night. The sight of the bag made our dog bark from the time he appeared at The Turn until he disappeared out of sight at Dunurgan. He lived in the end house then in Knocknacarry. His brother was called 'The Gager'.

"Old Mrs McDonnell and her son Dan were, I think, the last occupants of that house. Mrs McDonnell's other son was James 'The Bear' and, like Dan, also a top hurler, lived for a time at the top end of The Row, before emigrating to the east of Scotland to open a B & B in the Perth area. Sally McAfee lived in the next house to McDonnell's. Sally, Dan McAfee's mother and an aunt of May Leavey, was a McIlheran of Layd. She was related to Maggie Cameron, Jim O'Neill's mother, and old Charlie 'Heery' McAuley's wife - Mary McAuley's granny. Sally was hard working, kept a pig or two which she fed on wrack carried from the shore. She also kept lodgers.

"An aunt of old Hugh Murray, Rosie 'Van' Magee, lived in the next house. She was a sister of old Mary 'Van' - who lived in Dunurgan. In the house in which wee Sarah McAuley died, and later Madge MacBeth lived, Jamie 'Scotland' and his mother stayed in it while they were getting their own house on the hill slated. Granny O'Hara told me that her husband, old Alex O'Hara always ceilidhed with the old Katie Scotland. One night, perhaps during Halloween time, the young boys - among them his own sons Alex and John, stuffed the chimney with a bag of straw. Inside they were nearly suffocated. They tied the door, too, and when old Alex O'Hara came home later he was like a chimney sweep.

"After Katie and Jamie Scotland returned to their newly-slated house on the hill, above Knocknacarry village, Tommy Ross, wee Sarah McAuley (found dead there), Barbara and James McDonnell and Madge MacBeth lived there. Also in Knocknacarry then was some kind of character who maintained he was married to Queen Victoria, and had a large family living under the 'Diamond' - a triangle of grass opposite Charlie McCann's pub, later 'Pat's Bar'.

"When Alex 'The Sod' O'Mullan married Jeannie Ross he and his family lived in the third house for years, until the 'labourer's' cottages were built.

Jeannie's brother, Tommy Ross occupied the first house in The Row, next to where the telephone kiosk is. He was a small man, and handy. He helped my husband Alex put the barn onto the top of the byre. He also did a lot of work for Mrs Dr Dan McSparran ('Cross Auntie'). He built the big rooms to the front, and made the wooden framework for her climbing plants outside. The house occupied by Anne McSparran was occupied by the MacCormack's - Charles and Bella, and their three children, Charles Jnr, Dan and Mary." Charles and Isabella died in early 1939, seven years after their son Daniel Henry. Charles Jnr - christened Charles Stuart MacCormack spent most of his life in the United States, and was in the US Army during World War Two. He died in February 1973, while Minnie's faithful friend, Mary Catherine MacCormack died in September, 2001, aged 96.

Minnie added: "Next is the two-storey double house with the unique windows in the second storey. Some think it was built for a police barracks, and the lower window in the second house had iron bars in it. Granny O'Hara said a policeman and his family, named McNally, lived there in the early days of this century (20th). The house occupied by Dr Joe Kennedy was the police barracks. When John McKay married Annie McKillop of Tyban they lived there, and started a shop in the room. Later, they bought Kennedy's barn, renovated it into a dwelling, also with shop.

"When McKay's had their first shop I remember coming down from school at lunch and buying a bun in the shop. Coming out through the porch where there was a big open barrel of treacle - and dipping my bun in the treacle, which I loved. I have that theft on my conscience. I'm sure many more girl pupils did the same. Mrs McKay never suspected what was going on. Master Doherty never allowed the boys outside the school yard, but Miss Wilde gave the girls their freedom at lunchtime.

"Mary MacCormack lived next door to that shop. The part next to the wee houses hadn't an upper storey until the early 1930's. Mary's brother Dan, my brother Hugh, and Alex McKay of the Milltown were great pals. They used to tell of one night they tormented Mary's mother Bella, by climbing up to the bedroom window and meowing like a cat in the open window. Bella and husband were sitting at the fire in the kitchen. Bella, on hearing the 'cat' in the bedroom, climbed the stairs and started looking for it, but went back down to tell old Charles that it must have got out the window. The boys heard all this and started meowing again to have poor Bella thinking she had missed the rascal, and raced up the stairs again. This carry-on was repeated several times. Some neighbour came along and chased them.

"Most of Knocknacarry at one time belonged to the Kennedy's. They owned the Post office and shop where Sarah McKay now lives. They also owned the Row, which the Ballycastle Council bought from Miss Kennedy. The McSparran's bought the farm and the houses across the street, except Mary MacCormack's - which belonged to Mary's mother's people, the McLarnon's. But the McSparran's bought their farm, where Malachy's big house stands, and his sisters - and also where the new St Ciaran's School is.

"Where Peggy and Dr John McSparran live were two houses. In the first lived Anne and Mary Jane McGreer, whose mother was a Butler from Carey, and therefore they were relations of my mother. Their headstone is beside O'Harra's in Killavalla. Next door to Mary Jane McGreer lived Charlie and Kate McAuley - 'The Heerys'. To enable them to build their big house on this site, the McSparran's bought a corner off Pat McCormick's field, and built a small cottage for the 'Heery's' - where their daughter Mary now lives.

"The O'Hara's house was one-storey, until the mid-1920's. Attached was the stable and 'coach house' for big carts and drays used in their transport business. It was converted to a dwelling house in the early 1930's. Dan McCollam of Cushendall was the builder. About that time the McCollam's also built McGaughey's bungalow. At the bottom of Layd Road lived Maggie Cameron, and her son Jim O'Neill, in a small house in a very big neglected garden. Father Lynch bought part of the garden from Jim O'Neill, and built the Parochial Hall in the mid 1940's. The four houses behind it were built on the site of Jim's house, and the remainder of the garden.

"When I was at school, a jaunting car owned and driven by Archie McCambridge of Cushendall brought the mail from Cushendall to Cushendun, and also copies of the *Irish Weekly*. The postmen were 'Fisty' James McAllister and Pat Hamilton, who lived in Cushendun and whose sister Fanny delivered the letters in the village. They all carried the letters in canvas bags, wore uniforms, and walked. One man served the head of Glendun, while the other travelled to Torr. 'Fisty's' father was Welsh McAllister. His mother was McLarnon, an aunt of Mary MacCormack.

"James McAllister was called 'Fisty' because he had only one arm, his other having been lost in an accident in America. But, with one arm he could use a spade and plant potatoes in his garden. He was married to Annie Cochrane, a half-sister of Loveday's. They had one son, Johnnie, who emigrated to America very young. Annie became blind, and when Fisty retired they moved to Larne, where they died. On leaving Knocknacarry, from the cottage where Alex McIlhatton now lives, he gave my husband his saw and other things that he wouldn't need in Larne. We have that saw yet."

Ireland's Census of 1911 lists a number of families in Knocknacarry. They include Bridget McKinley (50), Annie Ball (23) - a niece of Anne McLarnon (66), and her brothers Pat and Stuart. The Presbyterian family of Kennedy owned a slice of the area, and the leader of the family then was Margaret Kennedy (77), with daughter Margaret Ann (37) and son Joseph Moore Kennedy (45). Also there was Maggie Cameron (44) and son Jim O'Neill (21).

The O'Hara's featured Alex (50) and his brother Dan (65), Alex's wife Kate (40), and their family of Mary (16), Alex (14) and John (12). Across the way were the McGreer sisters Anne (63) and Mary Jane (61); Dan McIlheran (58); Sarah McAfee (69) and Dan McAfee (29); Charles McAuley (64) with wife Ann and son Charles Jnr (26); James McGreer (39) - wife Lizzie (29) and daughters Mary (8) and Lizzie (1) and sons John (5) and

Sam A. (3). They worshipped at the delightful little Church of Ireland building close to Cushendun beach.

Charles MacCormack (44), with wife Bella (47), sons Charles (10) and Dan (7), and daughter Mary (5) were also prominent residents of Knocknacarry during the turn of the 19th and 20th centuries. On the edge of the village lived the Stewart sisters - Jane (33) and Margaret (38). Nearby dwelt the McMullan's - James (72), his wife Kate (65), and sons Archie (24) and James (21). Down the road a little piece in this cosmopolitan gathering was the McIlreavey family of John (50), Mary (40) and Sarah (30), who were listed as of the Presbyterian faith.

Nearby, at Agolagh, was Kathleen Brogan (24) and brothers John (22), Edward (10) and Maurice (8). On the south side of this compact special place was the McSparran family. Registered that day of the 1911 Census taken at Cloney were James McSparran (19), and servants Edward Magee (18) and Dan McLaughlin (38). On the high ground overlooking the valley basin were the McKay and McIlheran families.

# THE HUB

JOHN McKay, a close friend and hurling team ally who lived on the seaward side of our house in Knocknacarry, was born on September 4, 1933, and affectionately known as 'Wee John'. An electrical engineer, he became one of the most accomplished caman wielders, either as a goalkeeper or wing forward, to come out of the Glens, and was a major cog in the fabric of the village.

John, who lives with wife Pat (nee Lennon) at Milltown, Cushendun, retains an emotional connection with those past times. "There was no place like Knocknacarry," he declared, "When I was growing up there you had a list of everything you needed, including B & B at Annie Ball's. She kept boarders. Next door, the McGreer sisters did stitching. They lived where Dr Dan later resided.

"There was the Forge, always a centre for great craic. Next door, there was always something exciting happening in McKay's back yard. More often than not Bach (Jim McMullan) and Stoots would be trying to fix an engine of some sort or other. If the hammering wasn't there it would be down the street at Bach's yard, where a car or tractor engine would generally be hanging by pulleyblock to a tree.

"Directly across the road from the Forge, Annie Ball also owned a wee wooden hut where Denis Hamilton had a barber's shop. He later moved to Ballycastle. Annie Ball then sold minerals and sweets from the hut. Mick McAuley lived in the wee house at the end of Charlie McCann's pub and was also a barber. He was the first man to cut my hair. The McAuley's went to live in Ballyvoy, Carey. His son was 'Wee' Mick, whose sister married Dominic O'Loan of Glenravel.

"I didn't go to Knocknacarry until 1944. My life started when living in Ropework's Row, or sometimes called The Wee Row or Crommelin's or Gamble's Row, beside the Cushendun Hotel. Jamie McKendry, an uncle of Pat and Harry, lived beside us. Nearby, on the laneway to Cave House, was the home of the Andy's - Jamie, Pricilla and Henry. Their mother was a Jamison from Carey. John McAuley of Glendun's wife was also a Jamison. I spent the first three years of my life in and out of the 'Andy' house. They kept me when my mother and father were out working. Henry 'Andy' was an amazing character, a one-off. Jamie was qualified in Horticulture - and was the main gardener for Crommelins, and I believe also at Glenville.

"My father (Danny) and mother (Sarah Huggins) worked for the Walsh family, and so we lived at Rockport for three years during the Second World War, from 1941 to 1944. I especially remember Mrs Walsh's 'Bring and Buy' sales at Rockport. We moved to Knocknacarry in '44, to a house in Kennedy's Row. My mother was a first cousin of Miss Magaret Ann Kennedy. She had brothers John, Joe, who was a solicitor in Dublin, and Hugh, who owned a draper and hardware shop in Ballycastle.

"We lived at McGreer's end, before the McDonnell's arrived from the Cottages on the Crooked Line. Next up then was Bunty (the McMullan family), then Alex McGavock, and at the top end was Tommy Ross. My uncle Alex McKay was there, when he married Molly Mort, before Alex McGavock arrived to live in Knocknacarry."

The McKay family soon moved across the road to the Post Office, run by Miss Kennedy and then John's mother, Sarah. His new home once burnt to the ground in 1907, and was rebuilt in 1909. John also remembered some travelling troubadours who materialised in the valley: "I recall a tented show arrived after the War. It was named *Fair Enough* that was in McBride's field at the top end of Cushendun Village.

"I believe there was also a tented show in Alex McKay's field, in front of the Cottages, and with special talent competition for locals. The *Fair Enough* show included a talent competition. I believe, one time, there was a bit of a fuss following one of the shows at Cushendun. Apparently, Mary Margaret McDonald, daughter of Smith McDonald of Cushendun village, lifted her skirt to show her ankles during the entertainment at *Fair Enough*. Somebody snitched, and afterwards Parish Priest Fr Lynch threatened to excommunicate her!"

John's better half, Pat held warm recall of a special time at Knocknacarry Primary School when a Sister Cecilia was in charge. She said: "Headmaster Peter Paul Delargy was away on a course, and Sister Cecelia had us singing and spending most of our time learning parts for a play that was staged in the new Parochial Hall. The play was *The Roses of St Dorothy*. I had to play the part of St Dorothy. The late Alex White was one of the Centurions, along with Danny McNeill. Una McKendry was also in the play. 'Deck' (O'Hara) was the principal male player, who sent St Dorothy (me) to her death.

"I recall Sister Cecilia having this special coach down to tutor us for the play. We had a great time then at school. I also remember May Hernon, who died on St Patrick's Day, 1967, coming in from New York, and holding a 'Bring and Buy' sale and also introducing the parishioners to an American game of chance, called 'Housey-Housey'. Later this was better known as Bingo."

Malachy McSparran also regarded the people of Knocknacarry as special. Of this enchanting place, he argued: "There was always something going on. We had Cloney Sports in 'Kennedy's Field'. Knocknacarry was a marvellous social centre. We had a collection of men gathering on summer evenings to talk late into the night - about hurling, farming, or whatever. They were usually perched on the railings and steps outside my uncle James 'The Barrister's' house. The building of the Parochial Hall added to all the excitement.

"I grew up there. I recall a terrific time in Knocknacarry - of things happening in the Hall, Whist Drives, Yankee Nights, Scottish Nights, Plays, Kitchen Comedy and Variety Concerts. Mammy ran one of those fund-raising concerts, after Fr Lynch sectioned off the Parish to make money. I remember Gerard Neeson of Belfast singing. He stayed on holiday at Bonavor. I think he was with the Vienna Boys' Choir. We also enjoyed other singers such as Cliff Ledger, a Slim Whitman imitator who came over from Ballymoney with Hugh and Kathleen McGavock for the concerts."

Malachy resurrected other stirring memories of long departed institutions of that Post-War era: "I recall the wee wooden hut at the Chapel, where papers were sold on a Sunday morning. Schoolteacher Miss Healy ran it, until the hut disintegrated. It was a Catholic Truth Society stall. There were other distinct characters about the place then, such as Jamie Douglas coming down from his farm in Layd. One of his brothers was John 'By Gum Though' Douglas, who always wore a blue suit and lived at Straid. I think John had been at sea. Another man I recall was Pat Keenan, who was also a bachelor and lived in wooden structured house at the bottom of Layd Road. He was the eldest of the Keenan's from Glendun, went to sea for a while, and then rented land for grazing above Knocknacarry Primary School from Mrs McLarnon. He also rented fields near Bonavor that 'The Master', Peter Paul Delargy, later purchased. Pat was an independent farmer, and produced good cattle.

"I spent half my life in Knocknacarry, which always seemed to feature some very interesting people. We had, for example, Jim O'Neill who worked for my father. He was a very strong man yet with peculiarly poor eating habits. Then there were the varied poker sessions in the valley. 'Big Bob' McKay used to hold poker sessions at Agolagh. Also involved were folk such as Paddy Lynn and Danny McKiernan. Jim Spiers also ran poker, and games of '55'.

"However, in my view, Knocknacarry was the centre of the Parish then. There are certain wee things that stick in the memory. In the middle of youngsters playing hurling in the street, Eddie (Brogan) would come up from Agolagh to feed, from a bucket, his Rhode Island 'Reds', and then collect the eggs in the bucket. He also had big Hereford cattle. When it became too wet to play hurling after school shut, I remember sitting in a hut at Cloney where we'd dream up a quiz to pass the time . . . asking each other the numberplates of some local cars.

"We also had a retired First World War Navy man, Mr Oscar Wayne Walker. He married Kitty Cleghorn, who became Mrs Nicholas Crommelin in 1938. She married Walker after Crommelin died. They first lived at Linton Lodge, Tyban, before moving across the valley to Knocknacarry, to reside in wee end-house at Charlie McCann's pub. She lived many years after Oscar Walker died."

Walker was one of the pioneers of explaining in book form the various techniques required to play the game of golf at top level. He had a high pedigree as a proficient golfer, a winner of County amateur titles in England. He wrote *Round the Clock Golf*, an impressively illustrated booklet printed in 1949 by J. & S. Scarlett of Ballycastle, and costing two shillings and sixpence.

Malachy added: "Oscar Walker was quite a character. We also had the 'Admiral', Dan Magill, a local-born who went to sea and lived in a bungalow at Tyban, where Fred McCormick is. After Magill, the Garrity's (James and Rosie (nee O'Neill) came back from the States to live there. Archie O'Neill, a brother of Mrs Garrity, also was a long time in America."

Fred McCormick remembered the eccentric Walker, and said: "I recall Oscar cleaning a chimney at Linton Lodge by simultaneously pulling the triggers of both barrels of a shotgun up the chimney - and all the soot coming down all over the room. What a mess. Everyone was black with soot. I recall Oscar saying, 'When I was in the British Navy we cleaned the funnels of the boats by firing a gun up the barrel.' Oscar seemed to be well-heeled at that time."

Oscar Wayne Walker was involved in one of the most tragic events ever to smash the relative quiet calm of Cushendun. On the early evening of Tuesday June 22, 1948, the brothers Liam and Paul O'Hara found a metal object that washed either down river or up the river. They took the cylindrical object to an outhouse near their home at Knockacarry. It would appear Paul, who was nine years of age and a primary school pal of mine, dropped the cylinder. He was instantly blown to pieces. It seems the object was a hand grenade, left over from the War.

The *Irish News* publication of Wednesday, June 23, 1948, had the ghastly incident printed on the front page. The headings read: 'ANTRIM COAST EXPLOSION. Boy Killed, Brother Injured.' The report stated: 'A tragedy in which 10-year-old Paul O'Hara was killed and his eight-year-old brother Liam seriously injured, startled the little village of Knocknacarry, about a mile from Cushendun

## Antrim Coast Explosion

# Boy Killed, Brother Injured

A TRAGEDY, in which 10-year-old Paul O'Hara was killed and his eight-year-old brother, Liam, seriously injured, startled the little village of Knocknacarry, about a mile from Cushendun on the Antrim Coast, at about 8-30 last evening.

The boys, members of a family of eight, were in an outhouse at the back of their home at Knocknacarry Cottages, when an explosion occurred with some object which they had picked up. It is surmised that it was washed up from the sea.

Dr. A. M'Sparran, M.O., Cushendall, attended the injured boy, who was removed to Ballycastle Hospital.

on the Antrim Coast, at about 8.30 last evening. The boys, members of a family of eight, were in an outhouse at the back of their home at Knocknacarry Cottages, when an explosion occurred with some object which they picked up. It is surmised that it was washed up from the sea. Dr A. McSparran MO, Cushendall, attended the injured boy, who was moved to Ballycastle Hospital.'

Paul, of course, was nine years of age while Liam was the older brother by two years. Liam was severly injured, his life hanging by a thread, but miraculously saved by the quick thinking and actions of Oscar Wayne Walker, who arrived at the ghastly scene moments after hearing the explosion. He used all his experience gained from many years in the Royal Navy. He knew First Aid drill - fortunately for Liam. Walker placed a tourniquet on Liam, to prevent the 11-year-old from bleeding to death, before a doctor and ambulance could reach the carnage. Liam, despite horrific shrapnel wounds, survived to become one of the top hurlers in the Glens, and with County Antrim teams. He died in his Clady, Cushendun, home in late 2009.

There were many shattering setbacks of early-age deaths in the Parish, and none moreso than that of Paddy Hamilton, team skipper of the 1963 Antrim Junior Hurling Championship triumph. A bank official, he was tragically killed at 21 years of age. The son of Dan Hamilton, he was one of Cushendun and Antrim's greatest hurling prospects, and died on January 5, 1965, at Blackrock, County Dublin. I knew Paddy very well, having played with and against him.

He featured not only for Cushendun Emmets but also with Ballycastle McQuillan's, where he figured prominently in Under-16, Minor, Junior and Senior teams until the Emmets club was resurrected in 1962. Paddy was unflappable at half back. He made the game look simple. His displays in Antrim Minor teams were outstanding, including an eye-catching exhibition against Tipperary legend-to-be Michael 'Babs' Keating. There were even better days to come when he excelled in an All-Ireland Under-21 semi-final at Casement Park, lording over such icons of hurling as Dan Quigley, even though Antrim lost to Wexford on that occasion.

Other heartbreaking hurling team fatalities that fill the Emmet's Club history were the tragic deaths of 1931 Antrim Senior Championship winning team's captain Dan McCormick, of Bonavor, and the exceptionally talented 19-year-old goalkeeper Johnnie 'Baker' McNeill of Riverside, Cushendun. Both featured in North Antrim teams. Dan McCormick died in late 1932. Johnnie McNeill, an uncle of former Emmet's and Ballycastle player Seamus 'Baker' McNeill, died on May 11, 1930.

Seamus said: "I remember Tommy McGreer of Knocknacarry telling me he was with Johnnie on the day he died. They went up Glenariffe to collect hurley sticks from Black's sawmill. On the way back, Johnnie, who was on a new bicycle, suddenly decided to test his bike up the steep hill from the Cloughs crossroads to Cairns, at Cushendall. When he didn't return, Tommy went up the hill, and just around the bend he found Johnnie lying on the ground where he was dying. The strain on his heart proved too much.

"Tommy told me uncle Johnnie whispered before he died, 'I wanted to see if the bike could beat the hill. Instead the bike beat me.' Johnnie, who was a gardener to the Parry family at Rockport, was just into the Antrim senior squad when he passed away. He was my mother Mary's brother. She was McNeill, son of John and Rose McNeill, and married a McNeill. My father was known as Johnny 'Archie', and had brothers Pat 'Archie' and Jim 'Archie' - and a sister Mary, mother of Bert McAuley in Cushendall."

# McMULLAN

LITTLE Big Man. The unique Jim McMullan deserves a special slot in this trip down the memory trail, because he was such a great part of my formative days in Knocknacarry.

My older brother Alex held an unwavering affection for this little man with the giant heart, who had such an impact on many happenings. Affectionately known as 'Bach', he was not a tall man yet a collossus among the people of the Cushendun Parish. A fanatical follower of the indiginous game of hurling, he was dedicated to the playing of the sport through undying devotion to his beloved Robert Emmet team.

A measure of his influence is the continued telling to the present day of all those tales of colourful adventures. I hold the forever-image of this feisty straight-backed Bach, with his cloth cap always at a perky jaunty angle, strutting up the street in Knocknacarry to purchase a packet of cigarettes in McKay's shop.

Inevitably, it became a case of 'stop the clock' as he also checked on the well-being of 'Wee' John, 'Stoots' and 'Gus' McKay, and 'Deck' O'Hara, if they were fit and ready for an upcoming hurling game. I can still see him rummaging through a top pocket of his blue 'boiler suit', to select an appropriate cigarette butt, and then light up without having to stop in his stride. The craic in McKay's kitchen, just over our hedge, was always mighty, all farming plans placed on hold. Life was unhurried in those days, placed in proper perspective when Bach was around. People had time to talk.

This was an era before the intrusion of television on daily living. There was also sometimes a Walter Mitty-like approach to life by McMullan. He'd say: "One of these days I will finish the job, take the remains of that ash tree out from the side of Sharkey's dub and make a few hurls for the club."

Perhaps a better and more lasting image is that of McMullan with a 'protective' hurley stick at his side during a match, always at the ready as he rigidly refused to back off when facing recurring adversity before, during and after hurling games. While hurling was his sporting hobby, and he played for the club during the late 1920's and into the early 1930's, he was also notoriously attached to dismantling and rebuilding old motorcars, tractors and motorbicycles.

He was constantly tinkering to try and solve mechanical puzzles. "The big end's gone," he'd declare. Amid his farming enterprise he once built a special buggy with attached trailer from an old Morris Cowley engine, and front and back chassis, and named the hybrid vehicle 'Lizzie'. More often than not an engine block would be seen dangling on a suitably strong pulley chain attached to a tree near the entrance to his farmyard.

The famous tree was the focus of attention for nosey passersby. It is no longer there. Perhaps a preservation order should have been hung on the tree, after the last eight-cylinder engine block was lowered from the creaking branch. I have also warm recollection of his accepted offer to build a lightweight cart in O'Hara's backyard. He spent a couple of summer months trimming and making shafts to suit an axle and adjoining rubber wheels he acquired from a disused car. There was constant advice from 'over the hedge', mainly volunteered by Stoots and Gus.

It was like a scene from *Last of the Summer Wine* during those stress-free times before the Bach 'invention' was ready for a test run. Placed between the shafts was Alex O'Hara's lightweight animal, known as 'Walsh's Pony'. There were other lasting memories, perhaps some mixing fiction with fact. One thing is sure, both McMullan and another iconic character of that era of resiliance, Henry 'Andy' McNeill were involved in working for building firms in Taunton, Devon, and more significantly in Dublin where they helped the La Scala Theatre rise from the aftermath ashes of the 1916 Rising.

Sean 'The Rock' McNeill's aunt Maggie was landlady to Jim and Henry in Dublin. He said: "When they worked in Dublin they stayed with my Aunt Maggie. She was Mrs Neil Bonner. My father's sister married a Bonner from Donegal. They had a boarding house in Dublin somewhere, and Henry and Jim were definitely boarders there. The motorbike was taken up and down . . . clunk, clunk, clunk, the three steps at the front door. Bach's motorbike lived in the hallway."

The Dublin adventure was part of a landmark enterprise that resulted in the launching of the La Scala Theatre and Opera House on August 10, 1920. The theatre, which had two balconies and numerous private boxes, could accommodate 1,400 patrons. It also featured a restaurant, a bar and a ballroom, with the interior doors and paneling brought in from Belfast.

Henry Andy and McMullan worked on the building site that once housed the office of *Freemans Journal* newspaper in Princes Street, off Sackville Street - the name then used for Dublin main thoroughfare, and later changed to O'Connell Street. Most of this area was badly damaged or completely destroyed during the period from 1916.

In 1927, Paramount Pictures of Hollywood took over the lease, and changed the name to The Capital Theatre. The last stage show there was on October 29, 1953. It remained a cinema until 1972, when demolished along with the nearby Metropole Cinema. The site was then developed by British Home Stores, and later changed hands to the Irish group, Penneys.

One of the many notable productions in the La Scala history was the staging of a major boxing match for the World Light-heavyweight belt. On March 17, 1923, defending champion Battling Siki, born in Senegal - then French West Africa - lost his World title over 20 rounds to County Clare-born, US-based Mike McTigue.

The ring action took place while Civil War gunfire raged outside along the River Liffey. Days before the historic fight, the last 20-rounder for a

World Championship, a bomb blew up the nearby Customs and Excise building. The skittish Siki, his Dutch-born wife, and his manager Charles Brouilett were given police guards during their stay in Dublin. Despite given merely an outside chance of dethroning the fearsome punching Siki the date was in McTigue's favour, St Patrick's Day. Born on November 26, 1892, this farmer's son from Kilnamona, near Ennis, County Clare, become the first Irishman to win a World boxing championship on Irish soil.

McMullan, who died on May 6, 1975, was world-travelled, with an array of exciting memories that ranged from adventures in Rotterdam docks to unwittingly wandering into and surviving 'the toughest street' in New York's notorious 'Hell's Kitchen'. Both Bach and Henry Andy also worked for a spell in England, in Devon. Henry, who died in Glenmona House on August 5, 1978, also kept in touch with top sportsmen of the day in England. He went to see his soccer hero, the legendary Alex James playing, and also top British lightweight boxer Ernie Rice in action. Once on the way back home to the Glens, Henry was on the pillion of Bach's bike from Taunton to Liverpool docks. Jim claimed the always laid-back Henry slept the whole way.

Bach's niece, Rosemary McKay, along with her sister Peggy and brother John, was not immune to the constant toing and froing, the vehicle repairs, the revving of engines. Her mother Mary was bachelor Jim's sister. They lived on the edge of Knocknacarry village.

"How could I forget the tree in our yard. Uncle Jim had, from time to time, car, tractor and motorbike engines slung up there," recalled Rosemary, "Of course the game of hurling was his big interest. He was besotted with hurling, and always had a store of hurls and hurley balls in our house, at the ready for the Cushendun team. The Diamond was a hive of activity, a focal point for the bus to take the hurlers to a match. The camaraderie in those days was great. It was an era that will never come back. One helped the other. You don't get that now."

She retained a special memory of Knocknacarry: "The wee houses, Kennedy's Row, in the village were gorgeous - the lovely windows they had. So beautiful, those houses, and with the water pump at the bottom of the row, beside Dan McDonnell and his mother's house. I also remember the small empty house owned by Eddie Brogan at the end of the Diamond. Monica McSparran and I went there for Irish lessons. Eddie was our teacher.

"He used to come to the house with his two buckets, after feeding his Rhode Island Red hens. We sat on bags of meal, and the likes, when he gave us language and written Irish lessons. Knocknacarry Primary School also holds great memories. I was in the same table in the old school, with yourself, Alex White, and some others. I remember the folding doors that divided the old school into two rooms. One unhappy memory was of having to drink the third of a pint bottle of milk that had been thawed out and warmed beside the big school fire. The taste of that luke-warm milk was awful."

Rosemary has no idea how or why uncle Jim was nicknamed 'Bach'. Minnie O'Hara once suggested it may have been borrowed from a Paddy 'Bach' McMullan, a Carey Faughs' hurler of olden times. "That is probably an explanation, yet our McMullan family had no relations of that name in Carey. We came from the Terrace at the Bay, Glenariffe. My grandfather, Jim McMullan was from there, and went off to sea. He went to Scotland, and joined a boat when only 16. He also worked in Scotland for a while.

"Granda McMullan married Rose McKay from Ballylaughan, Torr. They lived in Glasgow. I believe uncle Jim was born in Scotland. My mother Mary, who was a couple of years older than uncle Jim, was born there and baptised in St Mary's Church, Glasgow. She died on January 20, 1979, and my father Jack (John) died on May 14, 1968. There were three in the McMullan family. A sister Margaret died of meningitis at seven years of age in Scotland, and is buried in Glenariffe. My sister Peggy is called for her.

"Sadly, my granda McMullan was drowned at sea. His remains were brought back to Glenariffe, and buried there. The family returned from Scotland. Stoots' father, John McKay, who came back from Australia, and his sister, my Granny McMullan, bought what is now Scally's farm. John McKay then married Annie McKillop, and consequently Grandma couldn't keep it, the farm, on her own. I believe a Polly Hamilton bought the farm, and my grandmother came to Knocknacarry.

"We, the McMullan's, bought the house and farm from the Stewart's. Keenan's of Glendun provide the connection, making the Stewarts relatives of the McMullan's. James Stewart, whose brother owned the farm next door - later to be Brogan's farm, married a McBride of Glenshesk - Rose McBride. He was a Sea Captain, went to Killyleagh, bought a pub, and subsequently got married. Their son is Fr John Stewart, a relative of mine. When they had the house in Knocknacarry, a Cushendun Parish curate stayed in the house. Fr Small lived here. It was just a box room. There remains a wee cubby hole in the house where the Blessed Sacrament was kept."

Mary McMullan, Rosemary's mother, married Layd farmer Jack (John) McKay. "My father's brother was Charlie McKay of Gortacreggen. I never met my uncle Charlie, but certainly knew my cousins Danny, Dominic, Patrick and Charlie. Daddy McKay died at 70," added Rosemary, whose late brother John was affectionately known as 'The Cub', a moniker attributed to him by his uncle Jim.

The 'Cub' learned a few tricks of the mechanic trade in 'The Yard' - and was a useful man around a car engine. He later became a house builder, and gave me first option on the new building project at Agolagh Heights. Like me, John spent many happy hours in hurling practice near the Primary School, and was in a small team organised by Cushendun Parish Curate Fr Vallely. We togged out in Kilkenny colours, and played against other primary school teams in the Cushendall and Glenariffe.

The 'Antrim' hurling team that competed in the New York league featured many young men from the Glens of Antrim who emigrated to the United States to find employment in the early 1920's.
This photograph was taken at Celtic Park, New York, on July 24, 1927.
BACK ROW (l to r)-Con Meeghan, Pat Carroll (both Randalstown), Hugh Harvey, John McDade (both Glenariffe), John McAlister (Glenaan), John McElheran (Torr), Dan McKeown (Cushendall), Neil McKeegan (Glenaan), Neil Darragh (Ballyeamon).
FRONT-Dan Moore (Ballyeamon), Archie McLean (Carey), John McCurry (Ballyeamon), John McMullan (Cushendall), John McAuley, James Quinn (both Ballyeamon), Dan McCormick (Ballycastle) and Malcolm McCambridge (Cushendall).

Cushendun Emmets squad members and backroom boys pictured at Healy Park, Loughguile, before beating Belfast St John's in the Antrim Junior Hurling final of 1963.
BACK-Hugh McCormick, Raymond McHugh, Jim McMullan, Paddy O'Mullan, Alex McKay, Mickey Quinn, Hugh McKeegan, Johnny White, Hugh O'Hara, Alex McGavock, Kevin McKendry, Alex White, Malachy McSparran.
FRONT-Kevin McClements, Daniel O'Hara, Paddy Hamilton (capt), Seamus McNeill, John McKay, Terry O'Hara, Tim O'Hara.

*The wedding of John Joe Blaney and Lizzie McGavock. Right is best man Willie Blaney and left is bridesmaid Miss Mary Scally. The picture was captured by the L'Atelier Studio, Main Street, Portrush.*

*Tough work in a Lint dub near Knocknacarry.*

*Minnie taking her first born, Alexander, for a pram ride in 1938.*

*Minnie and her eldest son Alex.*

*Fascinating study of 1930's Portstewart Junior Division, St Colum's Primary student during lunch break.*

*Minnie at Cushendun Mass Rock Procession, June 1991.*

*Minnie's pupils of Junior Division, St Colum's Primary School, Portstewart, taking a break.*

*Minnie's four sons - Denis (trying to confuse by wearing Daniel's glasses), Daniel, Alex and Hugh.*

*Minnie's brother-in-law John O'Hara with nephew Hugh O'Hara.*

*Minnie with sons Alex, left, and Daniel.*

*Paddy Hamilton, centre, one of Antrim's great hurlers, takes a day trip with the O'Hara brothers, Alex and Daniel.*

*Nieces of Minnie . . the youngest of the Blaney sisters, Jacinta and Ruth in 1960.*

*Minnie attends baptism of grand-child Orla O'Hara at St Brigid's Church, Belfast, in 1971. Included are Godparents Jim and Marie Hendron of Portadown, Orla's brothers Eamonn, Sean and Cormac, her sister Catherine, and parents Denis and Elizabeth.*

*Blaney sisters, Brigid and Eileen at older brother Sean's wedding.*

*Danny McKay on his motorbike, May 1931.*

*Alex and Lizzie McGavock.*

*Alex McKay, one of the heroes of the 1931 Emmets' hurling team, pictured with his new car.*

*Postman James 'Fisty' McAllister at Kennedy's Row, Knocknacarry, in 1930.*

*Jim 'Bach' McMullan takes a rest on Miss Kennedy's Post Office summer seat at Knocknacarry, 1930.*

*Willie Blaney, son of Minnie's sister Lizzie, relaxes at Legge Green, Cushendall, with Sean Mort.*

*In the swing is the legendary Henry 'Andy' McNeill, watched by Danny McKay as he hams it up with a golf club.*

Glens historian Denis McKillop bringing in the hay crop at the Big Bridge, the Glendun Viaduct.

Hats on, as always - Alex O'Hara (right) with cousins Thomas Nelson Brogan and Katie Brogan on a day out at the White Rocks, Portrush.

Chocks Away! Undeterred by her 'plane crash shock at Portstewart, Catherine 'Kathleen' McBride again takes to the air for a week in Paris in 1960. The owner of Cushendun Hotel brings along her niece Marie Kelleher, nephew Randal McDonnell, and her sister Mary McBride, mine host of 'Mary's Pub' in Cushendun.

Tessie McIlhatton, later to be Mrs Ned O'Neill, is pictured right with her older sister Jeannie outside their brother Alex's shoemaker shop at Dunurgan.

The Tacoma McGavock's. The gathering, believed to be in the late 1920's, features Minnie's uncle Hugh C. McGavock (second right) with sons (l to r) James, Hugh John, and one-time US Senator Leo.

Grannies day out . . . Minnie and Mrs Mary Stewart, Elizabeth O'Hara's mother from Comber, County Down, inspect vestments during the 1971 baptism of Elizabeth's youngest daughter Orla at St Brigid's Church, Belfast.

W.M. 2.

**AUTHORITY TO WEAR**
**WAR MEDALS FOR THE MERCANTILE MARINE,**
Awarded by H.M. The King
through the Board of Trade.

*Alexander O'Hara*

ISSUED BY THE BOARD OF TRADE. (Dis. A No. 842895 R.S.2 No. 3767 H ) is authorised to wear the undermentioned medals and ribbons against which the signature of a Board of Trade officer and an official stamp have been affixed.

Marine Dept. C. HIPWOOD,
Board of Trade. *Assistant Secretary.*

| | Authorised. | Signature of Superintendent of issuing M.M.O. with office stamp. |
|---|---|---|
| British War Medal ribbon | 18·10·19 | 18 OCT 1919 |
| Mercantile Marine Medal ribbon | 18·10·19 | |
| British War Medal (and clasp ) | | |
| Mercantile Marine Medal | 27·10· | AUTHORISED 27 OCT 1925 |

(545ve) (53122) Wt. G512 100,000 1-19 W b & L

*Signature of holder.* *Alex O'Hara*

Alex O'Hara's First World War medals awarded in 1919, but not processed until October 1925.

*Knocknacarry Primary School's nine-man hurling team of 1949.*
*Back (l to r)-Brian McQuillan, John McKay, Ian McElheran, Denis O'Hara, Pauric Scally.*
*Front-Alex White, Patsy McGarry, Liam O'Hara, Danny McNeill.*

*Jim 'Bach' McMullan and Jack Hernon, the latter retired to Knocknacarry after working for decades in the United States.*

*Captain James Redmond*

*Confirmation Day at Portstewart on May 30, 1933, for Minnie's 'God Children' - Mary O'Neill and Janie McLaughlin.*

*Minnie takes time out from her kitchen*

*Eddie 'The Farmer' Brogan, right, with his near neighbour, a young Jim 'Bach' McMullan.*

*1930 marked the tragic death of 19-year-old Cushendun Emmets' goalkeeper Johnnie McNeill. An exceptional talent, he was a North Antrim team player and promoted to the all-county panel.*

*Fabled Glens of Antrim landscape artist Charles McAuley, whose talent was early recognised by James Humbert Craig,*

*The 'Tin' Chapel in Portstewart*

*An early Cushendun scene*

*Hard men in Burberry overcoats. Pictured in 1954 at The Diamond, Knocknacarry, are prominent Cushendun Emmets hurling stalwarts (l to r) Dan McDonnell, the brothers Dominic and Charlie McKay, and a 21-year-old 'wee' John McKay.*

*Alex McGavock and wife Lizzie (left) enjoying a special celebration at Harold's Cross Road, Dublin, for Lizzie's brother-in-law Nick Bohan, a leading Dublin Fire Brigade officer. Right is Nick's wife Mary (nee Redmond), and centre is another of Lizzie's sisters - Susan Redmond, who played camogie for Cushendun in the 1930's.*

*Oscar Wayne Walker, who saved the life of Liam O'Hara*

*The cover of colourful Oscar Wayne Walker's illustrated booklet on how to play golf, priced two shillings and sixpence. It was printed in November 1949 by J.S. Scarlett & Son, Ballycastle, County Antrim.*

*Licking ice cream sliders outside Hamilton's 'Store' in Cushendun village during the 1930's, and looking like bootleggers on a day off, are Alex O'Hara, Charlie Brogan, Maurice Brogan, Joe Morgan, Eddie Brogan and John James McKay.*

*Sharing a joke at Knocknacarry are local hurling team members Denis 'Deck' O'Hara, 'wee' John McKay and Brian McQuillan.*

# SHORT RATIONS

DURING and immediately after World War Two a process of rationing was imposed on all citizens of the United Kingdom. In this time of austerity there was a curb on the amount of petrol, clothing and food you could purchase, and only if you had an allocation of official Ration Coupons.

Rationing was introduced at the beginning of 1940, following National Registration Day on September 29, 1939. Identity cards were also issued. Ration Books, regarded the key to survival and to make sure everybody received a fair share of the items available, were issued to each family, and contained a number of tickets to match the allowance for the number of adults and children in each household.

Each family or individual had to register with a local supplier from whom the ration would be purchased. These details were stamped in the book. The coupons were handed to and signed by the shopkeeper, and it meant people could only buy the amount they were allowed. The O'Hara butcher's shop at Knocknacarry had to maintain a meticulous watch on Ration Books when selling meat.

Minnie retained the intriguing inventory of the people then residing in the Parish of Cushendun who purchased meat from John O'Hara. The booklet reveals, in clear handwriting, the names of families, and their respective ration allowances. The first preserved O'Hara list of meat rationing is dated July 1941. Here are the names and Ration Book allowances.

M. J. Laverty, Cushendun (3 books), Mrs James McGreer, Knocknacarry (3), Mrs Walsh, Knocknacarry (5), Miss McNeill, Glendun Lodge (1), John McKay, Milltown (3), Mary Walsh, Milltown (2), Miss Erskine, Milltown (1), Alex McKay, Corrymellagh (8), John O'Hara, Ardicoan (2), John McNeill, Rockport (2), John McCormick, Dromore (1), Mrs McKay, Knocknacarry (3), Cassie McKillop, Tyban (1), Bob McKay, Agolagh (2), Mary McAllister, Whitehouse (3), John Hadden, Cushendun (2), Mrs McKenty, Knocknacarry (2), James McMullan, Agolagh (1), Margaret McKay, Cushendun (2), Miss Healy, Cushendun (2), Mrs Leavey, Cushendun (3), John McLarnon, Cushendun (6);

Miss Kennedy, Knocknacarry (2), Mrs Dan McKay, Knocknacarry (3), Hugh McGavock, Dunurgan (5-two children), John McGreer, Knocknacarry (2), Rob McGregor, Knocknacarry (1), Joseph McLarnon, Knocknacarry (1), John McCrystal, Knocknacarry (5-three children), Mick McAuley, Knocknacarry (4-one child), Mrs Heaney, Cushendun (2), Mrs Bell, Cushendun (2), John McNeill, Riverside (3-one child), Mrs Brown, Cushendun (4), Mr McMullan, Knocknacarry (2), Dan McAfee,

Knocknacarry (1), Miss McCleary, Cushendun (2), James McNeill, Sleans (2), James McNeill, Park (9-one child), Maggie Cameron, Knocknacarry (2), Mrs P. McKay, Agolagh (4), Rev P. Courtney, Knocknacarry (2), Miss McGaughey, Knocknacarry (1), Alex McGavock, Dunurgan (2).

The list continues and includes fabled landscape painter James Humbert Craig, Rockport (3). Also-Mrs Parry, Rockport (3), Mrs Lilburn, Bonavor (3), Mrs Doherty, Cushendun (3), Dan McDonald, Cushendun (2), Smith McDonald, Cushendun (2), Mr Calder, Cushendun (3), James McKendry, Cushendun (1), Alex McNeill, Cushendun (1), Mr Walker, Linton Lodge (3), Miss Wylde, Innispollan (2), Mrs Boyd, Cushendun (6-two children), Mrs Cox, Agolagh (3-one child), Mr T. Creary, Agolagh (1), Mrs McCann, Knocknacarry (2), Mrs John McDonnell, Ardicoan (3), Mrs Charles McAuley, Knocknacarry (3), Pat O'Hara, Clady (3), Mrs Hernon, Knocknacarry (2), Mary McKillop, Brablagh (2), Mrs Darragh, Cushendun (1), Mrs Charles McNeill, Cushendun (2);

John Murphy, Aughnasilla (1), Mrs Lennon, Milltown (5-one child), Mrs Cochrane, Cushendun (4-two children), James McNeill, Ballycleagh (8), Willie O'Hara, The Cottages (10-four children), Mr O'Hara, Ballycleagh (1), James McAllister, The Cottages (2), Annie Ball, Knocknacarry (3), Mrs Trainor, Knocknacarry (5-two children), Mrs James McDonnell, Knocknacarry (3-one child), Dan Clarke, Knocknacarry (1), Mrs Sharkey (5), Mrs Alex O'Hara, Knocknacarry (6-two children), John McNeill, Tournamona (1), Mrs McLaughlin, Knocknacarry (1), Mrs King, Knocknacarry (4-two children), Mrs Flynn, Bonavor (3-one child), Mr McNeill, Glendun (2), Mr McCann, Glendun (1), C. Gibson, Glendun (1), McBride's, Glenmona (2), Fred Muir, Dunurgan (1), McAlpine, Cushendun (2);

Walter Finlay (1), Rosemary Lillburn (1), McLarnon, Rasharkin (3), Mr Magill, Whitehouse (1), Mrs Harrison, Bonavor (1), Pat McCormick, Bonavor (2), Archibald Laverty, Ballyteerim (1), Mrs Keenan, Cushendun (4), Harry Scally (2-one child), Mrs Hynes, Agolagh (6-one child), Mrs Breheny, Cushendun (6-one child), Mrs McCluskey, Milltown (2), Curry, C/O Annie Ball, Knocknacarry (2), Mrs McHugh (1), Maggie Cooney (1), John Douglas (1), Mr McHugh (1), Rev P. Murphy (1), Alex O'Mullan (2), Mrs Murray, Cushendun (3-two children), Mrs Harrison (2), Mrs McQuillan (3), Mrs Evans (3), Boyd's, Cushendun (3), McLaughlin, Bonavor (1).

The recording of registered customers continued through to 1954. Some names disappeared, some new names appeared - including in 1942/'43 Mr J. McSparran (7), Mrs Lundy, Knocknacarry (6-one child), George Harvey, Cushendun (1), McFetridge, Castlegreen (1), W. McGarry, Straid (2), and landscape artist Maurice Wilks (1). The 1947 registry included Mrs Blaney, Cloughs (3), Alex McCurdy, Tournamona (4), Mrs James McSparran, Knocknacarry (4), Mrs P. Maher, Barrmean (3), Polly McAllister, Whitehouse (2), A. McSparran, Cloney (7), Mrs M. Convery (1), Mrs Spears (2), Archy McKay, Tops (5), Dan McNeill, Ligadaughtan (1), Mrs Dan McSparran (2), George McElheran, Straid (3), Mrs White (2), James Martin (1), Mrs Johnston (2), Mrs Archy O'Neill, Dromore (3), Annie McQuaid (2), Mrs Delargy (3), John Roy Hamilton (3), John Carey (4), Mrs

C. Graham, Calishnagh (2), Bella McKay, Ranaghan (1), Henry McKay, Ranaghan (1), Harry McHenry, Cushendun (5-two children), Tommy and Mrs McGreer (2).

* FOOD rationing lasted for 14 years, and came to a halt on July 4, 1954, when restrictions on the sale of bacon and meat were lifted.

# A PENAL PLACE

THE MASS ROCK at Innispollan was a major religious factor in the meticulously ordered mind of Minnie, who was 14 years of age when she attended a typical Sunday celebration in the wood at Craigagh. She was honoured to be a part of the annual Corpus Christi Procession to the old altar. The occasion elevated to a top news item in the Belfast morning daily - the *Irish News*, was in early June 1918. The Cushendun Parish Priest then was the Rev Tom Blacker.

The report included: 'It was the spot that Mass was celebrated in the Penal Days and the altar, which is still preserved, is held in great reverence by the sterling Catholics of the historic district.' The reporter also noted: 'The Sacred Host was carried by the Very Reverend J. McCartin P.P., VF, Cushendall. The rosary was recited by the Rev J. Small P.P. Culfeitrim, who was Master of Ceremonies. An eloquent ceremony appropriate to the occasion was preached by the Rev P.J. O'Kelly CC, St Patrick's, Belfast.'

Minnie once remarked: "Cardinal O'Fee says that St Oliver Plunkett visited this parish (Cushendun), and said mass at the Mass Rock. A Crucifix carved on rock at back of old Altar was taken from Scotland - maybe Barra as priests here had jurisdiction over some Scottish parishes. Boats crossed from Cushendun and also from Layd Monastery. A ferry service was in operation between Cushendun and Dunaverty in the Mull of Kintyre up to 1843."

In 1891, Cushendun curate Fr William Kelly organised a first Corpus Christi procession from the church at Craigagh to the Mass Rock Altar at Innispollan. Opposite the main gate to St Patrick's Church, renovated and rededicated in April 2010, rests 'The Gloonan Stone' - St Patrick's Well. Just inside the Church gate is a special tree. A Miss Foster (a relation of Vere Foster) gave the rhododendron bush which grows there, and conveniently blooms around Mass Rock Procession time. Minnie gained confirmation of this from Mrs Nellie McKay (nee Hernon), who lived at 'Mickey's Corner' on the road to Cregagh and was a sister of the infamous Dan 'The Duck' Hernon.

Minnie wrote: "Mrs Nellie McKay told me the beautiful rhododendron bush which grows inside the gate to the graveyard at St Patrick's Church, Cregagh, in the townland of Killavalla, was planted there by Miss Foster - who stayed in Glendun House as a guest of Miss Ada McNeill. Nellie was once a maid there." Minnie also remarked the small plant for this tree came from the grounds of the fabled Mussenden Temple at Downhill - and was a goodwill gesture to the Catholic parishioners of Cushendun from the people who worshipped at Castlerock and were friendly with Lord Cushendun and his relatives.

Mussenden Temple is perched on a clifftop that is 120 feet high. The 18th century building, built in 1785 and along similar lines to that of the Temple of Vesta at Tivoli outside Rome, is in the grounds of Downhill Demesne and lies one mile from the seaside village of Castlerock. It was built as a summer library by Frederdke Augustin Hervey, Bishop of Derry and Earl of Bristol, and dedicated to his cousin Frideswide Mussenden. Vere Foster, born in 1819, died in Belfast on December 21, 1900. He was an educationalist, and also became the first President of the Irish National Teachers' Organisation. Born in Amsterdam of an Irish-born father, he founded the Irish Feminist Migration Fund in 1852, to assist young women to emigrate to Canada, the first ship sailing in that year.

The link between St Patrick's Church and Downhill was through the influences of Lord Cushendun's friends. The area along Cushendun Bay held a magnetic attraction for the 'landed' gentry, and was also a constant source of curiosity and enjoyment for landscape artists, artistes, poets and writers. Taking parochial pride of place in Minnie's singing was the inevitable -

### CUSHENDUN

*O far distant hills of my own native home*
*I see you again in my dreams*
*'Tis Antrim I long for and dear Cushendun*
*with its wee winding roads and its streams.*

*The path by the Dun to the top of the glen*
*where the grouse and the wood pigeon dwell*
*The little white farmhouses tucked in the folds*
*of the mountains that nurse them so well.*

*I long for the splash of the trout in the Dun*
*and the hoot of the owl in the trees*
*The sound of the wee chapel bell in the glen*
*brought to me on the wings of the breeze.*

*I hear the storm rising to rush down the gap*
*I see the hills crowned with a pall*
*The mountainy streams are caught up by the wind*
*and turned into mist as they fall.*

*God grant me once more a sight of this spot*
*may I wander again through the wood*
*may I look for the faces I loved long ago*
*and find them God grant that I could.*

*O, maybe some day I shall find my way back*
*and you can sure, if I do*
*In that tiny wee chapel that calls us to pray*
*I'll thank God that my dreams have come true.*

During her retirement Minnie was accorded the utmost respect by her past pupils, and none greater than near-neighbour Elizabeth McGreer. In the 1980's, Liz spent a lengthy sojourn in Australia and Bali, yet remained devoted to Minnie - sending letters to describe her journey 'Down Under'. For a person who refused to board an aeroplane, nor sail in a boat ('I never flew nor floated', she loved to declare) Minnie enjoyed hearing of 'far-away places with strange sounding names', and was an avid viewer of television programmes on geography, holidays abroad, sport, the world at large, and such like.

Letters from the ever-faithful 'Liz' McGreer were welcomed with great relish, and in return she would send a perfectly written reply in her most wonderful handwriting, detailing all the latest innocent information from the village of Knocknacarry. Here's a sample, when she was 85 years of age. The letter is dated Sunday the 18th of June, 1989: "A very belated 'thank you' for the beautiful card you sent me from the island of Bali. And, how lucky I was to get speaking to you on the 'phone yesterday morning."

Later, a stickler for detail, she refers to a busy day - 'Last Tuesday, the 13th, I had an appointment with Dr Adrian McWilliams (eye-specialist) at the Waveney Hospital, at 10.20 a.m. and wasn't home until 1.30p.m. Then, at 3.30p.m. I headed off with Master and Mrs Delargy, and also Mrs McKay, to a function for Retired Teachers in Garron Tower. I wasn't home until 9.15p.m. This lovely weather is suited for Denis's golf. He goes to Ardglass tomorrow, and then on Tuesday - and for the rest of the week, he'll be in Portmarnock reporting on the Carroll's Irish Open golf tournament."

Minnie was always at peace when relaying to her grandchildren stories of the past, or reading an item from a newspaper or magazine that might improve their education. This was a source of deep joy to her. A shopping day trip to Ballymena was 'heaven sent' as she related her times past in that market town. Here is a little limerick Minnie loved to tell to the kids .
. .

### THE DANCER

*Thomasina from Ballymena*
*Could dance on her toes like a ballerina,*
*BUT..........*
*She married a man from Cushendall*
*And now she doesn't dance at all.*


Her shopping needs were minimal, the day trips monumental. Always hopeful of meeting people she knew, having a bit of craic, and enjoying a good strong cup of tea in a restaurant were all important. Forever picking up and also formulating witty sayings, one of her favourites on the occasional shopping 'spree' was - 'People are buying things they don't need, to impress people they don't like."

The youngsters on the trips did not get off lightly. When they arrived back at Knocknacarry they had to write down their thoughts on the day's adventure. Once, her grandson Cormac Denis O'Hara (aged 10) had to produce some doggerel on trips with Minnie to Ballymena, in June 1979, with writings scrutinised by Granny. Here is a sample from . . .

### EVERY OTHER DAY

> She gladdened our hearts by saying to us
> 'I think, to-day we'll all travel by bus.'
> Orla and I, and Denis McKay
> Went to the kiosk to spy
> and call to Granny when the bus was coming
> but, just as the clock read half-past two,
> the two of us ran back to say:
> 'Who do you think is coming round the corner
> but Maggie Gore in her light blue car.'

Minnie also encouraged some doggerel in 1975 from another grandson, Sean, upon his anxious elevation to become an altar boy at St Patrick's Church. "Sean's keen-ness on becoming an altar boy is reminiscent of his uncle Daniel Vincent, who, at an early age, forced his way onto the altar - only to get 'the boot' after a while from Father Tom McKillop, because he couldn't be kept from talking and looking round him during Mass," added Minnie.

"As soon as Father Tom's successor arrived (Fr Frank McCorry - a member of the Antrim 1946 All-Ireland football final team, and also a North of Ireland amateur golf champion) the outcast angel wangled his way back. During Father McCorry's short sojourn here, Daniel was his right-hand man, accompanying him on journeys to Torr and Toomebridge to exchange dogs, and to Ballycastle when Father went to Mrs Downey to buy the cloth for a new suit, and then across the street to Mr Morton, the tailor, to have it made."

Sean O'Hara's first time to serve as an altar boy in Cushendun was at First Friday Mass held at 8.00pm on November 7, 1975. Minnie kept this detail, and afterwards helped the young man with the following flow of words . . .

What a night to remember
The seventh of November
I had every intention
That evening to mention
My one great desire
To come down from the choir
And serve on the altar
With big brother Eamonn
And friends Dominic, Seamus and Raymond.

So, the first thing to do after school
Was to get permission from Father Laverty.

*After three times finding the Parochial House empty*
*At last I was lucky to gain an entry*
*On hearing my request, Father was quite sympathetic*
*And assured me of a welcome at Mass that very night*

*All out of breath to Granny I trotted*
*Who was pleased to hear that I was allotted*
*A place on the posh panel who serve at the altar.*
*Proudly I walked that night*
*With Eamonn, Dominic, Seamus and Raymond*
*And in the Sacristy I found a surplice and soutane*
*Left there by one who is now a man*

*To crown my happiness I accompanied Father Laverty*
*As he distributed Holy Communion*
*By holding the paten for what seemed to be hundreds of communicants*
*My right hand sometimes felt the strain but I hardly noticed the pain.*
*I just felt real proud at being allowed on my very first night.*

Sean entered a footnote to reveal he went after Mass with his older brother Eamonn, Minnie, her brother Alex and his wife Lizzie McGavock, to a Glens of Antrim Historical Society meeting in the Bay Hotel, Cushendun. The lecture was by Lady Antrim, speaking on the life and times of Sir Randal McDonnell.

# DUN DEALINGS

O N MAY 14, 1991, Minnie offered her thoughts in this intriguing special place, Cushendun. "The area at the beach is now owned by the National Trust, but was previously owned by two landlords. The land and houses on the south side of the river were owned by the Crommelin's. The land and houses on the other side were owned by Lord Cushendun, whose father was Edward McNeill - called 'Long Eddy', who was a native of Craigdoon, outside Ballymena.

"Ronald McNeill (Lord Cushendun) was married to a girl from Cornwall, and when he had the houses built in The Square, the architect, Clough William Ellis, designed them in the beautiful Cornish style. The date on them is 1912. Ellis also designed the Maud Cottages at a much later date, and they were called for this lady, whose name was Maud. The Crommelin's were descended from the French Huguenots, and built the Cave House. One of their daughters was married to the famous poet, John Masefield, who often stayed in the Cave House. The mound above the fascinating entrance to the isolated Cave House is known locally as 'Crommelin's Hump'.

"Lord Cushendun lived in Glenmona, and his cousin, Miss Ada McNeill lived in Glendun Lodge. She was born on September 27, 1860, and died on July 10, 1959. Miss Ada's famous visitors included Roger Casement and Francis Joseph Biggar, the latter the 7th son of a 7th son born in 1863 on Belfast's Antrim Road. Biggar was involved in the Gaelic League that started in July 1893, with a first meeting held in Lower O'Connell Street, Dublin. It was a non-political, non-sectarian gathering, and involved people of different politics and religion in a common cultural effort to revive the Irish Language and preserve Irish culture. The inaugural meeting was called by Eoin MacNeill. It progressed to have 550 branches. The first Chairman and also later the first President (until 1915) was Douglas Hyde.

"Many other prominent people came to stay on holiday with these aristocrats. In each house there were servants, both male and female. Usually each house of the rich employed three servant girls, two or three gardeners and a coachman. Once a rich linen merchant from Belfast occupied a house in the area, and drove his own coach from Belfast. He went through Knocknacarry and other villages so fast the inhabitants called him 'Flash Finlay'. I am not sure which of the 'Big Houses' Flash Finlay occupied, but I was told he had a light in every window to welcome home his two sons from a boarding school in England for their Christmas holidays.

"One of them was named Walter. As a married man Walter lived in a wooden shack in a corner of a field on a very sharp corner of the 'Crooked Line'. The shack is still there. The other Finlay brother owned the salmon fishery, and his wife kept boarders in what was the Anchorage Hotel, a hostelry later renamed the Glendun Hotel when purchased by the Elliott family in 1927. This Finlay family moved to Cushendall. The Elliott's launched the Bay Hotel in 1936."

The Bay Hotel, part of the property linked to the Glendun Hotel, became a regular stop-off for Fawcett's bus tours that created summer cavalcades of post-War holiday seekers travelling from Larne to Portrush. This was a very busy and bustling place. I can recall the Gregg brothers, Robin and Alex, coming on summer vacations from Ballymena, to stay with their uncle Bertie Gregg at the hotel. Bertie was married to an Elliott.

The teenage Gregg boys were fitness fanatics, outstanding athletes who trained daily on Cushendun beach, and regularly swam across the bay. Alex became a noted javelin thrower who gained representative honours, while Robin developed into an exceptionally talented rugby player for Ballymena, Ulster and Ireland. Incidentally, after leaving Cushendun, Mr and Mrs Bertie Gregg took up the catering franchise at Knock Golf Club in east Belfast.

The flat-roofed Bay Hotel since changed owners on a few occasions - to Tommy McKenna of Ballymoney, to James McAllister of Glenavy, to the Quigg family, the McCartney's, and finally to Danny and Pearl McQuillan before being sold to a development company. The 'Bay', a haven for weddings, special meetings, and social club dinners was sentimentally demolished and replaced by 46 apartments. Minnie, however, was in a better place when the iconic building was flattened. I prefer her memory of olden times in Cushendun, when all varieties of artistes, such as actor, songwriter and film producer Richard Hayward, settled for long and short-stop periods. She wrote: "Famous people like Robert Lloyd Praeger and his sister, Rosamund - a renowned sculptress, came each year on holiday. A wild rose is name after them. There is also the Praeger Institute, established in Coleraine University.

"The Crommelin's employed many local people in their Mill, in which ropes were made. It was just a wallstead in the early years of this century (20th). Then in the 1920's, Mrs McBride bought the ruin, and had it roofed by James McGreer. In November 1926, Daniel McBride made a successful application to open a new hotel in Cushendun. The *Northern Whig* of Saturday November 13, 1926, reported "NEW HOTEL FOR CUSHENDUN". Mr McBride, grandfather of Randal McDonnell - later the proprietor of the Cushendun Hotel with its 'Blue Room' bar, was represented by James McSparran B.L.

Minnie added: "From the bridge down past it is a lovely piece of road along the river bank which was called the 'rope walk' - where workers twisted the ropes. Rockport House is where the Higginson's lived. One of their daughters was the famous poetess, whose pen name was *Moira O'Neill*, and her many writings included *Songs of the Glens of Antrim*. Her real name was Agnes Shakespeare Higginson."

Born in 1865, she became Mrs Agnes Nesta Skrine, and died in 1955. The Irish-Canadian poet and author wrote novels, her first was *Elf-Errand* in 1893, but mainly ballads. She was inspired by the beauty of the green Glens of Antrim, especially the Cushendun area because of where she lived. She also used the name Nesta, and followed the 1901 *Songs of the Glens of Antrim* with *More Songs of the Glens of Antrim* in 1921. Her daughter was Mary Nesta Skrine, born at Newbridge, County Kildare, in 1904, and educated at Bray, County Wicklow. She married a Bobby Keane, and was the Irish writer/playwright known as Molly Keane and also M.J. Farrell. She wrote eleven novels, and died in 1996.

Rockport House was once occupied by the Parry family. Mrs Parry was a cousin of Roger Casement. The long row of low buildings at Rockport House was used by Customs. A flat stone in the corner of the hurling field was where the money was paid to the Customs men. A few years ago, when the 'Rigs' - the old uneven hurling pitch, had to be levelled, a paved road was found close to the shore. Horses and carts would use this to bring cargo from the boats after paying Custom duty. The name of this field is Liganergat, which means 'field of the money'.

Minnie wrote her tribute poem/song to the Rigs, and based it on the air of *The Bells of Aberdovey.*

### LIGANERGAT

*They say the swans of Lir so Royal*
*Banished to our northern shores*
*Settled on the Sea of Moyle*
*Not far from Liganergat.*

*When once they saw this fair Glen*
*They flapped their wings*
*And flew right in*
*To the field of Liganergat.*

*When Cushendun possessed a ferry*
*Which daily plied to Scotland's shore*
*With lithe Glensmen and their stock galore*
*They sailed from Liganergat.*

*See all their sails*
*White as snow*
*Carry vessels as they go*
*from the pier at Liganergat.*

*A change of scene takes place again*
*Instead of ships are hurling men*
*Upholding the name of their dear Glen*
*in the Rigs at Liganergat.*

*In black and green*
*How they play!*
*And many trophies came their way*
*From the Rigs at Liganergat.*

*On we come to a later date*
*To be precise - 1968*
*The Rigs were now quite out of date*
*They bulldozed at Liganergat.*

*Such a great change*
*Where Emmets range*
*You would think it Croke or Casement*
*This park at Liganergat.*

Minnie held a special affection for this magical place at the beach. It seemed a forever personal family connection, and perhaps that obvious distant link to the Scottish Lowlands. Sheltered anchorage was one of the old-time attractions of Cushendun, and became a focal point for traders such as Minnie's grandfather, Hugh McGavock. She took a extra-special interest in any place or situation her relatives were involved.

Her take on the background to this charming Bay included: "As lately as the middle of the 19th century, Tiree and Shetland ponies were brought across the Sea of Moyle by Irish horsedealers, and landed in Cushendun. At that period it was a small village of thatched fishermen's cottages, and a Coastguard Station. The Bay was a convenient landing place for pre-historic man, Excavations carried out in McBride's Field some years ago proved this to be the case. In later years, the McDonnell's of the Scottish Isles landed here, and over-ran the McQuillan community of Dalriada."

# ROCKPORT

GUARDING the inlet at the north end of Cushendun Bay was once the home of fisherman Sean McNeill. The waves almost lapped up to his front door. He had another more romantic take on the money background to the Irish word, Liganergat.

He said: "My father, John, once remarked that possibly 300 years ago a highwayman, who was eventually caught and hanged. Apparently he buried his money, his gold, in the Rigs - the field known as Liganergat. That was a story handed down. However, Minnie's theory could have been right.

"I was also given some history on the trading route from Cushendun to South End or Dunavarty. Garron Ponies were wild, and were rounded up once a year. They may have been shipped out from here, too. The boats came in at Rockport, and also at Cushendun. Sometimes the boat could get into one and not into the other, during periods when the river was in flood. The boat was hauled in slowly by a rope, right into the inlet at Rockport. There wasn't much room. They were probably 40-foot boats, able to take a dozen horses. Campbeltown had 12 distilleries at one time, and exported the whisky. Some of it came here too, as well as the majority exported to North America.

"Of course, there remain many rocks guarding this area, and it was the understandable reason we became known as McNeill of the Rocks. The old Custom House buildings lie close to my old home. The houses were more than likely once owned by HM Customs, and then sold. The first folk I recall living there were the Parrys, then Mr Archer, who was Town Clerk of Belfast."

This special place of natural beauty became a magnet for celebrated oil and watercolour landscape painters such as Maurice Wilks, James Humbert Craig, the locally-born Charles McAuley, and later on Larne's Sam McLarnon. Also there was the renowned poet *Moira O'Neill*. Incidentally, I recall as a youngster delivering butcher's meat packages to Mr Wilks when he spent summer months after World War Two living in a green-painted temporary cottage made of a corrugated roof and iron sides - and situated at the bottom of one of Harry Scally's fields, at the start of the road to Torr Head.

Wilks, born in Belfast in 1910, was an exceptionally gifted oil and watercolour landscape painter. He died in 1984. During the early part of his career he was encouraged by James Humbert Craig, the latter born in Belfast on the 12th of July, 1877. I never met the great man, who had a studio in Cushendun, and died on June 12, 1944. Sean McNeill has childhood recollection of being tutored by Humbert Craig.

"When I was a very small child I used to paint along with the great Humbert Craig, the first real artist to come to Cushendun. He lived at Rockport, beside the house where I was reared. I used to be in Craig's house. He showed me how to paint, but that was as far as I progressed. Dr Flora Maher now has the bungalow that Craig once owned. I can vaguely remember the bungalow being sold and bought by Dr Marion Brogan.

"It was a pleasant place at Rockport, to sit on a summer's day with an easel and look across the Bay. Craig died quite unexpectedly. He was 'waked' in Belfast, where he had a house off the Antrim Road, and was buried in the Church of Ireland graveyard in Cushendall."

Obviously, the 'well-to-do' and landlords seemed to favour living around and along the seaside setting, mainly in the Cushendun village. The name translates from the Gaelic as 'foot of the Dun', or 'beside the Dun'. The word Dun means brown, and anyone who has seen the river in flood will realise how apt the name is. It flows from Orra mountain at the top of Glendun, from which it carries much brown moss.

The mouth of the River Dun was a popular landing place and ferry point between Scotland and Ireland since man first settled on the north coast. The picturesque village is situated on a raised beach at the end of the glacial valleys of Glendun and Glencorp.

Minnie wrote: "Part of Cushendun village and surrounding lands were owned by Ronald McNeill, later to be Lord Cushendun. Rockport and the north side of the Bay was owned by the Whites, while Sleans on the south side was owned by the Crommelin's. They also owned the secluded Cave House. The Caves provide a perfect example of a raised beach, through the middle cave is a road leading to the House."

On the mound above Cave House lie the ruins of Sleans Church, built in 1834 as an Orthodox Congregational Meetinghouse. Like the Church of Ireland, on the other side of Cushendun village, it faces east, and a tablet on the west gable proclaims: 'Orthodox Congregational Meetinghouse - And the Lord said I have hallowed this house which Thou hast built to put my name there forever, and Mine eyes and thine heart shall be there perpetually. MDCCCXXXIV.'

In 1830, a plan was put in motion by a local businessman Nicholas Crommelin to develop the harbour commercially, so that it could cater for the surrounding district and industrial centre of Ballymena. Architect, Sir John Rennie was commissioned to design the harbour, but the project failed when the government pulled out of funding it. Crommelin was from Huguenot extraction, from a long line of French refugees that included the distinguished Louis Crommelin, who was appointed royal supervisor of linen manufacture in Ireland. The Census of 1911 included the imperious sounding name of 50-year-old Nicholas De La Cheron Crommelin, the lord of Sleans. Listed is his wife Katherine, aged 20, who is also named a worshipper at the nearby Church of Ireland. Servants named from local Catholic families were Mary O'Neill (19) and Mary McLarnon (22).

In the village area then were 52-year-old Bessie Banks and her sons Thomas Joseph (15) and John James (13). Also there at that time, probably on holiday from Dublin, were Kate Redmond (28), her daughter Mary (2) and infant son James. Named in the Census is the family of Charles McLarnon (50), the Finlay's - who worshipped at the nearby Church of Ireland, and the Andrew McNeill (46) family that became better known as 'the Andy's' - and included then was a four-year-old Henry Joseph, later to become famous as a fisherman, hunter, boxing aficionado and raconteur.

Minnie added: "Besides the rope factory there were a few water-driven mills erected by Scottish planters. Some years ago there was an old man named McGregor, who lived beside McIlreavey's in Upper Agolagh (near Knocknacarry). His people once owned what is now known as Carey's Mill in Tyban. Sharkey's Mill up Dunurgan Road had been owned by an old man who lived near Rockport, and who used to come up to visit the Sharkey's riding a big tricycle."

In the 1830's, it was recorded in an Ordnance Survey of Layd Parish that Cushendall was a post town, with the mail carried through it on horseback from Ballycastle to Glenarm twice a day. Also noted was: "There are no manufactories in the Parish of Layd. Unlike most parts of the North of Ireland they make no cloth for market, though almost every family makes what linen and woollen cloth is required for their own use. The population of this Parish amounts to about 4,000, 129 families are Protestants and the remainder, without exception, Roman Catholics."

In the Griffiths Valuation of 1848-'64 the area of Agolagh, Cushendun and Sleans included names such as Adam Bartley, Duncan Black, Alexander Blaney, Hugh Collins, Patrick Connor, Nicholas D. Crommelin, Finton Doolan, John Doughey, John Harvey, the Rev Walter Johnston, Catherine Magill, John and William McAllister, Patrick McCaughan, Catherine McElheran, John McIlreavey, Charles McLernon, James McMullan, Alexander, Neal and Daniel McNeill, Patrick McVeigh and William Moore.

Cushendun's quaintly English-style village owes a good deal of its character and architectural heritage to the whims of Ronald John McNeill. He became the 1st Baron of Cushendun in 1927. Born on April 30, 1861 he died on October 12, 1934.

In his memoirs, Lord Cushendun stated his affection for the place. Close to his Glendun House, the area and path from his Gate Lodge and through what is now a Caravan Park, was the small townland, one long since forgotten, of 'Drumnadrissoch' and on the sea side, the field running down to the shoreline - the famous Liganergat. He claimed he might have used a different personal title, and wrote: "It crossed my mind to take one of these names for my title, when I became a Peer." In 1912, on the site of fishermen's cottages, he commissioned renowned architect Clough Williams-Ellis to design a village square featuring seven houses.

Minnie remarked: "The elegant houses became known as 'The Square'. Their tall white chimneys and slate-covered gables bear testimony to the genius of their famous architect. Above the door of the central house is the date 1912 in Roman numerals, together with the initials R McN and M McN (Ronald McNeill and his wife Maud). Elizabeth Maud McNeill died on January 30, 1925. Also included in the progressive plan was a public hall, but this was never completed. In 1923, Williams-Ellis, famous for his quaintly unique village production at Portmeirion near Portmadoc in north Wales, was invited back to the Glens to design the Maud Cottages - demolishing the Coastguard Station, and Glenmona House. The Cottages were built in 1925. Williams-Ellis, who also designed a school and a church at the Giant's Causeway for the McNaughton family, died on April 8, 1978, aged 94.

"Further along the beach, at Rockport, raiding Scottish clans landed their boats near Carra Castle, the ruin of the keep of the castle still to be seen. Shane O'Neill was slain there in June 1567, during a quarrel with with the MacDonnell's at Crosscreene - an old church site in the townland of Ballyteerim and close to Castle Carra. Shane's remains are said to have been buried close by, after his head was taken to Dublin and placed on public display. In 1908, a 'Cairn' was erected on ground overlooking Cushendun Bay, on the scenic Torr Road."

CUSHENDUN BAY, I feel, is a delightfully appropriate setting to close Minnie's memory trail. She had such a clear and uncluttered manner of recording things past that truly mattered. Her knowledge was greatly respected. She was the fulcrum to all passages of family endeavour, starting with her McGavock roots in the Glenarm area. Minnie maintained a pride in her beloved Glens of Antrim, and a faithful geographical link with the adventures of her bloodlines. Her recall brought us around the globe from Dunurgan to such far off places as Tacoma, Libertyville, Chicago, Nashville, Fox Lake (Illinois), Waukegan, Beloit, Galveston, Perth (Australia), Panama, Rio de Janeiro and right back to her grandfather's favourite place, Liganergat.

FIN

DENIS O'HARA, a journalist from Knocknacarry, Cushendun, is the second eldest of Minnie and Alex O'Hara's four sons. This is his fourth book, following the release of . . .

*The Remarkable Kyles* (December 2006) - athletics biography,

*Candy Men of '54* (December 2009) - recall of a famous Derry City soccer side,

*Hooked on the Jab. The B.J. Eastwood Story.* (March 2010) - the acclaimed authorised biography of bookmaker/ boxing manager Barney Eastwood.

The other surviving member of the O'Hara family, second youngest Daniel - an accountant in Dublin, joined Denis in assembling the unique historic recollections of their mother Minnie, and their maternal grandfather Alexander John McGavock.